Shaky Colonialism

A John Hope Franklin Center Book

SHAKY COLONIALISM

The 1746 Earthquake-Tsunami in
Lima, Peru, and Its Long Aftermath

Charles F. Walker

DUKE UNIVERSITY PRESS

DURHAM & LONDON 2008

Printed in the United States of America on acid-free paper ∞
Designed by Jennifer Hill
Typeset in Quadraat by Tseng Information Systems, Inc.

Library of Congress Cataloging-in-Publication Data
appear on the last printed page of this book.

Duke University Press gratefully acknowledges the support
of the Spanish Ministry of Culture and the Program for Cultural
Cooperation between Spain's Ministry of Culture and United
States Universities at the University of Minnesota, which
provided funds toward the production of this book.

Tables

Acknowledgments

When I began this project I naively believed I wouldn't depend on so many people as I had in writing my first book. I was wrong. I have no regrets, however, as friendships and intellectual debts grew in tandem.

Arnie Bauer and Andrés Reséndez read this book chapter by chapter, giving me their advice and support at delightful coffee meetings in Davis. Peter Guardino, Adrian Pearce, and Rich Warren did not flinch when I sent them the completed manuscript. Their comments dramatically improved the book. I also inflicted chapters on Mark Carey, Margaret Chowning, Rebecca Earle, David Garrett, Lyman Johnson, Kathy Olmsted, and Karen Spalding, who provided important feedback. Carlos Aguirre and Mirtha Avalos continue to be important supporters and dear friends, helping me in numerous ways. Extended conversations with Iván Hinojosa brightened Lima winters and taught me xii

a great deal. Ramón Mujica shared his knowledge of the baroque and much else with me and I have only the best memories of our lunchtime "seminars" at his apartment. Víctor Peralta has been an important comrade for years, and I want to thank him and Marta Iruruozqui.

At the beginning of this project, I was fortunate to hook up with two young Peruvian historians. Ricardo Ramírez Castañeda began as an archive assistant, and we ended up publishing together. José "Google" Ragas is a constant source of insights and bibliography. Both Ricardo and José inspire me. In Lima, I've also counted on the friendship and support of Yolanda Auqui, Ruth Borja, Gisela Cánepa, José de la Puente Brunke, Javier Flores Espinoza, Pedro Guibovich, Lizzie Haworth, Fernando López, Hortencia Muñoz, Aldo Panfichi, Marisa Remy, and Raúl Romero.

Claudia Rosas and Nuria Sala I Vila took time off from their research to provide me with copies of obscure archival material that proved very important for this book. Kathryn Burns, Ryan Crewe, Jeff Hergesheimer, Willie Hiatt, Ruth Hill, Al Lacson, Jorge Lossio, Matt O'Hara, Scarlett O'Phelan, Rachel O'Toole, Stuart Schwartz, Adam Warren, and Toni Zapata helped me clarify issues and answer questions. John Coatsworth, Nils Jacobsen, and Eric Van Young have supported me for well over a decade, and Tulio Halperín-Donghi has been an inspiration since my undergraduate days. Pablo Whipple aided me with research, particularly in the final stretch.

My family and I would not have had such a great year in Sevilla if it were not for the help, humor, and support of Antonio Acosta. Luis Miguel Glave and María José Fitz were and are also dear friends. Ernesto Bohoslavsky contributed with his erudition, research skills, and take on life. I also benefited from the friendship and support of Jesús Bustamante, Pilar García Jordán, Pilar Latasa, Ricardo Leandri, Ascensión Martínez, Alfredo Moreno, Pablo Emilio Pérez Mallaína Bueno (an eminent scholar on the earthquake of 1746), Guillermo Pastor, and Mónica Quijada. An ACLS-SSRC International Postdoctoral Fellowship allowed me to launch the project. My research in Spain was supported by a National Endowment for the Humanities Fellowship. Grants from the University of California, Davis helped with trips to Peru. I have presented papers on eighteenth-century Lima in many places. I received particularly valuable comments from Jurgen Buchenau, Susan Deans Smith, Paulo Drinot, Antonio Escobar Ohmstede, Virginia García Acosta, Mark Healey, Jobie Margadant, Ulrich Muecke, Mauricio Pajón, Alexandra Puerto, and William Taylor. Alessa Johns talked me into giving a paper years ago, starting me on this project. Bill Ainsworth, Emily Albu, Tom Holloway, Ari Kelman, Victoria Langland, Ted Margadant, Kathy Olmsted, Ben Orlove, Jaana Remes, Alan Taylor, Stefano Varese, and Louie Warren help make Davis both a pleasant and stimulating place. Nara Milanich and Nicola Cetorelli are still honorary Davisites. I have also been blessed by outstanding students who have made me think and rethink cities, catastrophes, and other topics.

I want to thank Chris Brest for the maps (and for his patience) and Kevin Bryant for his technological skills (and patience). Miriam Angress and Valerie Millholland took me through the steps once again at Duke University Press with their characteristic enthusiasm and charm. Mark Mastromarino did a wonderful job overseeing the production stage, as did Larry Kenney with the copyediting. I would like to acknowledge Fernando López, Luís Nieri, Pilar Morín (Imprenta Ausonia), Ramón Mujica, and José Ragas for their help with the illustrations.

My family continues to think it's fine that a grown-up spends his days reading old papers and writing on curious topics. Thanks Mom, Maggie, John, and Mary for all your love. Zoila Mendoza supported the project in many ways. Her enthusiasm for Sevilla allowed for a wonderful year and many returns to that city. My children, Maria and Samuel, are everything to me. Although I know they tire of accompanying me to Peru and Spain, I hope one day they will appreciate this book.

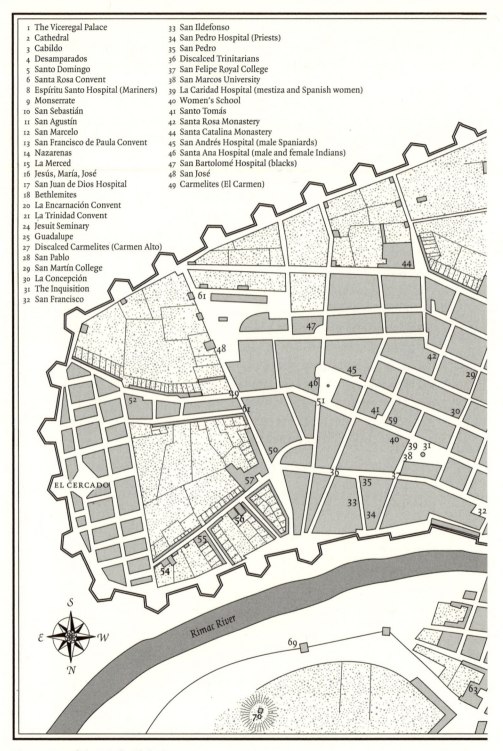

1 The Viceregal Palace
2 Cathedral
3 Cabildo
4 Desamparados
5 Santo Domingo
6 Santa Rosa Convent
8 Espíritu Santo Hospital (Mariners)
9 Monserrate
10 San Sebastián
11 San Agustín
12 San Marcelo
13 San Francisco de Paula Convent
14 Nazarenas
15 La Merced
16 Jesús, María, José
17 San Juan de Dios Hospital
18 Bethlemites
20 La Encarnación Convent
21 La Trinidad Convent
24 Jesuit Seminary
25 Guadalupe
27 Discalced Carmelites (Carmen Alto)
28 San Pablo
29 San Martín College
30 La Concepción
31 The Inquisition
32 San Francisco

33 San Ildefonso
34 San Pedro Hospital (Priests)
35 San Pedro
36 Discalced Trinitarians
37 San Felipe Royal College
38 San Marcos University
39 La Caridad Hospital (mestiza and Spanish women)
40 Women's School
41 Santo Tomás
42 Santa Rosa Monastery
44 Santa Catalina Monastery
45 San Andrés Hospital (male Spaniards)
46 Santa Ana Hospital (male and female Indians)
47 San Bartolomé Hospital (blacks)
48 San José
49 Carmelites (El Carmen)

EL CERCADO

Rímac River

Map 1   Map of Lima. *Credit*: Christ Brest.

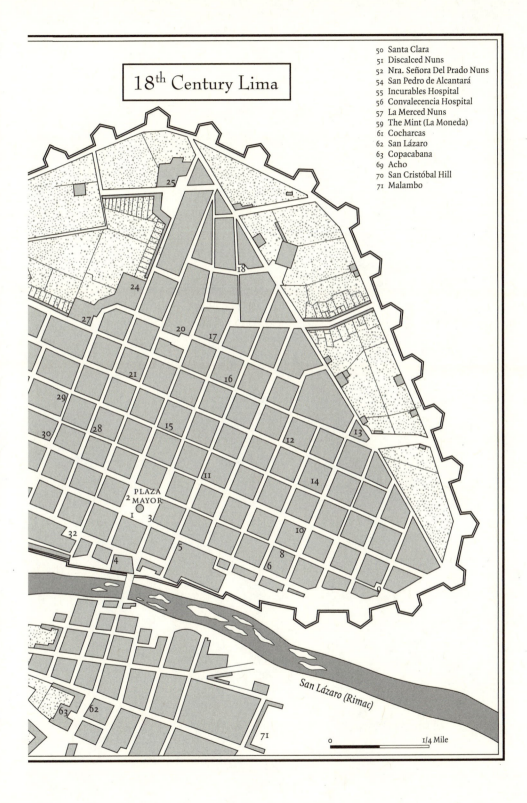

18ᵗʰ Century Lima

50 Santa Clara
51 Discalced Nuns
52 Nra. Señora Del Prado Nuns
54 San Pedro de Alcantará
55 Incurables Hospital
56 Convalecencia Hospital
57 La Merced Nuns
59 The Mint (La Moneda)
61 Cocharcas
62 San Lázaro
63 Copacabana
69 Acho
70 San Cristóbal Hill
71 Malambo

PLAZA MAYOR

San Lázaro (Rimac)

0   1/4 Mile

Contents

Contents

For Three Cool Guys,
My dear friend, Arnold Bauer
My brother, John Walker
My son, Samuel Eduardo Mendoza Walker

Earthquakes, Tsunamis, Absolutism, and Lima

What man can remain steady when the mountains tremble? If the earth shakes, what will hearts do? —ANONYMOUS, *El Día de Lima*, 61

Dogs, hunched next to cadavers and with their eyes to the sky, gave such great howls that even the most insensitive broke into tears.
—JOSÉ EUSEBIO LLANO ZAPATA, "Observación diaria," 146–47

One

On October 28, 1746, at 10:30 P.M., a 220-mile stretch of the Nazca tectonic plate lurched under the continental plate about 100 miles off the coast of Peru, causing a massive earthquake that ripped open the city of Lima, capital of the Viceroyalty of Peru.[1] Like all earthquakes, this one struck with a one-two punch. Danger came from below and above. The shaking earth knocked people to the ground, and the intense but irregular tremors kept many lying there and terrified everyone. The quake shattered walls, roofs, facades, and furniture, hurtling them down upon victims. Heavy adobes crushed many people who did not make it out of their residence. Others were trapped inside and were not rescued. Danger also awaited those who made it outside, as they were threatened by tumbling balconies, beams, the walls that surrounded the city, and the heavy bells that graced churches. Some people who rushed back inside to save family members or retrieve

2   valuables died when a beam or adobe toppled over on·top of them. Those who survived suffered with uncertainty about their loved ones as well as with the horrible sight of the devastated city and the sounds of wailing victims and collapsing structures.

As the underwater fault surged, it not only sent shockwaves into the ground but also abruptly pushed up parts of the sea floor. This motion generated waves that moved across the Pacific at the speed of a jet airplane. The waves appeared small in the depths of the sea, then became magnified in power and height as they reached shore. Multiple waves merged in a looming, destructive tower of water. At 11 P.M., half an hour after the earthquake, eerie sounds of receding water indicated imminent horrors just before the wave, a tsunami, hit. Some claimed that the largest wave that struck Callao, Lima's port, was over eighty feet high, although most put it at fifty feet.[2]

The earthquake and tsunami wrecked much of central Peru, its swath of destruction stretching from Trujillo in the north to Pisco and Ica in the south. It was felt over six hundred miles to the northwest in Guayaquil and about four hundred miles south in Cuzco. It destroyed buildings in the Amazon, shook the mines of Huancavelica, knocked down churches in Huarochirí, and coincided with a volcanic eruption in Lucanas, to the south of Huamanga. The massive tsunami shattered the port of Callao and struck areas up and down the coast, from what is today southern Ecuador to central Chile. Though harmless, large waves reached even Acapulco, Mexico, some two thousand miles away. In Callao, the waterline suddenly rose twenty-four feet, and the water reached three miles inland.[3]

Lima, located six miles inland from Callao, quickly became "a frightening place, like a war scene put to the sword and set to fire, its beautiful buildings turned into piles of dirt and stones."[4] The bustling, multiracial city of fifty thousand, the heart of Spain's territories in South America, lay in ruins. José Eusebio Llano Zapata, the best chronicler of the Lima disaster (and a fascinating self-taught Renaissance man whose accounts enliven this book), noted that a city that had taken 211 years to build was destroyed in a little over three minutes. He glumly predicted that Lima could not be rebuilt in two centuries or with two hundred million pesos.[5]

Don Francisco José de Ovando y Solís (the Marquis of Ovando), the commander of the Spanish navy's Pacific fleet, had just sat down to dinner when the earth began to rumble. He fled to an inner patio that contained a hut made out of reeds designed to withstand earthquakes. Ovando had

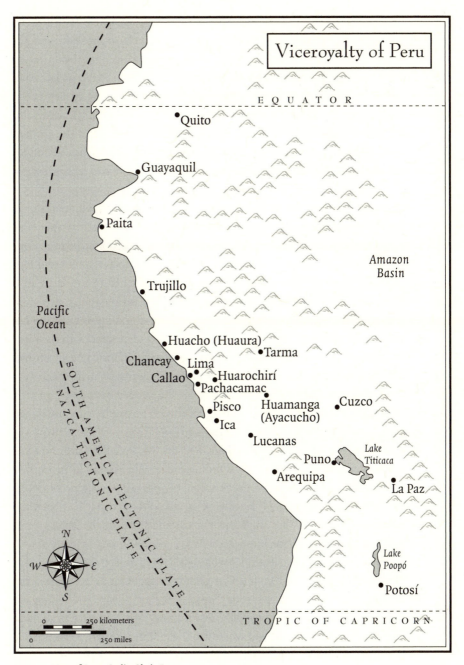

Map 2   Map of Peru. *Credit*: Chris Brest.

4   just made it out the door when much of his house collapsed. The earth, "a robust beast shaking the dust off itself," shook so hard that he could not remain on his feet. Expecting the worst, he gathered his family from among the ruins and found that only one young black man, probably a slave, had minor injuries. The rest were unharmed. They prayed in the garden patio, realizing from the eerie screams they could hear, the din of collapsing buildings, and the clouds of dust that swirled about them that the city had been devastated. Despite objections and his own misgivings, he ordered his family to go back inside the house to gather food and water, recognizing— as a smart sailor would—that difficult times lay ahead.

Ovando lived in the northeast corner of the city, in the Santa Ana parish, next to the Indian quarters of El Cercado. He gathered three members of his family to aid the nuns in the neighboring Discalced Mercedarian convent. Although no one there would open the doors, the sacristan told him that all had survived. The rescue party then proceeded to the vast Santa Clara convent, which housed almost a thousand people, nuns, servants, and seculars. He was not allowed in there either and so returned to his house, where he saddled up a horse and a mule and proceeded to the Viceroy's Palace in the Plaza Mayor. His passage through Lima's streets, strewn with "roofs, doors, balconies, and furniture," underlines the physical presence of the Catholic Church in Lima. If he had headed east, down Maravillas street and toward the Indian neighborhood, he would have passed the Mercedarian convent, the Santa Toribio hospital run by the Bethlehemites, also called the Refugio de Incurables, and the San Pedro de Alcántara *casa de convalencia*, none of which are standing today.[6] But instead he proceeded west toward the Plaza Mayor. On this walk of approximately nine blocks he would have passed the Discalced Trinitarian convent (what had been the Beaterio de Nerias), the San Pedro church and hospital for priests, and, with a slight detour to the Inquisition Plaza, the La Caridad hospital as well as the Inquisition office itself. He would have then passed the majestic San Francisco church, which consists of San Francisco el Grande, larger in the eighteenth century than it is today, as well as the Los Milagros (Miracles) and La Soledad (Solitude) chapels. From there he would have proceeded two blocks to the Plaza Mayor, where the Cathedral, now with a gaping hole in its nave where its towers had fallen, stood.

After a long wait, Ovando visited the viceroy, José Manso de Velasco, and also checked in with other dignitaries, helping them select areas where the survivors might take refuge. He described the confusion and fear of

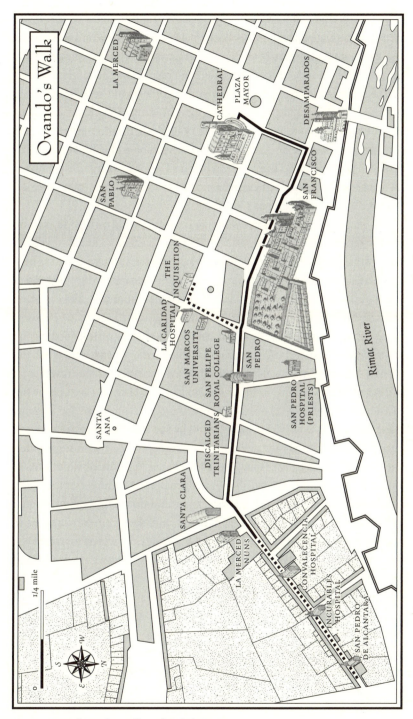

Map 3   Map of Ovando's walk. *Credit*: Chris Brest.

more destruction and social mayhem, especially at the hands of "the plebe, thrown together in packs." The marquis was overjoyed to find his friends and associates, members of the Lima patriarchy, alive. This changed when he reached the Conde de Villanueva del Soto residence. The mother, father, and sister of Pablo Olavide, who in years to come would be a figure in the Spanish Enlightenment, were visiting that evening. They had made it to the doorway but were killed when the house collapsed on them. Two of Olavide's sisters were dragged out of the ruins, one with a broken leg. The marquis gave them the water he carried and went in search of what was most needed, doctors and confessors. He found neither—they were all overwhelmed with incessant pleas for help.[7]

The sun soon rose, and the marquis recognized his own good fortune and the terrible state of Lima: "No hyperbole can evoke so much tragedy in such a short time. The pleas for divine mercy and the sobs and cries for help alternated with the aftershocks, muddling the pained cries of the wounded and the appeals for help from those trapped under the debris, like prisoners in caves, begging for aid with their last cries. Many died this way." He compared Lima to Troy after the Greek war.[8] Chroniclers of the catastrophe emphasized the disturbing mix of noises and the heightened fear when the ground shook again. Aftershocks would torment Lima for months.[9]

Father Pedro Lozano, a Jesuit who was not in Lima at the time of the earthquake but received several reports, wrote a letter about the tragedy, a document that would be widely quoted by succeeding generations. It led generations of scholars to attribute to him incorrectly the more detailed and much-translated *True and Particular Relation of the Dreadful Earthquake*, which he did not write.[10] While Lozano's report, a summary rather than an eyewitness account, provides more general information than personal experience might have, he struggled to find suitable terms or metaphors to portray the gravity and magnitude of the disaster. After summarizing the basic information and reporting exaggeratedly that only twenty-five houses remained standing, he began his second paragraph by claiming that "few examples in history can be found of such a pitiful event; and it is difficult for even the liveliest imagination to depict such a calamity."[11] He described the damage in Lima's sixty-four churches, including the destruction caused when the Cathedral's two towers toppled. Lozano depicted the distressing sight, reiterated by many other observers, of dazed nuns forced out of their monastic seclusion walking the rubble-strewn streets of Lima in search of food and shelter. Curiously, this, rather than the thousands of dead and wounded or the legions of traumatized survivors, would become the major rhetorical symbol of the unthinkable horrors of the earthquake. Lozano also tallied the damage to principal buildings, including the Viceroy's Palace, the Inquisition, and the Royal University, all reduced to a "sad reminder of what they had been."[12] The frequent aftershocks, the cries of help from people buried inside their houses, and the uncertainty about the extent of the damage and what would follow nourished people's fears. The panic that gripped the city on the day of the earthquake continued for weeks.

Viceroy Manso de Velasco toured the city on horseback, returning periodically to his camp in the Plaza Mayor to coordinate emergency efforts. He moved quickly to restore the city's water and bread supply. Workers fixed the channels that ran from the Rimac River to different plazas as well as to flour mills and adobe ovens. The viceroy ordered that wheat and other basic supplies be brought in from neighboring towns. Before dawn, he gave orders to shoot or hang looters. He worried that the architectural damage—the destruction of so many houses, churches, and public buildings—would lead to a complete breakdown of social codes and ensuing chaos. In the sixteenth century, the Spanish had laid out the city in such a way as to reinforce its order and hierarchy. Yet after the earthquake, not only had many elite and lower-class residences shared the same fate, destruction, but distinguishing among the classes became difficult. It pained the viceroy to see nuns and patriarchs in rags, his own palace as well as the Cathedral in shambles, and the checkerboard layout converted into serpentine paths of rubble.

The earthquake damaged Callao more than Lima. That area's softer, sandier soil increased the intensity of the shaking ground, and fewer houses there had wood frames.[13] This mattered little, however, as it was the massive tsunami that killed most of the port's population and devastated its buildings and ships. The wave exploded along the shore and pushed inland, rushing over the city's walls. Warned by the rumble or sight of the growing wave, some people attempted to flee toward Lima or sought refuge in one of the nine bastions of the city's outer walls. Others desperately grabbed wood or simply panicked, unable to get keys into locks or move their legs. Many of the sailors, aboard their vessels for the evening, survived the first crushing wave but were then knocked overboard by the ensuing rush of water back toward the ocean and by subsequent waves. Boat parts, lumber, and debris from the city finished off many of those thrown overboard, dragged into the sea, or engulfed by the surging water. Some had no inkling of their fate until the deadly surge crushed them.

The wave sunk nineteen ships and, having snapped their anchors, hurtled four into and beyond the walled city, "farther than a cannon shot" in the words of the mariner Ovando. The warships *Fermín* and *San Antonio* landed almost a mile inland, the *Michelot* on the grounds where a hospital, now flattened, had stood, and the *Socorro* closest to shore, behind willow trees just beyond the Indian fishing village of Pitipiti.[14] The *Socorro* (meaning Help or Aid) provided a bit of good news and sustenance, as the wheat and lard it had just brought from Chile remained on board and helped feed the population in the following days. The Augustinian Church was reportedly carried virtually intact out to sea onto an island.

Fewer than two hundred of Callao's five thousand to six thousand residents survived. Most of the survivors resided outside the port city's walls, including fishermen and twenty-two prisoners sentenced to hard labor on the rock pile on San Lorenzo Island. One fervent believer in Saint Joseph grasped ahold of a large painting of him and floated to safety hours later. Others made their way on driftwood to San Lorenzo Island or to the beaches south of Lima. Two men and a woman washed up in Miraflores almost twenty-four hours after the wave had struck, exhausted yet wishing to take confession after their harrowing experience. Twenty-two people reached the top of the Holy Cross bastion of the walls and, partially shielded by a large painting, hung on. One man climbed the flagpole atop one of the bastions and threw himself into a canoe as the water surged. He reported hearing many pleas for mercy, but once the wave had struck "all the cries were immediately silenced, and it was then that all the inhabitants suddenly perished."[15] Other tragic stories were told. A Jesuit priest, Father Iguanco, reached a ship, the aptly named *Asombro* (astonishment), but at four A.M., five hours after the tsunami had struck, another wave broke its anchor line. The boat capsized and the priest drowned. Another priest reportedly could have fled but refused to leave. On October 30, two days after the disaster, survivors spotted four exhausted men floating on a piece of wood. The rough current and dangerous driftwood prevented a rescue. A priest dolefully read them their last rites from the cliffs. The few miraculous happy endings paled next to the deaths of thousands.[16]

The Lima population had turned to Callao in hopes of finding solace

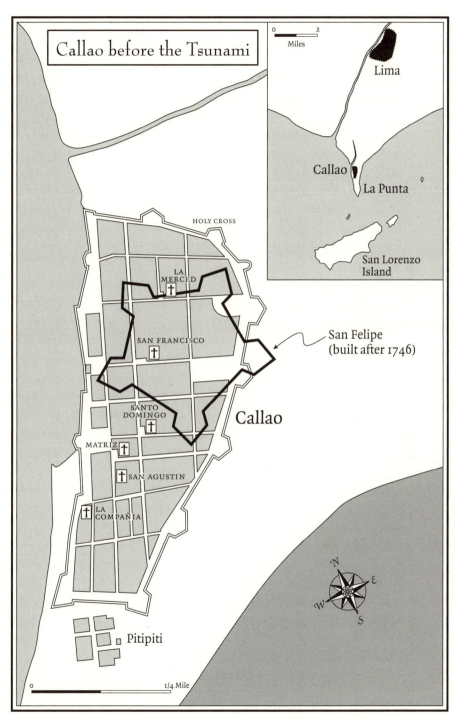

Map 4   Map of Callao. Credit: Chris Brest.

and perhaps some much-needed supplies, but it found only greater tragedy and a bit of food. Lozano was probably exaggerating when he contended that the site of the former town could not even be distinguished amidst the devastation, but Ovando noted more precisely his difficulties in finding the property where his second house had stood. He described stepping over cadavers of both sexes "in the most violent scene that a rational person can imagine."[17] Viceroy Manso de Velasco observed bitterly that only some remnants of the wall's towers remained, such as the Holy Cross bastion and two gates; the walls themselves had been flattened.[18] The tsunami shattered the battery of bronze and steel cannons that defended Callao and Lima, and for months people salvaged military goods up and down the coast and inland. The catastrophe devastated the port's important warehouses, which meant the loss of "wheat, lard, wine, brandy, cables, timber, iron, tin, copper and the like."[19]

Bodies washed up on shore for weeks. In his "Desolation of Lima," written just weeks after the calamity, Victorino Montero del Aguila commented that the bodies of the dead served as "birdfeed."[20] Another commentator wrote, "The sea vomited bodies for months, the naked cadavers half eaten by fish."[21] The floating cadavers included not only those killed by the tsunami, but the remains of the dead unearthed from the shallow graves in churches by the impact of the wave. Less morbid remains also washed ashore. The day after the earthquake people lined up at nearby beaches to gather valuables such as wood furniture and framed pictures and searched through the wreckage for goods. Some claimed that thieves were stripping the dead of jewelry and clothing.[22]

Limeños' fervent religiosity was on full display after the earthquake. Barefoot members of the Mercedarians brought out the image of the Virgin Mary and the Virgin de las Mercedes from their church two blocks from the plaza. One priest exhorted the crowd, "Lima, Lima, your sins are your ruin." In the following days worshipers carried images of the Virgin of the Rosary, Nuestra Señora del Aviso, Santo Cristo de Burgos, el Jesús Nazareno, and the very limeño Señor de los Milagros. The urns of three Peruvian saints, Santo Toribio, San Francisco Solano, and Santa Rosa, each of whom had some earthquake miracle story, were also displayed.[23] Guilty penitence gripped the city, and dozens of processions snaked through Lima's streets. One prelate received lashes on his bare back from a lay brother who shouted, "This is the Lord's justice for this vile sinner."[24] The Franciscans sold thousands of shrouds to cover the dead.[25] Members of this order, whose numbers in Peru had been increasing in the early eighteenth century, practiced a particularly public, physical form of devotion. Observers lauded their zeal as they led "blood processions" and preached seemingly nonstop in the days after the earthquake. Friars Thomas de Cañas, Juan Matheos, and Joseph de San Antonio, Franciscans who emulated Christ by walking barefoot, donning thorned crowns, and dangling ropes around their necks, called for mass penitence and emphasized God's obvious desire that Lima give up its sinful ways. They preached in the streets for months.[26]

Stories were told about religious people who had foreseen the catastrophe. A Franciscan account mentioned that the abbess of the Carmelite convent postponed 7 P.M. choir until 9. When the nuns entered, she gave them the opportunity to turn around and save themselves from the impending punishment that she foresaw. Seven or eight stayed, waiting for God's will to be done. They died. A Dominican friar, Alonso del Río, was taken to be crazy when he walked the streets of Callao that same evening warning of the calamity. He, too, perished.[27] In the aftermath, reports of miracles improved people's spirits. Both Llano Zapata and Ovando told the story of a woman and her nursing baby who survived after four days trapped under rubble. Even the far from pious Llano Zapata exclaimed that divine providence "at the same time that it extends its punishments, propagates its pity."[28] The less holy also were lucky. A ruptured channel flooded the Inquisition dungeon, and only the efforts of Inquisitor Inspector Pedro Antonio Arenaza saved the prisoners from drowning.[29]

In the following days and months, epidemics, hundreds of aftershocks, and the gruesome discoveries of buried bodies added to the anguish. The stench from rotting human and animal flesh, a crime wave, and the shortage of food and water made life miserable. Alarming reports about the destruction of the heart of Spanish South America crossed the Atlantic, entering Enlightenment debates about nature and power, particularly after the Lisbon earthquake of November 1, 1755. The disaster also sparked much discussion in the City of Kings, as Lima was also known in this period, and in Madrid about urbanism and Spanish rule.

Panic and Opposition

The earthquake and ensuing tsunami cracked open Lima and provided a snapshot, albeit a dreadful one, of the city at 10:30 P.M. on October 28, 1746. This book builds on a trend among historians of homing in on a particular event, a specific time and place, and following its broader repercussions, what Robert Darnton has baptized "incident analysis."[30] In particular, the earthquake-tsunami granted a novel perspective on how Lima was organized—who lived where, for example—and how different groups believed the City of Kings should be rebuilt. Disagreements among the Spanish, the Church, and Lima's multiracial population emerged immediately, race, class, and gender playing their typically vital roles.

Lima was a fervently Catholic city prone to earthquakes, and people reacted to the tremors by invoking saints and joining in religious processions. They brought out virgins and crosses from Lima's numerous churches as well as the urns of saints. Beneath this seemingly unanimous turn to the Church, however, lay simmering tensions about the role it should play in Peru, concerns about its internal structure and members' behavior, and disagreements about the proper form of devotion. The chaotic aftermath of the disaster of 1746 revealed deep disagreements about religion, guilt, and redemption as survivors sought explanations and culprits. In the succeeding phases of shock, disarray, mourning, and rebuilding, people attempted to identify the causes and, if possible, correct them. A few erudite souls discussed natural causes, replicating the worldwide division in this era before the dawn of plate tectonics between those who deemed subterranean gases to be the cause of earthquakes and those who stressed water seeping underground and weakening the earth.

The vast majority of Lima's inhabitants, however, saw the calamity as a sign of God's wrath over the city's well-known decadent ways. In speeches, masses, processions, and publications, groups and individuals expressed their opinions about the immorality of Lima and how to correct it. They reproached women's independent ways and risqué clothing with particular vehemence. Some individuals lived these fears and had frightful premonitions about the imminent destruction of the city. The catastrophe thus illuminates the uncertainties and guilt of the Lima population, themes at the heart of this study.

The earthquake developed into a virtual referendum on Lima. Viceroy Manso de Velasco devoted much energy to rebuilding and improving the city. He and his French aide, Louis Godin, both central characters in this book, drew up an elaborate plan to "rationalize" Lima, to create a more manageable city along the lines of European urban reform of the period. They envisioned an organization and layout that would increase the viceroy's power and weaken that of the upper classes, the Church, and other corporate groups. They proposed widening streets, tearing down the top floor of two-story buildings, and limiting the number of facades and bell towers. Such measures would not only facilitate the circulation of goods, people, and air (an eighteenth-century obsession), allowing light to reach areas of "shady" behavior, but also clip the power of the upper classes and facilitate controlling the lower classes and Lima's famously independent women. Viceroy Manso de Velasco sought to regulate (but not eliminate) the Church's presence, attempting to limit the number of churches, convents, and monasteries that could be rebuilt. This campaign brought to the fore deeply felt opinions that the Church, particularly the religious orders (Franciscans, Jesuits, Dominicans, and others), had become decadent and condoned too many wayward priests and too much focus on money and power. The viceroy disliked the ostentation and wealth of the Church and the upper classes. He believed that vanity was the ultimate source of Peru's problems, as it prompted wasteful spending and perhaps sparked God's wrath. He also tried to rein in the rambunctious lower classes and tame religious celebrations.

Yet to Manso's great surprise and frustration, he encountered opposition and resistance from all sides. Much of this book examines these debates and controversies. The Crown was at best lukewarm to the viceroy's plan, accepting the objectives but refusing to spend resources on a distant city, even such an important one as Lima. To the imperial officials in Madrid, the earthquake seemed like an unfortunate setback in the effort to increase revenue from their American holdings and to keep other European powers at bay. In 1746, the Spanish were again fighting the British, in the oddly named War of Jenkins' Ear. Manso's and Godin's proposals, which, as noted, echoed European urban design of the era, did not persuade the Madrid court. Lima was a colonial capital and entrepôt, not a Spanish city proper that deserved or even required magnificence. But money was not the only problem. The contradictions of the Bourbons' policy in the Americas, what became known as the Bourbon Reforms, ensnared the rebuilding efforts.

The enlightenment project imposed by the Bourbons and other absolutist governments such as Frederick the Great of Prussia, Catherine the Great in Russia, and the Habsburg Emperor Joseph II implied some notion of social homogenization or simplification, although not equality: a divi-

14 sion between nobles or the elite and the common people was to replace the multiple forms of identity characteristic of the ancien régime.[31] The Bourbons and other absolutists sought to streamline power relations, envisioning vertical ties that moved from groups or individuals to the Crown and its representatives rather than through multiple intermediaries. Thus the Crown and the viceroy targeted corporate groups, weakening the prerogatives and group identity of guilds, the Church, and caste groups such as Indians. Yet these corporate identities had deep roots in Spanish America, buttressing social divisions and political organization. They were at the heart of Spanish colonialism. Dismantling them and centralizing rather than delegating power would be difficult and potentially dangerous. Questions such as where Indian nobles fit in the new scheme and how to control American-born Europeans, Creoles, without losing their allegiance vexed the Spanish and the viceroy in the earthquake's aftermath and well beyond. The Bourbons also sought to change family and gender relations. These policies proved equally ridden with contradictions and difficulties, in Spain as well as in Peru.[32]

Moreover, the groups the Crown sought to control had their own ideas. The upper classes, the mendicant orders, the secular clergy, the lower classes, and surrounding Andean areas had very different notions of what a new Lima should look like, who should pay for it, and how political relations should be recast. The viceroy found it much more difficult to impose his vision of Lima on the population than he expected, a preview of what would take place in the following half century or more as the Spanish struggled to tighten their hold and, later, merely to keep it. The earthquake allows us to examine the limitations of Spanish absolutism and the obstacles to reform. The period also illuminates how power and change were negotiated.

Disorder and Order, Baroque and Bourbon

In the disputes about who was to blame and how to rebuild, two issues loomed large and marked opposing sides. First, individuals and groups presented divergent understandings of the concepts of order and disorder. Everyone agreed that the earthquake had caused pandemonium: collapsed buildings, a vanished presidio and port, eerie noises, putrid smells, ragged patriarchs, floating cadavers, scary animals, and thousands dead. Yet they

disagreed about what the worst consequence was—what abhorrence epitomized the wretched chaos—and thus what needed to be done first. What
most distressed the viceroy was the breakdown of Lima's geometric preci-
sion, as debris blocked streets, crumpled towers and balconies distorted
the city's crisp right angles, and people slept wherever they could find a few
square feet of space. This upheaval of urban codes seemed to motivate him
more than the thousands of dead or the continuing misery of survivors. He
sought to straighten up, quite literally, the city and to staunch the excesses
of baroque public life. Some members of Lima's lower classes, however,
saw the destruction and disarray as a sign of the tottering power of the
Spanish. In a period when political rule so depended on ritual and display,
many interpreted collapsed palaces and churches and patriarchs dressed
in ridiculous rags as signs not only of a temporary suspension of normal
rules and codes but perhaps of impending change and even revolution.
These differing understandings of order and disorder, of what Lima was
and should or would be, clashed in the earthquake's aftermath.

Many observers pointed to the high number of dazed nuns walking the
streets, unable to return to their cloistered life, as the most horrific symbol
or effect of the disarray prompted by the earthquake. The displacement
of these religious women, their forced exile into Lima's bustling streets,
meant different things to different people. For the viceroy, they personified
the breakdown of the primordial spatial division between the cloistered
and secular worlds, the sacred and the profane. He sought to restore that
divide, seeking limits on the number of nuns and priests and making sure
they focused on monastic life. Others in Lima saw the nuns as heartbreak-
ing signs of God's anger about the city's immorality, a poignant warning
of possibly more apocalyptic events to come. Many pointed their fingers at
women or at the Church itself, blaming its own internal disorder and loss
of purity. Some of the pious believed the viceroy's timid efforts to limit
the presence of nuns and other religious people had prompted or boosted
divine wrath. What for the viceroy and others was a solution to the nuns'
terrible situation—fortifying the profane/secular divide—was for others
a cause of this abhorrence. Although the displaced, wandering nuns became the widely shared symbol of the earthquake's ghastliness, people interpreted them in various ways, indicating broad disagreements over why
Lima lay in ruins and what could be done.

The second and related fault line was the battle between baroque

16   Counter-Reformation governance and Bourbon "enlightened" colonialism. *Baroque* refers to an architectural and artistic style which "materialized the spiritual world," particularly through the ornate and abundant religious images and icons that had been at the heart of the Catholic world at least since the Council of Trent (1545–63). It was an urban phenomenon, epitomized in magnificent buildings, churches, plazas, and avenues that held luxurious festivities and were the scene of an ostentatious social life. In terms of religiosity, the word denotes "devotion radically separated from the workaday world, engaged less with the intellect than direct, emotional experience of the heavenly realm through dazzling displays of holy objects and the fine arts."[33] At the core of the baroque lay the juxtaposition of piety and sensuality. Nuns and other religious women had an enormous presence in Lima, constituting in 1700 about one-fifth of the city's female population. At the same time, however, covered women, the *tapadas*, flirted energetically, affairs and concubinage were common, and libertinage marked the city.

Eighteenth-century Lima was an eminently baroque city, and reformers saw the earthquake-tsunami as an opportunity to rid it of certain elements of its ornate architecture and to tame its elaborate religious festivals and social practices. The struggle between baroque and enlightened colonialism was most evident in the efforts by the viceroy to weaken the presence of the Church and to wean people from baroque piety. The viceroy was a religious man, but he believed nevertheless that the Church should neither flaunt its wealth and power nor promote ostentatious forms of religiosity. Devotion should be internal and private rather than external and public. He was an early example of "enlightened Catholicism."[34] Reformers targeted the lush, heterodox nature of religious devotion, what they considered "baroque excesses," and the city's festivals and plazas.[35] Yet not only did the Church defend its position, but the people of Lima demonstrated their allegiance to the public displays of religiosity that defined the baroque and Lima in particular.

The conflict moved far beyond the question of the role of the Catholic Church, manifesting itself in clashes over urban design, religiosity, sensuality, and centralized political rule. It appeared in discussions and controversies over two-story houses, premonitions, bread, clothing, parades, and other seemingly unconnected topics. The baroque/Bourbon absolutism fault line thus transcended overtly political struggles about the relative

power of the viceregal state, marking the multiple controversies about how
to rebuild and reorder Lima.

The confrontation between the reforming viceroy and the many opposing groups ended, I contend, in a stalemate. This standoff foreshad-
ows the haphazard implementation of the Bourbon Reforms. In order to
tighten control and increase revenues, the Spanish centralized political
rule, modernized fiscal and administrative systems, and invested in the
military. While most scholars date these changes from Spain's costly defeat in the Seven Years' War (1756–63), particularly the reign of Carlos III
(1759–88), I join others in probing the earlier decades of reform.[36] The
Crown and the viceroy vacillated about policies regarding Indians, Creoles,
and the Church and fretted about the high cost of administrative reforms.
These and other groups fought certain aspects of the reforms. This irregular implementation and broad resistance marked the decade following the
earthquake-tsunami studied here as well. In fact, the rebuilding struggles,
in which virtually every group opposed the viceroy, but for different reasons and with distinct alternatives, also augured Peru's peculiar position
in the Wars of Independence of the early nineteenth century. Most sectors
(classes, ethnic groups, regions) disliked Spanish rule, but they could not
unite. Fragmented opposition also marked the decade of rebuilding after
the earthquake.

The debates about rebuilding were not limited to Lima, Callao, and the
hinterland. They entered transatlantic and European discussions about
earthquakes, colonial rule, and divine wrath. The viceroy and the Crown in
Madrid wrote back and forth about the earthquake and the many controversies surrounding the rebuilding, but in addition accounts of the earthquake appeared in Mexico, what would become the United States, France,
Holland, Portugal, and Spain. Many luminaries of the period, including
Voltaire, Immanuel Kant, and Benjamin Franklin, referred to the Lima
earthquake. In following this paper trail, I pay special attention to the relationship between what Europeans wrote about Lima throughout the eighteenth century and discussions in the city itself about the city's grandeur
and flaws.

Perceptive studies of travelers, scientists, and other writers have taught
us a great deal about how Europeans perceived Peru and how these ideas
were perpetuated. In fact, we may know more about these European notions
than about how Lima and the surrounding hinterland felt about themselves,

18   that is, about the images and concerns that circulated through the city and its environs. The question of how colonial peoples reacted to, questioned, ignored, or incorporated Western discourse promulgated by travelers, scientists, and others—what in the context of Eastern colonies Edward Said deemed Orientalism—constitutes a crucial question underlined by a variety of scholars.[37] I show that Peruvians debated classic Enlightenment themes such as luxury and consumption, progress and decline, and social hierarchies and sovereignty. Some of these discussions emerged in response to harsh European criticism of Lima's moral order. This was, however, only one of several motivations or reasons. Since the late seventeenth century at least, many Creoles sought to distinguish themselves from the European-born, staking their claim in large part on literary and artistic renditions of the grandeur of Lima and other cities. In addition, people in Lima had expressed concern (or glee) about their city's supposedly sinful ways well before Europeans wrote their reproachful, patronizing condemnations. I show that these debates and discussions in Lima were not just reactions to Europe—they intersected and paralleled them, particularly travelers' insistence about Lima's libertine decadence. At times, Peruvians responded to this discourse; often they were developing their own perspective, building on European social debates as well as Peruvian sensibilities and preoccupations. The earthquake brought these to the surface.

Natural Disasters?

This book also builds on other fields of enquiry. The study of natural disasters has boomed in recent years, as writers have used them to enter normally cloistered areas, to probe mind-sets, and to examine reactions to adversity.[38] Many explanations can be found for this trend. Most simply, earthquakes, hurricanes, floods, droughts, and other catastrophes continue to devastate and make headlines. While I was writing this, the tsunami of December 2004 ravaged Southeast Asia. Scenes of people being dragged out to sea and through towns that suddenly ceased to exist captivated the world. Eight months later, the Katrina hurricane showed us a side of the United States that the media rarely portray, the poor, and brought into light a theme stressed in much of the literature, including this book: the ability (or inability in the case of Katrina) of the state to respond to disasters. Governmental reactions serve as a revealing test of a government's powers and its relationship with the governed, and the fallout from these efforts often radically transforms political arrangements. Regimes throughout history have fallen because of their failure during and after disasters, and these events have changed societies in profound ways.

The Southeast Asia tsunami and Hurricane Katrina confirm that distant countries, usually impoverished areas, often gain the attention of the U.S. media only during a catastrophe. In fact, the seemingly secure, regulated life of much of the first world makes natural disasters even more dreadful and enthralling. The fascination with disasters as sudden jolts to faith in progress and order dates from the Enlightenment (with precedents going back thousands of years). The Lisbon earthquake prompted Voltaire to question in *Candide* and "Poem on the Lisbon Disaster" the notion of the progressive control of nature and the optimism ("the best of all possible worlds") espoused by Alexander Pope and G. W. Leibniz among others.[39] It also ushered in a drastic rebuilding of Lisbon, under the leadership of the Marquis of Pombal. Occurring nine years before Lisbon, the Lima earthquake and tsunami offer wonderful grounds for comparison.

Organization of the Book

In chapter 2 I examine how people reacted to and understood the catastrophe. While a few writers proposed scientific explanations, most believed it was caused by God's wrath. The chapter focuses on a panic prompted by visionary nuns whose premonitions indicated that the earthquake and tsunami were just the beginning—further, more severe divine punishment was imminent. Their premonitions and panic illustrate how people envisioned and experienced the earthquake, interpretations which shaped the city's rebuilding. In chapter 3 I outline the development of Lima from its founding by Francisco Pizarro in 1535 until October 1746, particularly the question of how this precisely planned city became a teeming, multiracial metropolis. I also examine the horrors and chaos of the hours and days following the earthquake.

The earthquake destroyed churches and major buildings, damaged food and water supplies, and suspended normal social codes. In chapter 4 I review the urgent efforts by Viceroy Manso to impose order and to rebuild the city. In chapter 5 I focus on the battles between the viceroy and the upper classes, a struggle that epitomizes the obstacles to imposing reform.

20   At the heart of these confrontations lay contending notions of order and propriety. Viceroy Manso blamed the garish ways of the Lima elite not only for his difficulties in creating a more manageable, rational city but, at one point, for the disaster itself. In his eyes, their ostentation and immorality prompted God's wrath. The Limeños disagreed both with this interpretation as well as with his efforts to change the city's architecture. Debates about and within the Church, both among the regular mendicant orders and the seculars, are the subject of chapter 6.[40] For the viceroy, the calamity was an opportunity to weaken the presence of the Church, part of the eighteenth-century secularization campaign. The Church fought back energetically, stressing the need for its services in this time of destitution and turmoil. The struggle over the role of the Church moved back and forth from material issues—the Church was a major property owner and lender—to moral issues such as indecency and piety.

Many pointed their fingers at one group in particular as the cause of Lima's supposed moral demise and resulting divine anger: women. Ever since Lima's founding, critics had harangued the city's women for their immoral dress, particularly the covered *tapadas*, and their active social life. In chapter 7 I explore the campaign by the Church and state for new dress codes and for changes in the residents' behavior. Although many residents blamed women, the implementing of these changes proved difficult. I discuss the reactions of the lower class to the earthquake and its chaotic aftermath in the following chapter. A crime wave, a conspiracy in Lima, and a violent uprising in the nearby Andean province of Huarochirí petrified many people in Lima, especially the authorities, and brought to the surface debates about the loyalty and trustworthiness of Afro-Peruvians and Indians. These events not only highlight racial thought and policy, but also demonstrate that the dark-skinned lower classes had very different ideas about the meaning of the earthquake and about what Lima should become. In the epilogue I consider the implications of the earthquake and the ideological and political battles it prompted in Peru in the eighteenth century and beyond.

Balls of Fire: Premonitions
and the Destruction of Lima

You only I have known
Of all the families of the earth;
Therefore I will punish you
For all your iniquities.

Is a trumpet blown in a city
And the people are not afraid?
Does disaster fall a city,
Unless the Lord has done it?

Surely the Lord God does
Nothing,
Without revealing his secret
To his servants the prophets.

The lion has roared
Who will not fear?
The Lord God has spoken
Who can but prophesy?

AMOS, book 3

Two

José Llano Zapata provided lucid summaries of reactions to the earthquake. He noted that people could not speak because of their shock, declaring that "it wasn't life that we were living but death that we were passing through." He depicted the horrid rumbles of aftershocks; the desperate pleas for help; the "ridiculous clothes" that people were reduced to wearing; and sobs, cries, shrieks, sighs, moans, and groans. He chronicled the panic, disbelief, agony, and mourning that gripped the city.[1]

Llano Zapata also developed his ideas about seismology. In the wake of the devastating Lisbon earthquake of 1755, he wrote a report to King Ferdinand VI of Spain in which he summarized his ideas about the causes of earthquakes and possible preventative measures. He contended that subterranean fires in large caverns prompted massive winds and rising air pressure that shook the ground, a view proposed by Nicolas Lémery and Martin Lister, distinguished European scientists, and developed by Georges-Louis Leclerc de Buffon in his *Histoire naturelle* (1749). In this period, two schools of thought clashed: one, followed by Llano Zapata, emphasized underground fires and air pressure, and the other contended that water seeped underground, weakening the earth's shell and prompting tumultuous changes.[2]

Whereas Llano Zapata proposed natural causes for the Lima calamity, the vast majority saw it as a sign of the wrath of God. They evoked and in many cases brought into the streets the city's hallowed group of saints and religious images. The praying, processions, and nonstop masses in the days following the tragedy supported the observation that earthquakes were "collaborators with the Inquisition," as they persuaded seemingly everyone to decry the city's sinful ways.[3] Guilt and fear about the prospect of further divine wrath due to Lima's errant behavior paralyzed much of the population. Some took consolation, however, in the belief that the punishment could be prevented if they amended their sinful ways. Divine, rather than natural, explanations of earthquakes have their advantages.

The anguish over the earthquake continued for more than a decade, illuminating differing notions of why God was angry at the City of Kings. The fact that the Lima population ascribed the earthquake to God's wrath does not mean, however, that they agreed on the causes or solution to this divine predicament. People disagreed deeply and publicly about why God was angry and how to appease him, blaming a variety of groups: women, the upper classes, the Church itself, and others. To the chagrin of reformers, Lima reacted in utterly baroque fashion.

Interpretations of earthquakes, however, cannot be neatly divided between those who allege natural causes and those who interpret them as divine acts. Although in the 1750s Immanuel Kant would ridicule those seeking divine explanations—declaring that "we stand with our feet on the cause"—most mid-eighteenth-century writers combined divine and natural explanations.[4] In the aftermath of the Lisbon earthquake, for example, which also damaged Seville and other parts of southern Spain, Father Josef Cevallos argued that while all earthquakes are God's work—as is everything in the natural world—only some were providential punishments. He thus claimed that Lisbon and Seville had not been castigated for their sinful ways; the earthquake was "entirely natural."[5] Yet in Lima, few ascribed the catastrophe to natural causes, looking instead to heaven. Anguish and debate about the city's decadent ways and the possibility of divine wrath marked the decade or so after the catastrophe, shaping the understanding and implementation of emergency measures and rebuilding plans.

Cloistered Voices

On November 7, 1756, ten years and ten days after the earthquake, the Franciscan priest Joaquín Parra gave mass in his order's main church, San Francisco. The first Sunday of each month was dedicated to the Sacred Heart of Christ and usually attracted a large and prominent crowd. Among those present were Mateo de Amusquíbar, the head of the Peruvian Inquisition, and the eminent lawyer Manuel de Silva y la Banda. Father Parra stunned the audience and prompted a citywide panic and years of judicial wrangling by relating the premonitions of a small group of nuns and other religious women. All had a common theme: because of its inhabitants' licentious ways and disregard for previous warnings, the City of Kings would soon be the victim of God's wrath in the form of balls of fire falling from the sky. Although forewarned, few if any would survive the flames. While spreading the blame widely, the nuns targeted the failings of the religious community, particularly the orders, and the sinful customs of the city. The earthquake of 1746 was seen as an unheeded warning, a staggering first blow. News about the sermon spread through the city's well-developed rumor and gossip circuits, bringing to the surface profound fears shared by most of the population. Father Parra himself became the subject of an extended inquiry, as the Inquisition, the archbishop, and the Franciscans fought over who should try him for disseminating these possibly heretical visions.

Parra's trials are an enlightening entryway into the hidden struggles among these institutions. The inquisitor Amusquíbar locked horns with the irascible archbishop, Pedro Antonio de Barroeta. The Franciscans, in

24 turn, gingerly attempted to keep the investigation internal and thus shield Father Parra from the judicial arms of the Inquisition and the archbishopric. Much more interesting, however, are the premonitions themselves and the panic they prompted. The Inquisition records include detailed accounts of both the nuns' painful experience of these visions and their chilling content. Each woman envisioned different forms of God's wrath, including various types of fireballs, fire-breathing bulls, and wretched demons who obscenely taunted women. Some also encountered a mournful Jesus walking the streets of Lima as well as talking statues and images and messages in the sky. Their visions display both immediate obsessions as well as more enduring fears and nightmares.

The premonitions defined a decade-long cycle that began with the severe and obvious warning of the earthquake of 1746 and would end with even more devastating catastrophes. Within this cycle, the visions included references to actual events, such as revolts that had taken place in Lima and in the nearby Andes in 1750, the ongoing Juan Santos Atahualpa uprising in the jungle to the east, and, across the Atlantic, the Lisbon earthquake that had taken place on November 1, 1755, a year before Parra's mass. Yet the nuns' accounts also reflected longer-term concerns or patterns. The nuns shared with many of the city's residents the belief that Lima had been hexed since the late seventeenth century. A previous earthquake, in 1687, subsequent agricultural decline (what was called sterility of the fields), an epidemic in 1718–23 that killed over two hundred thousand people, and intermittent pirate attacks were also signs of God's rising anger with the City of Kings.

From the 1680s to the 1750s discussions about Lima's sinful ways were intertwined with discussions of the city's decline. It lost its political hegemony in South America with the creation of the New Granada (1739) and, subsequently, Río de la Plata viceroyalties (1776), while the emergence of Atlantic ports such as Buenos Aires threatened Callao. Its population had grown slowly in the eighteenth century. Economic and political worries surfaced in the premonition panics. While modern analysts might see the premonitions and widespread fear as a manifestation of the concerns about the waning position of the city and a display of baroque religiosity, contemporaries had the opposite explanation. They blamed the city's social and political stagnation and feared the imminent destruction of its sinful ways.

The debates over the premonitions transport modern readers into the world of the cloistered nuns and the city's deep religious fervor. It is deliciously ironic that nuns—women who cloistered themselves or retired from and minimized communication with the mundane world—provide these insights. While the voices of the nuns are filtered—the testimonies are almost all from their spiritual fathers, or confessors—their premonitions and the deep concern about the implications of what they were saying for the safety of the city offer uniquely vivid testimony on eighteenth-century Lima. They bring to the fore the misgivings about the weakening division between sacred and mundane spaces.

Sins, Saints, and Earthquakes

In 1600, four future saints lived in Lima: Santo Toribio Alfonso de Mogrovejo (1538–1606, archbishop from 1581 to 1606, canonized in 1726); San Francisco Solano (1549–1610, also canonized in 1726); San Martín de Porras (1579–1639, not canonized until 1962); and Santa Rosa de Lima (1586–1617), who had the distinction of becoming the first American-born saint in 1672 and the "principal patroness of the Americas, Philippines, and Indies."[6] San Juan Macías (1585–1645, canonized in 1975) arrived in Lima a few years later. In the seventeenth century, the city also housed many candidates to sainthood, including the Mercedarian Pedro Urraca (1583–1657), who reportedly ran through a wall to escape the devil dressed as a woman, the Indian Nicolás Ayllón (1632–77), and the mystic Ursula de Jesús (1605–66). These three were not canonized, but they plied their religiosity in Lima and the hinterlands, gaining devoted followings both before and after their deaths.[7] Peru produced forty candidates for canonization in the seventeenth century, a dozen of the cases reaching Rome.[8] The link between the city's religiosity and its seismic woes makes saints and disasters inseparable in Lima.[9]

Solano, a Franciscan born in Spain, was renowned for his street preaching. In December 1604 he beseeched Limeños to change their sinful ways, cautioning that "the city is so full of souls with vices and sins that it has reached the point that if God's ire is not placated, it will have to be destroyed with the three punishments that Saint John refers to in his Canon."[10] The sermon prompted a multitude of devotees immediately to beg for mercy and flagellate themselves. The city's churches and confessionals overflowed

1 Santa Rosa Venerated
by Indians, Blacks, and
Mestizos. *Source:* Ramón
Mujica, *Rosa limensis*, 61.
Anonymous, Eighteenth
Century, Convento de los
Descalzos, Lima.

that evening. One woman, Isabel de Flores, later known as Rosa de Santa
María, or, more commonly, as Santa Rosa de Lima, a member of the Third
Order of the Dominicans (and thus not a nun), took Solano's preaching to
heart. She increased her already rigorous flagellations to the point that her
family wondered whether she would survive. Over time, Santa Rosa de Lima
was attributed with saving the city, and her bones and other relics were
brought out after the earthquakes of 1687 and 1746. Luis Antonio Oviedo y
Herrera's epic poem, *Vida de la esclarecida virgen Santa Rosa de Santa María* . . .
(1711) lauded her protection: "He who gives law to all laws / And boasts of
bringing armies down / will not allow them to destroy the City of Kings, /
For it has Rosa as its Star and crown."[11] Santa Rosa would have a prominent
place in the nuns' premonitions.[12]

Devotion to an image called El Señor de los Milagros, which still inspires
processions involving hundreds of thousands, was also inextricably tied to
earthquakes. In 1650, an Angolan slave (or mulatto) painted the image of
Christ on the crucifix in some slave quarters in Pachacamilla, in the west-

ern part of the city. Unlike the buildings around it, the painting survived an earthquake on November 13, 1655. Its miraculous nature was confirmed a decade later when authorities, presumably concerned about the boisterous reverence of its largely African and Afro-Peruvian devotees, demanded that it be whitewashed. In carrying out the order, one painter fainted, the next found himself paralyzed, and a third refused. The sun then burst out of the clouds, and the sunshine was followed by rain, extremely unusual for Lima. The image survived.[13] El Señor de los Milagros remained one of many earthquake saints in colonial Lima. Survivors in October 1746 also rallied around the images of Nuestra Señora de las Lágrimas (Our Lady of the Tears) and Nuestra Señora del Aviso (Our Lady of the Warning), both deemed patrons of earthquakes. Subsequently, the Apostles Saint Simon and Saint Judas (whose feast day is October 28) became additional patrons, and people turned to other images as well.[14]

Saint Francisco Solano's sermon of 1604 indicates the long history of equating Lima's earthquakes with God's displeasure. A Franciscan account of the earthquake in 1687 presents more evidence. It describes how God had revealed to a nun, Madre Angela, his will to obliterate ("acabar de una vez") Lima because of its continual offenses. As in 1756, the testimony is from Madre Angela's confessor, who passed it on to Father Galindo, a Mercedarian. It stressed four offenses: the injustices of "judges, their ministers, and the powerful" against the poor in exploiting and belittling them; profanity and vanity in men's and women's dress and houses in marked contrast to the "naked and unadorned temples"; the greed for property and honors, which prompted usury and tricks by laypersons and clergy alike, without respect for the Church and the threat of excommunication; and the sin of lust or lechery, "not only [of] men with women but men with men and women with women," forgetting completely about "God's severe justice and punishment."[15] Another account described how multitudes witnessed an image of the Virgin of the Candelaria crying repeatedly in July 1687, deeming this a sign of an imminent earthquake, which in fact occurred on October 20. In response to the catastrophe, survivors took this image as well as the relics of Santa Rosa and of the Jesuit Fray Francisco del Castillo (1615–73) into the streets to placate God's wrath.[16]

Ever since Lima's founding in 1535, earthquakes, sins, and saints were so intertwined that much of what occurred in 1746 and 1755 seems almost timeless, not confined to that period but rather possible in the sixteenth,

2 San Francisco Solano
Preaching in the Plaza Mayor.
Source: Ramón Mujica, ed.,
Barroco en el Perú, 324.
Anonymous, Eighteenth
Century, Convento
de San Francisco.

seventeenth, or eighteenth centuries and beyond. Collective hysteria and
public pleas for penitence and redemption were common in this pious city,
which seemed to have more than its share of natural disasters. In 1664–65,
for example, anxious Lima inhabitants interpreted comets as signs of impending divine punishment.[17] The visions and premonitions in 1755 formed
part of a perceived cycle of crises dating from the late seventeenth century.
Luis Miguel Glave deems 1680–93 the high point of "baroque fatalism" in
Peru, listing a shocking array of epidemics, famine, earthquakes, and other
maladies.[18] In the late seventeenth century, authorities finished the construction of a wall surrounding the city. It embodied the growing anxieties
of the residents, or at least the authorities, and the splendor and fears of baroque Lima.[19] In the same year that the wall was completed, 1687, a strong
earthquake struck Lima. Writers in the eighteenth century, echoed in the
twentieth, blamed the earthquake for Lima's agricultural decline, claiming it had sterilized the land and forced open the door to Chilean competition, particularly for wheat. Eighteenth-century Lima residents experi-

enced other signs of crisis, decline, and, for many, divine ire. The epidemic of 1718–23 killed seventy-two thousand people just in the archdiocese of Lima, British ships attacked the coast in the early 1740s, rebellions began in the hinterland, and Lima's political and economic weight vis-à-vis Mexico and its South American competitors declined.[20] Apocalyptic thought and stern Counter-Reformation texts and evangelization reverberated in Lima, deepening the city's anguish and the residents' search for another sign of God's anger.

At the heart of the nun's premonitions was the decades-long debate about the sinful ways of Lima's inhabitants. This was the overwhelming message of their visions—that God had sent a severe warning in 1746 and was soon to inflict a much greater punishment. More than a manifestation of Lima's seeming political and economic decline, their visions focused on divine anger and the need for rapid redemption. Sermons and paintings that stressed the apocalyptic beliefs of Saint Augustine and Joachim of Fiora, both saints deeply rooted in the Americas, helped nourish these concerns about the end of the world.[21]

A unique source sheds light on the depth and meaning of the fear of God's wrath that people in this period felt. In the 1750s, a distinguished widow, Doña María Fernández de Córdoba y Sande, founded a House of Spiritual Exercise for illustrious women, which was managed by the Jesuits. She had earlier been instrumental in the creation of the Nazarene Carmelite monastery.[22] Until Fernández de Córdoba did this good deed, women had no such house and were forced to return home after a few hours of spiritual exercises in a church or convent. Two such houses had existed for men, the San Antonio Abad Noviciate, destroyed along with its rich art collection in the earthquake of 1746, and San Bernardo on the outskirts of the city. At the novitiate, a distinguished group of men stayed the night once a month to detach themselves from their mundane affairs. They performed acts of contrition, humility, and devotion, including flagellating one another and themselves and kissing the ground. Just as important as the modest meals and rigorous praying were the omnipresent reminders of the battle between God and the devil on the walls in the form of poems and paintings.[23]

Inaugurated in 1751 one block from the Jesuits' main school, San Pablo, the Women's House of Spiritual Exercise promoted spirituality and Christian mores not only through a rigorous regime of prayers and ascetic behavior, but also through visual reminders. Poetry and paintings covered

30   virtually every bit of wall space. Above the entryway was lettering that read, "Puerto al Cielo," or "entryway to Heaven." The entry hall had two large paintings, one an idyllic scene of people dancing as the devil enticed them toward hell and a Jesuit and a Capuchin tried to detain their descent. Below was the following poem:

Tente hombre, no te arrojes	Stop yourself, don't throw yourself away
A unos males tan inmensos,	into such immense evils
Mira, que si en ellos caes	Look, if you fall into them
No ay remedio, no ay remedio	There is no remedy, there is no remedy
Mira bien, a donde vas	Look carefully where you are going
Miralo bien, no seas necio	Look carefully, don't be stubborn
Y ten lastima de ti	And have pity on yourself
Que ahora ignoras lo que es fuego	Because you don't know what fire is
Al presente, Dios te espera	God now awaits you
Y piadoso te da tiempo:	And kindly gives you time
Si lloras ahora tus culpas	If you decry your sins
Subiras gozoso al Cielo	You will joyously climb up to heaven

The other painting showed a Jesuit sadly contemplating spreading flames. The painting and the poem below it represent the end of the world.[24] Beyond the entrance, room after room displayed large paintings with poetry about the devil's temptations, Jesus' suffering, and the rocky road to salvation. Many depict the wretched death of sinners. For example, a painting in the first patio portrayed two demons taking the soul of a sinner and throwing it into hell. The poem below it began,

La muerte del pecador	The death of a sinner
Aqui la ves retratada	Here you see portrayed
Si tanto asombra pintada	If it scares you so painted
En la experiencia, que horror!	In real life, how dreadful!

The paintings, more than 180 in all, portrayed dozens of saints, the sacred heart of Jesus, various torments, and scene after scene of the eternal horrors of the path taken by sinners.[25] The nuns of Lima had been trained in this type of devout, forbidding world in which reminders of the entrapments of the devil and God's punishment were omnipresent. In their dreams, visions, and premonitions, they lived many of the woeful scenes depicted in the Women's Spiritual House.

Women and the Franciscans

Since the Middle Ages, many believed that women had special communication powers and embodied true Christian piety. Saints such as Catherine
of Siena (1347–80) and Teresa of Avila (1515–82) were venerated in Europe
and became important figures in the Americas as well. With the Counter-
Reformation, the proliferation of the tales of saints and the fervent battles
against the Protestant north had further encouraged a female religiosity
that emphasized mystical experiences such as revelations and premonitions. Pierre Chaunu refers to a "feminization" of Counter-Reformation
religiosity.[26] Since the Council of Trent (1543–63), however, the Catholic
Church had also attempted to control female mysticism, questioning medieval notions of women's particular sensitivity to God's message and discouraging nuns' and other women's physical, almost sensual, experience
of the Lord.[27]

Female aesthetes — nuns, beatas, *alumbradas*, and others — had constituted a key element of Lima's population since its founding and were venerated by many and intermittently challenged by the Inquisition.[28] In the
eighteenth century, the Bourbon regalist program revived the campaign
against them. The divergent notions of female religiosity clashed in the
anguish and trials over the premonitions of 1755. Many of the testimonies
referred to the belief that women had a special gift and thus their warnings
should be heeded. They shed light on the heterodoxy of female religiosity,
which thrived in part because it took place offstage, in convents, worship
houses, and processions, and was nurtured by popular culture. Archbishop
Barroeta, however, dismissed this view, claiming the visions were a mere
reflection of women's weakness and simplemindedness. He understood
female mysticism as an unfortunate remnant of baroque and lower-class
religious practices that needed to be extirpated.

Church authorities were cautiously skeptical and thus demanded elaborate investigations into the veracity of the visions and proof that they were
divine and confirmed orthodox belief. Starting in the fifteenth century, officials in Spain and in Italy had developed an elaborate system to authen-
ticate the validity of revelations and visions: the discernment of spirits.
Alumbradas and others who claimed to have direct contact with the divine
were subject to the Inquisition, which searched for signs of diabolical influence and probed the visions and premonitions. The panic in 1755 prompted
such an investigation.[29]

3 Franciscan Friar, by Baltazar Jaime Martínez de Compañón. *Source:* Biblioteca del Palacio Real, Madrid. "Trujillo del Perú," tomo 1, folio 71.

In order to understand piety in Lima in this period, Father Parra's order, the Franciscans, must be taken into account. The Franciscans had assumed an increasingly important role in the missions in Europe and the Americas since the Council of Trent, particularly after the creation in 1622 of the congregation for propagating the faith, De Propaganda Fide. Moreover, since the end of the Thirty Years' War in 1648, a more vivid, theatrical style of evangelization had been used in poor, rural areas of Europe. In his study of these missions, Louis Chatellier refers to this baroque age as one of "divine fervor, apostolic zeal and prophetic enthusiasm."[30]

In the eighteenth century, the Franciscans shook up the languid state of evangelization in Peru, preaching in the streets and outside of the cities and emphasizing in explicit, physical ways the need to heed God's warnings. In 1708, Friar Francisco de San José arrived in Lima from Mexico and began "preaching penitence in all of its streets and plazas to massive crowds."[31] The Franciscans fostered "popular missions" sponsored by the Propaganda Fide in Rome. In 1725, they founded the Ocopa hospice in the Mantaro Valley to the east of Lima, an institution that was converted into an apostolic college in 1757.[32] Horrified by the fallen state of Catholicism and the sinful behavior of the viceroyalty's population, particularly its women, the Franciscans preached energetically and effectively throughout Peru. The Cathedral chapter lauded their accomplishments in Lima:

> The effects of their useful and fervent missions in Lima can be seen in the spiritual fruit that they have harvested. Penitent, unadorned ["desnudo"] people, without social distinction—the Nobility, the plebe, and particularly the Religious communities, regular and secular—have been present at numerous blood processions that the Franciscans have led; it was difficult to count the number of penitents and people in these processions, because no one in this city excused himself, all attended with exemplary devotion.[33]

Another section of the same report credited their procession and public preaching for "reforming profane dress, scandalous songs, and dishonest dances" and preventing robberies, adultery, and other sins. After the earthquake, the Franciscans preached tirelessly for months in the streets.

The Franciscans' efforts in Cuzco in 1739 highlight their highly physical and theatrical form of preaching and the possible impact this had on the Lima visionaries. Four Franciscans, including Friar José de San Antonio, who led the order's moralizing campaigns of the era, entered Cuzco on January 8, 1739, singing and preaching, crucifix in hand. They held mass in the cathedral as well as in the San Francisco church, exhorting the populace to pay heed. The following day, Father San Antonio burnt his arm in the midst of mass to shock his audience. In subsequent days, he brought a skeleton to the pulpit to emphasize his message of a coming plague, hung three well-lit skeletons in a funeral mass, and displayed an image of the devil. He preached in the streets of Cuzco, pointing out sinners, offering forgiveness, threatening those who participated in carnivalesque activities, and throwing himself on the ground to beg for forgiveness. The Franciscans' traveling evangelical group—their next stop was Potosí—broke with the staid nature of much contemporary religious ritual, moving their unusually long masses outside and incorporating props that included their own flagellated bodies. They continually stressed the urgent need for repentance.[34] Although the trials of the nuns included priests from several orders, Father Parra himself as well as some of the nuns and the other spiritual fathers were Franciscans. Their physical, denunciatory preaching style defined the nuns' world.

34

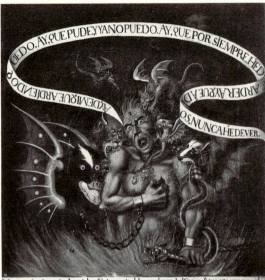

Caption within the image:

Dolores, ansias sin cuento Aqueste horrible tormento, Hoguera, hornos, bolcanes, A tu gusto amargas y cele
bolcanes, garfios, cadenas, Con la gran pena de daño, Bronses, yerros abrasa, dos, Devíboras y drágones,
Aunque son crueles penas No Serán penas de un año, Todos son fuegos pintados, Sapos, Sierpes, y escorpiones
No son el mayor tormento Siglos duraran Sin cuento Con las llamas Infernales, Te dataran verdugos crueles,
No verá Dios ni un momento Sin alivio de un momento Los torpes, y Sensuales, Side pen sarlo te dueles,
Esta es la pena sin par; Eternamente he de estar, A qui rabiando han de estar, Como lo po dras pasar,
en aquesta obscura Carcel Y en el fuego de este Ynfierno Yenã que este horrible Fuego Pue Con Fuego del yinfierno
Sin Dios, y Sin fin penar. Para Siempre He de rabiar. Para Siempre han de penar, PorfuerSa lo has de tragar.

4 Condemned to Hell.
Un condenado en el
infierno. Source: Ramón
Mujica, ed.,
Barroco en el Perú, 245.
Anonymous, Escuela
Cuzqueña, Eighteenth
Century, Convento de
la Merced, Cuzco.

Whom to Blame?

The news about Parra's shocking sermon disseminated quickly throughout the city. For some, it was a terrifying novelty; for others, it confirmed
rumors about premonitions and signs of God's ire. One testimony gives
insight into how the information spread: "Full of very Christian fears,
Manuel de Silva, being very persuaded and thus telling everything to everyone in his house, caused his wife great consternation, not shielding it from
her despite the fact that she was very ill, and the news reached her very extensive family and from there to others, so that by that evening there was
not a person who had not learned the news, affecting everyone differently
according to the state of his or her conscience."[35] Religious and secular authorities acted quickly, owing in part to their concern about the panic and
the threatened destruction of Lima and in part to their interest in avoiding
blame and assuring that their institution judged Parra.

The following morning, Archbishop Barroeta sent two clerks to sum-
mon Parra. Barroeta was not in Lima on the day of the mass and would

later be criticized for acting slowly. He was a controversial figure. Born in Ezcaray (La Rioja, Spain) in 1701, he arrived in Peru in 1748 and was archbishop until 1757. He fought incessantly with Viceroy Manso de Velasco and his inner circle, writing hundreds of inflammatory memos to Madrid. The viceroy bitterly noted that Barroeta had conflicts with "almost all the Tribunals, and he filled the city with edicts and mandates, greatly confusing the residents."[36] Part of the conflict was personal—Barroeta was a confrontational character who believed that Manso and his followers had slighted him ever since his arrival in Lima. He complained endlessly about breaches of etiquette (how he was greeted, where he was seated at receptions, etc.) and attacked Manso's supporters with shockingly personal insinuations about their dark-skinned lovers, black ancestors, and leprosy.[37] On the day of his departure, the bells in Lima's dozens of churches rang incessantly for five hours, a noisy celebration that no doubt irritated Barroeta, who had tried for more than a decade to tame the noisy City of Kings.[38]

Beyond his cantankerous nature, Barroeta's countless written complaints also demonstrate his role as a stern reformer of the Church. With the same vigor with which he took on the viceroy and the Inquisition, he battled the heterodox nature of Peruvian Catholicism, attempting to rein in the orders and homogenize religious practices. He campaigned against raucous processions and other religious celebrations, baroque sermons, profane music, sensual festivities, and other "excesses."[39]

The archbishop's clerks found Parra on their second trip from the Cathedral to San Francisco, and Barroeta interrogated him that same day. He was accused of spreading false and dangerous revelations or rumors and thus prompting a panic. This accusation hinged on whether the nuns and their premonitions were trustworthy, the focus of the investigation. Barroeta demanded to know the names of the visionary nuns. Parra was initially evasive about the identity of the religious women, invoking the secrecy of the confessional, from which much of the information he had shared in his sermon had been gleaned.

From the beginning, his defense rested on three points. First, he had consulted with "distinguished people," including Barroeta and the inquisitor Amusquíbar, before the mass. Barroeta did not deny this but, as will be seen below, shifted the blame to Amusquíbar. Second, Parra explained that he was not "making public" [publicar] or "breaking the news" about the premonitions but instead simply commenting on something quite well

36   known and much discussed in order to calm the nerves of the people. In other words, he was not the first person to bring the public's attention to the revelations. Parra developed this linguistic self-defense, contending that he did not preach or advocate ["predicar"], but rather was simply "spreading the news" [notiziar, hazer saber].[40] He insisted that before his mass "rumors were spreading in the city about several punishments."[41] According to Parra, therefore, he had not prompted the commotion—it had already existed, and he was attempting to calm it. For example, he asserted that some women were falsely claiming to have had premonitions and that he was trying to stem this rising tide of copycat visions.[42] Other independent testimonies confirmed that rumors were spreading in the weeks before Parra's sermon. In noting his skepticism about a woman who claimed to have had premonitions about the earthquake of 1746 as well as the catastrophe that Parra and others now predicted, Friar Juan Garro, a Franciscan, observed, "This year rumors were more widespread than ever, and it might be that hearing them would have enlivened her imagination."[43]

Finally, Parra and other priests who spoke about the premonitions justified their actions in biblical terms, contending that they were simply transmitting God's will. Parra cited Saint Paul ("Do not quench the Spirit. Do not despise the words of prophets, but test everything; hold fast to what is good") and chapter 3 of the book of Amos to support the notion that God did not punish his kingdom without a warning. Parra as well as his Franciscan brother Garro cited textually the lines from Amos: "Surely the Lord God does/Nothing,/Without revealing his secret/To his servants the prophets." Their reading of Jeremiah, chapter 5, made them wonder whether fire might be a mere symbol and that another form of punishment such as the plague was what God intended for Lima.[44] Parra cited the Bible to support his announcement of the premonitions. He and the other priests believed God sent warnings before destruction; they also understood from their readings of the Bible that the punishment would be gruesome.

On November 16, nine days after the offending sermon, Barroeta excommunicated Parra for his act and for his refusal to provide the names of his sources for the sermon. He continued to interrogate him into early 1757. The Franciscans refused to recognize Barroeta's jurisdiction and battled against the archbishop. The real dispute, however, was between Barroeta and Amusquíbar. The archbishop accused the inquisitor of being "the author or at least the principal promoter of the revelations, which prompted great fear in the city, as well as much censurable behavior, in light of the fact that someone of such rank and office would find himself mixed up in such flippancy ["ligereza"] and deeds of less reflexive people, above all nuns and beatas, who for their gender and weak condition, are so prone to understanding any dream or fantasy as revelations."[45] Barroeta accused Amusquíbar of frequenting the convents and becoming too close to Sor Andrea, a Capuchin nun "very tempted by everything to do with Revelations."[46] Elsewhere, he asked whether Amusquíbar was the "spiritual son" of Parra "or at least his intimate confidante and friend."[47]

The Inquisition looked into these accusations, finding that Amusquíbar as well as Father Gregorio Zapata had visited the Jesus, Maria, José convent of the Capuchins and learned about Sor Andrea's visions of Lima burning. Barroeta claimed they had visited her before Parra's mass, passing secret papers and fostering rumors. They denied these charges, contending that they had visited the convent after the mass in order to find out more about the premonitions.[48] Once again, Barroeta's battles combine personal with institutional struggles. Barroeta clearly disliked Amusquíbar and believed he had been taken in by foolish fantasies. Yet the archbishop was also locked in battle with the Inquisition as an institution over jurisdictional disputes. Throughout Spanish America, archbishops and the Inquisition fought over the extent of the tribunal's control of "causas de fe." Barroeta battled particularly hard, publishing edicts that forced all ecclesiastics, even the inquisitor, to receive his permission in order to take confession. He discouraged them from visiting monasteries without this document.[49] He also limited the inquisitor's right to name officials. In essence, Barroeta attacked the autonomy of the Inquisition from the archbishop's office. The court of Fernando VI, as part of its attempt to rein in the Inquisition, backed Barroeta on both accounts.[50] On the other hand, the Inquisition believed the archbishop was overstepping his authority and seconded the charge of the Franciscans that he was merely attempting to cover up his ineptitude in the premonition panic by pursuing these jurisdictional issues. The Franciscans also joined in the accusations that Barroeta himself led an overly lavish lifestyle. Skirmishes between the two built up until they came to a head at the Parra trial.[51]

While acknowledging the constant sniping between Barroeta and Amusquíbar, the formal inquiries focused on whether the premonitions themselves were trustworthy or fantastic and induced by rumor. A finding of trustworthiness would justify Parra's declarations. Parra abandoned his initial tactic of remaining silent and in the end gave lengthy testimony about his spiritual daughter (the nun whose religious life he oversaw) and also revealed the names of the confessors, who then testified. The testimony is detailed but indirect—the nuns themselves rarely talk (Parra's nun does at one point), only their confessors. The reliability of such testimony is a question of debate, but the trial records here support the view that the confessors and nuns could develop strong relationships and that the testimony of the confessors could reflect the nuns' point of view. The priests professed their compassion for and understanding of the nuns and, as we will see, opened up through their testimony the nuns' usually closed or cloistered physical and mental worlds.[52]

God Is Angry: Ashes as Punishment for Grave Sins

After initial denials, Parra admitted that one of the nuns with premonitions was his own spiritual daughter. His testimony as well as that of others emphasized her extreme spirituality and the painful suffering her visions caused her, qualities that added credence to her visions. She was about thirty-five years old, a *doncella*, or unmarried virgin, from a good family. She had vowed chastity at nine and lived a simple, selfless life in an unnamed convent. She slept little, prayed more than three hours a night, and left the convent only for mass or a religious duty. One of her examiners, the Augustinian friar Diego de Aragón, mentioned that ten years earlier the devil had tried to tempt her ("against her chastity, with horrendous propositions, against the faith") but that she had pledged herself to the image of Our Lady of the Rosary and no longer suffered such temptations. Another priest said he had never met such a pure soul, a compliment that left her worried that she would become vain.[53]

On August 14, 1756, the eve of the Assumption of the Virgin, the nun dreamed that God threw three flaming lances or arrows at each house in Lima "burning them all, leaving them in ashes as punishment for the grave sins committed, especially by members of the secular and regular ecclesiastic communities, including nuns." She woke up soaked in tears. The vision of Lima burning returned every time she prayed. She saw male and female saints pleading for Lima, including Saint Teresa and Saint Catherine of Siena, who "always accompanied her." She believed that the divine pun-

5 Santiago Matamoros, the Moorslayer, and Christ with Three Lances. *Source:* Ramón Mujica, ed., *Barroco en el Perú*, 228, Anonymous, Escuela Cuzqeña, Eighteenth Century, Private Collection.

ishment would occur on the eve of a celebration for the Virgin Mary, so her fears increased around these dates. After a "brother of hers, a theologian and a mystic himself," advised her to "empty her interior" and tell everything to her abbess or confessor, she decided to confide in Friar Parra. She worried, however, that she would end up in the Inquisition for being a "witch or delusional [ilusa]."[54]

This nun's core premonition, fire falling on Lima for the sins of the Church, is found in virtually all of the other religious women's visions, which, however, varied greatly in other details. Fire is, of course, a central Christian symbol. Passages from the New and Old Testaments declare that fire would be used in the final judgment of the Lord and in the punishment of the damned. The priests involved in this case joined the centuries-long debate about whether the fire was metaphorical or not. Although the prevalence in Lima of adobe and brick rather than wood houses meant that fire was not the grave danger it was in other cities, it nevertheless occupied a prominent place in the city's mentality. For example, Ana María Pérez, a

40 mulatta friend of Santa Rosa, noted how "God had wanted to bury this city in flaming spears [palos] for its sins but thanks to her [Santa Rosa] and another of the Lord's servants he had not done it."[55] The image of Christ with three lances was used extensively in colonial Lima.[56]

After hearing the nun's confession, Parra met with a fellow Franciscan to ask how he should proceed. The friar told Parra that if she spoke in Latin, her premonitions would be certain. The next day, Parra was flabbergasted when in the midst of her prayers she clearly said, "Iratus est Dominus," (God is Angry).[57] She explained that while praying, "I understood that God was angry, in the interior of my soul I felt a deep fear and at the same time I understood a few words: iratus Dominus and I believed and understood that God was angry."[58] This testimony prompted a spiritual crisis in Parra in turn. As a result, his encounters with this informant and his own revelatory experiences increased. The following day, for example, he suddenly burst out in tears while at the altar, feeling "a sensitive pain in the heart." He spent the night praying with another priest. The following day the nun asked him about his prayers, as though she had been there. Then, on October 31, the nun suddenly had a "grave impulse" to go to the San Francisco Church, where she met Parra. She described her pleas and prayers to God to not punish Lima, convincing Parra that "the revelation was certain, she had too much of a soul to be an alucinada."[59]

The account of the trial tells much more about the methods for evaluating premonitions and visions than the nun herself. Father Aragón examined her to verify whether her visions could be trusted, attempting to determine if she were humble, virtuous, obedient, and consistent in her spiritual life. He also evaluated her for any physical or external cause: "If she had any stomach or head ailment, if she slept little, if she fasted too much, if she mortified herself excessively, if she were prone to dreams, visions, and fear of the demons, if she were frequently tempted by horrible imaginations [sugestiones], if she had ever desired having revelations . . . if she suffered from melancholy, if she cloistered herself and was not prone to conversations, visits, and frequent commerce of people, if she read too many spiritual books, especially those that deal with revelations."[60]

In the end Father Aragón confirmed her proper spirituality, discipline, and distance from negative influences, particularly questionable people and books. He noted that women require more scrutiny because their "simpler nature and susceptibility to impressions" made them prone to revelations and visions. Aragón embodied the cautious ambivalence toward female mysticism of the Counter-Reformation Church described above. Women's nature made them superior recipients of God's messages, yet also made them susceptible to false impressions. The friar supported her, calling for further inquiry. He lauded her humility and benevolence, asserting, "If she ever fools herself it is not her fault, but rather God's providence, who orders it for more humiliation and knowledge."[61]

Friar Aragón also evaluated the nun's premonitions. He used two guidelines to verify them: did they contain elements known only to God and not to the "young woman"? and did the vision or revelation last in her memory? (divine warnings could not be ephemeral).[62] He noted that although choleric humors or some other physical explanation could have provoked the dreams of flaming destruction, the details about the lances and their targets indicated that they were God's determinations. As to the second point, her continual visions and fear in the approaching Virgin's festivals indicated that the premonitions were trustworthy. Even more convincing was her outburst to Parra in Latin. Friar Aragón cited Saint Thomas to argue that it could not have been the work of the devil, whose understanding did not have such great reach. Aragón emphasized her repeated visions in mass, her bond with Parra and other priests, the depth or "penetration" of her prayers, and her discretion in confiding only in her confessor, "admirable" in women, who are generally "talkative and simpleminded." He judged that "God's spirit resides in her" and that she was not "delusional" (ilusa). He finished by noting the similarities between her premonitions and those of the others: "Although the devil can fool this or that person, it is difficult to believe that God would allow him to trick nine." He deemed her visions "frightening."[63] She had, in short, passed Friar Aragón's lengthy "discernment of spirits" test.

Fires and Bulls

The trial also reviewed other women with premonitions: eight nuns, two beatas, a "virtuous woman," a doncella, and a married woman of "known virtue." They constitute an insightful cross section of female religiosity in Lima, and their premonitions and sufferings illuminate how religion was lived and the fears that enveloped Lima. Although the earthquake of 1746 represented in most cases the starting point, their visions hearkened

42   back into the past, across the Peruvian landscape and across the Atlantic to Europe.

As was the case with Parra's charge, only the name of the confessor is provided in the other women's trials. Fray Pedro Alcántara of the San Francisco de Paula order had a spiritual daughter whom he had known for twenty-five years. In his testimony, he emphasized her tolerance for pain and her dedication to serving others. In 1750, in the midst of an Indian conspiracy in the El Cercado neighborhood and in the Andean town of Huarochirí about thirty miles east of Lima, she broke out in profuse sweat, felt sudden anxiety, and pleaded in her prayers that priests be spared from the violence. She had no way of knowing about these events — she learned only later about the uprising and the deaths of Spaniards by "those barbarians." She and Fray Alcántara realized that at the very moment of their deaths, she had been praying to God for their salvation. On November 1, 1755, without understanding why, she found herself compelled to pray for the suffering of distant cities. Months later, she found out that her prayers had been offered at the same time as the Lisbon earthquake on All Saints' Day.[64] Fray Alcántara noted that she "feels in her spirit notable sorrow for the disorder and scandalous profanity of this city, and she has told me that in her prayers she experiences seeming lightning bursts, which distress her, as she takes them to be signs of the Lord's anger with this city." Her pains and sorrow had begun with the earthquake in 1746, and she had since begun to feel that Lima would be destroyed if radical changes were not made. She begged God for his mercy so that "the fire falls into the sea and mountains" and not on Lima.

Alcántara also told the story of another young woman he knew well, although he was not her confessor, who before October 28, 1746, saw in her dreams Lima devastated, with "trenches filled with cadavers." Once, when she was deep in prayer, the image of Jesus she had in her room talked to her: "He lamented sadly that his creatures had hurt and offended him." She was so upset that she became ill.[65] Fray Alcántara also discussed Doña María Ruíz Luna, a married woman who was the spiritual daughter of Fray Garro.[66] Alcántara adduced a long list of compliments, describing her as "exemplary, of known virtue, heroic humility, and constant prayer." When she saw profane women "she became inflamed in zealous defense of God's honor" [enardecida en el celo de la honra de Dios] and exclaimed in threatening fashion, "Our Lord, because of so many sins in this city, especially the obstinacy of these vices that scorn the divine wrath experienced in the ruin of the 1746 earthquake, will send fire to purify it of so much evil."[67]

The Franciscan friar Joseph Antonio de Santiesteban testified about a nun in an undisclosed convent (non-Franciscan) who led a life of tremendous self-discipline. Friar Santiesteban could find no sins in her conduct but described a unique style of prayer. She suffered "sweet and loving" ecstasy or rapture ["deliquios"] to the point that she had to be separated from the other nuns. She became impassioned and sobbed "tenderly" with abundant tears, becoming so tranquil as though "in a sweet, loving hug"; in these moments, she appeared "angelical." Besides this sensual form of worship, she punished herself brutally: she ate seeds and bark to get ill and applied hot wax, plants with thorns, and studded leather to her skin until she blistered and bled. Although self-mortification was common in this period, this behavior was extreme. Her torments were also internal and terrifying. Not only did the devil bother her, but she had visions of dead souls who asked for prayers. With one look she recognized people who were soon to die.[68]

Around 1750, in the midst of self-mortification ["disciplina de sangre"] in her convent cell, the nun looked out the window to see the San Cristóbal hill (then to the north of the city, now in its very midst) on fire, "with countless people of both sexes and all social conditions hugging one another." She thought it was punishment for her own sins, and she disciplined herself so brutally that she fainted. She believed that her penance had prevented the wrath of God, who was angry at Lima's affronts. Months later she had another "nightmare." She saw a large herd of bulls running through the streets, led by "many demons with ugly features and whips that made a thunderous din, who went along saying dishonest and horrifying things." The bulls smoldered and with one look incinerated countless passersby, who screamed dreadfully before dying. With the cross on his shoulder, Christ walked behind them, bleeding freely and lamenting that nothing he had done for the Lima population "made them refrain from offending him so much." The nun woke up soaked in tears and began to do her spiritual exercises. From that day on she cried for Lima. When bullfights were first held in the Acho bullring in the early 1750s, she asked Fray Santiesteban if they might be the bulls of her nightmare.[69]

Fray Santiesteban passed on a story about the nun told by another priest, who confessed to "a soul of great contemplation" who three times had been "snatched in spirit and placed in the presence of the Supreme Judge Jesus Christ." The first time she saw that Jesus tried to burn Lima to the ground she appealed to the Virgin Mary, who responded, "My daughter, plead to God with me for Lima" and then kneeled in prayer. The second time she again saw fire falling on Lima and again invoked the Virgin Mary. In the third instance, she saw fire in the form of "burning cotton balls" raining down on the city. She consulted with the Virgin, "our Queen," who recommended that she speak with "virtuous, zealous people who should plead for Lima and that its inhabitants make amends: she said that women's clothing, the bad lives of priests and the wife of his Majesty, the poor's clamor for justice and the widespread dishonesty and lasciviousness had irritated our Lord."[70] The Virgin's admonishment includes virtually the entire list of sinners (especially the religious community and profane women) as well as the sins that prompted God's wrath found in the other premonitions, including the scandalous clothing of women.

Friar Santiesteban closed his testimony to the religious tribunal with another story from his friend the priest. He knew a "very holy and simple religious soul" who in 1748 lived in Huamanga (between Lima and Cuzco, today Ayacucho). She claimed God had warned her several times about the imminent ruin of Lima and Callao, whose sins had given him no choice but to "scorch them." Twice in her prayers she saw Lima in flames as fire fell from the sky. The priest, Santiesteban's friend, was so moved by these stories that he returned to his hometown of Lima "full of terror." This case indicates how the fear moved from the nuns through their confessors and into the larger community. Everyone involved understood the earthquake of 1746 as a prelude or warning and dreaded that the balls of fire would fulfill the threat.

The major chaplain of the Concepcionist observant convent Descalzas de San José, Friar Joseph González Terrones, testified about the visions of Mother Theresa de Jesús, a black veil nun (a symbol of the deepest renunciation of the secular world) and twice abbess of this convent. Since the 1730s she had perceived that God was indignant over the city's sensuality and blasphemy and that he would ruin it with a "formidable earthquake." She denounced the servants' dress in the convents, deeming them "profane and indecent." Weeks before October 28, on her deathbed (Llano Zapata claims she was over one hundred years old), she envisioned the city and its temples ruined, with nuns walking the streets and men roaming the inner sanctum of the convents. With tears in her eyes, she begged people to take to the streets to preach and enlighten Lima's people about this threat. Father González Terrones consulted with others, and they decided not to do anything, more to prevent a panic than because of their skepticism about her premonitions.[71]

Mother Theresa de Jesús was the best known of the prophesying nuns discussed here. Two Franciscan friars, Luís Rodriguez and Parra himself, classified her as a successor to other holy people who had predicted Lima's earlier earthquakes, such as San Francisco Solano and Father Galindo de la Merced (1687) as well as the fishermen who saw Panama City in flames from their boats fifteen days before the actual fire in 1737.[72]

Llano Zapata, in one of his accounts of the earthquake of 1746, dedicated a paragraph to Mother Theresa. He noted her prediction that she would die before the earthquake, which she did thirteen days before the catastrophe, and criticized the authorities for dismissing her warning because of her age.[73] Although Llano Zapata's account might have increased her reputation in Lima, she was already a well-known and feared figure. Fray González Terrones provided anecdotes that no doubt fortified her fame.

One night, with González Terrones present, Father Nicolás Carrasco Palomino, the chaplain of the Discalced Trinitarians convent, went to the San José convent to take her confession. She told him she would die in his hands, not in those of González Terrones. He laughed because he lived three blocks away while González Terrones lived in the convent. Weeks later, however, Carrasco Palomino gave her the last rites because González Terrones, her confessor, had become ill. Both friars worried that this would mean her prediction about the destruction of Lima would also turn out to be true, which the events of October 28 in fact confirmed. But this was only one of several confirmations of her powers. She had tenaciously fought González Terrones's plan to build a *sala de profundis*, or prayer room, in the convent, regarding it as a waste of money and time. She prophesied that no matter how strongly built, it would be ruined in the earthquake. González Terrones went ahead with the project anyway and, to the delight of the contractor and masons, paid to have it heavily fortified. The earthquake destroyed the new building, including its normally resilient new wooden doors.

One night, weeks before the earthquake, nuns gathered around Mother

46   Theresa's cell to hear her predictions. Another nun, María Joseph de Mercedes, made fun of them. She was from the distinguished Jáuregui family—
her sister was married to the prosperous merchant don Martín de Olavide,
the father of Pablo de Olavide, an important figure in the Spanish Enlightenment.[74] Mother Theresa heard her jibes and according to several nuns
said, "Don't laugh, I guarantee that the first news you hear after the tremor
will be about the death of your people." María Joseph's sister and brother-
in-law would become two of the most distinguished victims of the earthquake when their house fell and crushed them.[75] Mother Theresa's story
indicates that premonitions about the destruction of Lima took hold in
the city before the earthquake. The aftershocks in the following months—
430 in the three-and-a-half-month span from October 28 to February 16,
1747—must have petrified Lima's population, who feared that each one
could be the final punishment.[76]

Friar Carrasco Palomino, the surprised provider of Mother Theresa's
last rites, told another story of one of "his religious women." One night in
1751, this woman saw large flames violently enter under the doorframe and
through the window of her convent cell. Her vision lasted for fifteen minutes or more, and she then called a servant to accompany her. This servant
stayed the night but saw nothing. The next night the nun observed that her
cell lit up with the reflection of fire, but again the servant saw nothing. The
third night the reflection from the flames was fainter, so the nun did not
call the servant. Her fear increased, however, a few days later, when another nun told her that she had also dreamed of flames falling from the sky,
boiling the water in the baptismal font and filling the convent with "bits of
fire." Fray Carrasco Palomino's testimony ended with those words.

Fray García de Moroña, a Dominican who served as chaplain of the Santa
Rosa convent, referred in his testimony to a doncella of "great purity" who
had frequent visions. She had proven her powers to him when he had asked
her to pray that two women would commit themselves to spiritual exercises. She told him in reply that one would continue and the other would
leave. She seemed to have been wrong, as the one who she predicted would
stay did not and vice versa. Soon thereafter, however, the two women re-
versed their behavior. In the months before the earthquake in 1746 she
had night visions. She saw with horror that fire rained over the city ("a
fine hail of fire"), inducing her to increase her daily prayers. Another night
she saw Jesus riding on horseback through Lima, with his sword in hand,

"as though he were threatening its inhabitants with a great punishment." She later saw Santa Rosa ("our glorious patron") humbly pleading before God for the salvation of Lima, "her patria," as well as to the Virgin. Santa Rosa "sheltered under her blanket all who came to her fearful of Divine justice." The young woman understood that Santa Rosa and the Virgin had postponed but not prevented the city's punishment; she was petrified at its impending arrival.[77]

Friar García de Moroña gave other examples in his testimony of premonitions and alarm. A "virtuous woman" whom he confessed knew a "servant of God" who had a figure of Jesus that talked, revealing that Lima was to be punished with fire and recommending that she "take refuge in a temple, because its angels will defend it and save all of the city's temples from the fire."[78] This anonymous virtuous woman also told about a priest who fled 40 or 50 leagues (120–50 miles) from Lima. There he confessed a doncella who had twice dreamed about the Lima earthquake. She described it in such detail and with such exactitude that the priest was shocked to learn she had never set foot in Lima. In the second dream, the doncella came to Lima to learn that God was going to punish it with "an even bigger earthquake." She saw "horrifying things such as huge trenches opening up in the ground and engulfing people." Her stories as well as those of the woman in Huamanga indicate that the fear spread far beyond Lima itself.

Fray Garro told brief stories of two women who had passed away. Ana María de la Concepción, a beata of the Santa Rosa de Viterbo beaterio, saw in 1747, 1748, and 1749 (the year she died) fire falling from the San Cristóbal hill and the ocean tumbling into the city. María del Rosario, also called María Terrones, a cuarterona (daughter of a Spanish man and a mestiza) whom Garro confessed, told him in 1749 that she was happy to die not only because she awaited the mercy of God, but also "to miss the fire that my Lord Jesus Christ told me he was going to send down on the city." When the friar asked her when this would occur, she answered ominously, "Soon."[79]

Garro also discussed a woman of "known virtue" who heard voices earlier in 1755, sometimes while awake and others when asleep, that told her, "I have to destroy this city of Lima with fire," although not specifying when. Another woman, who had lived for decades in a recoleta, or more reclusive monastery, in 1747 and 1748 had seen in the sky a powerful hand holding a sickle while a voice repeated, "I must devastate this city." Another nun he

48 confessed, who lived in a different convent from these women, dreamed in 1748 and 1749 that fire rained on Lima. A fourth nun told him that God had told her he wanted to "burn down" (acabar con fuego) Lima. Another had the same vision but saw it in more detail: the fire fell in the form of "burning golden bread," making the city smell like roasting beef. Finally, Garro mentioned two pious women who confided in him that they had seen Lima burn down in their dreams. At this point, Garro conceded that rumors about the destruction of Lima abounded, which perhaps stimulated people's imagination and nurtured the abundance of similar visions. Nonetheless, Friar Garro cited the prophet Amos as well as Saint Theodoret and noted, "With his infinite commiseration and compassion God always warns the faithful before a universal punishment." He implied that he doubted some of these premonitions but did not reject the possibility of divine punishment.[80]

In his testimony, the Dominican friar and prior of the Santa Rosa convent, Gregorio de Mendoza, stressed that God often employed women and female saints to reveal His mysteries. He cited the role of Mary Magdalene in the resurrection of Christ, despite the fact that Saint Thomas and Saint Buenaventura were alive. He told the story of a "noble woman," an open-veiled ["de hábito descubierto"] beata and a doncella, whose dreams months after the earthquake were filled with abundant fire falling on the city with such force that the horrifying screams, groans, and howls "broke hearts." She used an unusual metaphor: countless gold-plated books thrown into the sky and tumbling down onto the city. In the dream, Lima immediately fell into a nightmarish silence, as if there were no survivors. She also saw lots of smoke and noted that the city smelled like "burnt meat." Not surprisingly, she could not forget this nightmare and lived in constant terror. What is surprising is that Friar Mendoza, when asked if he had heard of other people with such dreams, answered no.[81]

In these same proceedings, Friar Rodriguez gave a brief account of a nun who had also correctly prophesied the earlier 1746 disaster, including details such as the flooding of Callao and the gathering of displaced nuns in plazas. Since early 1747, whenever she prayed she sensed another imminent punishment of sinful Lima. One time she saw fire falling from the sky and people kneeling and pleading for divine mercy when suddenly everything went silent. The smell of burning people spread, and fire continued to fall like "panes de oro batido" (loaves of beaten gold). She told the friar that the vision had recurred a year before and that she understood that God wanted to "destroy [Lima] voraciously."[82]

Friar Rodriguez then told the story that most scared him. He indicated that not all of the visionaries were women. He knew a deeply religious man who often seemed crazy but had extended periods of absolute lucidity in which he had "new enlightenment and intelligence about the things of God and the sacred mysteries." While praying one day prior to 1746 he saw that God and divine justice wanted to annihilate the city with fire. He was then transported to heaven, where he begged the Lord to punish him, "this vile sinner," and save the people. In response, he was turned over to the devil. In the months following the earthquake, this visionary repeatedly cautioned that Lima had avoided punishment once but would not be so fortunate in the near future. He blamed the city's disorderly and profane customs for the impending punishment.

The Franciscan friar Joseph de Pozo told a story about a priest who one morning before dawn in 1753 or 1754, while deep in prayer, had a brief but clear vision of Lima with its temples standing but their towers tumbled over and the city otherwise flattened and without people. Relating this to the vision he had had that foretold the earthquake of 1746 six or seven months before the event, he came out of his "abstract" state of mind fearing that Lima would soon be greatly punished again. Nuns were not the only ones in Lima who received disturbing warnings about impending doom.

Fears

The visions and premonitions that beset mid-eighteenth-century Lima are a wonderful entryway into the fears and mentalities of the era. A few common features are evident. They were not overtly political or subversive in nature, like those that starkly questioned power relations and prompted messianic or millenarian movements. Instead, they confirm Richard Kagan's point that "the vast majority of medieval and Renaissance prophecies addressed religious issues. The dominant theme was the reform of the church, which was accused of corruption and immorality."[83] With the possible exception of Mother Theresa and her threatening rejoinder to the upper-class nuns who teased her believers, none of the nuns enjoyed or took advantage of their special knowledge. As Parra's nun best demonstrated, they suffered terribly with the visions, both in the painful reception of messages about an impending apocalypse as well as in the ensuing anguish. Once they had the vision, they not only dreaded divine wrath, but also guiltily reviewed their own sins to see if they were perhaps personally culpable.

The nuns and much of the rest of Lima believed that the earthquake of 1746 had been a sign of God's wrath and that only a drastic change in the residents' behavior and piety could prevent an even more crippling punishment. Virtually all of the participants in the trial following Parra's sermon in 1756 shared this view. The nuns understood their visions as messages from God, while the priests cited the Bible to support the notion of prophetic warnings. In the trial, the inquisitors as well as the archbishop clearly assumed that women had a gift and that the warnings of necessity should be heeded. The decades-long debate and mass concern about Limeños' errant ways and the decadence of the Church was thus revived, if indeed it had ever died down.

Dread and guilt permeated Lima. The earthquake of 1746 had deepened the concern of most of the city's inhabitants about God's wrath, confirming the subtext in decades of discussions about Lima's sinful ways and its wayward Church: repent or calamity would strike. The nuns blamed the city, the Church, and themselves for God's anger. Certain symbolic elements stand out. The premonitions express particular horror and worry about women in Lima, especially their profane dress. The earthquake and the premonitions stimulated campaigns to tighten control of women's bodies, efforts that displayed fascinating notions about gender and race (see chapter 7). This interpretation of the earthquake and the fear it deepened shaped the city's rebuilding. No discussion or plan could avoid the issue of God's wrath and the search for its causes (the guilty sinners) and a solution.

What about the nuns and their visions? As was often the case in colonial Spanish America, the pitched jurisdictional battle, in this case between the archbishop and the inquisitor, ended in a rather amorphous tie, with no apparent winner. The final sentence does not clearly favor one or the other.[84] Barroeta continued this and his many other battles until his transfer to Granada, Spain, in 1758. Franciscans managed to move Parra out of the limelight, and his name and the case itself are not prominently mentioned in the newspaper La Gaceta de Lima or in documentation from the era. In 1769 he was transferred to Chile.[85] We know nothing about the nuns. They presumably took solace in the fact that the devastating blow they envisioned did not occur. The testimonies indicate that while they blamed themselves for the city's woes, they also recognized that their efforts could detain God's ire. They no doubt continued to be troubled by their special insights into impending events and fearful of divine wrath, pained by their own sins as well as those of their city. Nothing in the record indicates a reprieve from that fate. What is clear is that the debates about the causes and nature of disasters shaped the physical, institutional, behavioral, and social reconstruction of Lima.

The City of Kings:
Before and After

[Lima is made up] of such a variety of names and colors that it would be work just to list them. —FRANCISCO JAVIER EDER SJ, *Descripción de la Provincia de los Mojos en el Reino del Perú, 7*

Three

As Viceroy Manso de Velasco toured the devastated city in the hours and days after the earthquake, he mourned the loss of lives, tabulated the physical destruction, and lamented the breakdown of the city's precise layout and organization. For Bourbon authorities such as the viceroy, Lima had already been unacceptably disorderly and unruly, even before the earthquake. The regular, geometric street layout of 1535 that set in stone social divisions among classes (or "nations") and sanctified the place of the colonial state, the Church, the municipal government, and other institutions had been weakened by the city's racial complexity, the overindulgence of baroque religiosity, and the power accrued by the mendicant orders and Jesuits as well as the city's elite.

In the first half of the eighteenth century, authorities had attempted to make Spanish and Spanish American cities more manageable and place the Crown and its viceregal representatives firmly in control. The earthquake threatened to overturn these efforts, unleashing lower-class truculence, upper-class independence, and the Church's search for even a greater role. The viceroy saw it as his duty to impede these potential developments and restore Lima to its former self, albeit in new absolutist fashion. Viceroy Manso believed the city was at a crossroads. If his efforts to resuscitate and modernize the sixteenth-century sense of order failed, the city would fall into chaos and decadence.

The Capital

Having learned of the fabulous wealth of the Inca empire, in 1531 Francisco Pizarro and his forces climbed the Andes to confront the Inca leader Atahualpa in Cajamarca. To the Europeans' good fortune, the Incas were in the midst of a civil war between Atahualpa and his half brother, Huascar. In addition, they were already falling prey to the mysterious and ghastly diseases the Europeans had brought. Pathogens moved faster than human invaders, and the great Inca leader Huayna Capac presumably died of smallpox in 1527, years before the Spaniards' arrival, igniting the war between his two sons. Well experienced by their thirty-year presence in the New World, the Spaniards used the Incas' civil conflict and the ravages of disease to their full advantage. They captured Atahualpa and on a trumped-up charge executed him nine months later. Continuing to stoke the flames of the Atahualpa-Huascar conflict, the Europeans drove south to the majestic Inca capital of Cuzco in 1534. Following a number of battles and sieges, they gained control of the city but then faced decades, indeed, centuries of resistance. Inca rebels fled toward the jungle while the common people, suddenly lumped together and categorized as Indians, demonstrated great resentment toward the imposition of Spanish rule. Nevertheless, with astounding speed, Pizarro's forces took control of much of the vast Inca empire.

In contrast to Hernán Cortés, who built Mexico City literally on top of the Aztecs' capital, Tenochtitlan, the Spaniards in Peru did not establish their capital on the site of the pre-Hispanic center of Cuzco, but rather on the coast. Pizarro founded the City of Kings, Lima, on January 18, 1535, alongside the Rimac River, six miles inland from what would become the port of Callao. The area, a place where rivers brought water and rich soil

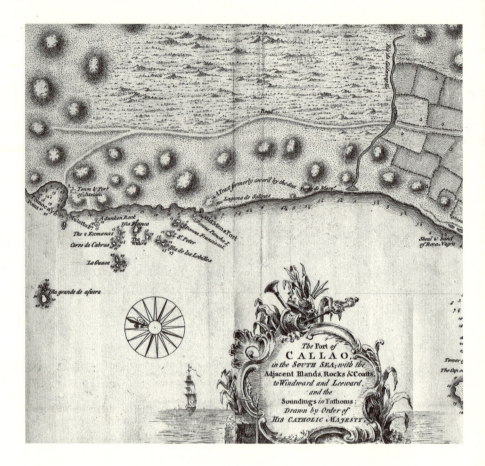

The Port of
CALLAO,
in the SOUTH SEA; *with the*
Adjacent Islands, Rocks &Coasts
to Windward *and* Leeward;
and the
Soundings *in* Fathoms;
Drawn by Order of
HIS CATHOLIC MAJESTY.

from the Andes, constituted one of the lush valleys formed in the otherwise desertlike coast. It formed part of the domain of the Indian *cacique* Taulichusco and was linked to the coastal religious center of Pachacamac. Pizarro took possession of the site, setting the first stone of the Cathedral on top of the Puma Inti temple. He then set out streets and distributed plots to his fellow conquistadors as well as to the mendicant orders of the Church and a hospital. Each perfectly square block was 450 feet on a side and was divided into four plots, or *solares*. The streets were 35 feet wide. The 13-by-9-street rectangle produced a checkerboard consisting of 117 blocks.[1]

For centuries, visitors to Lima would comment on the founders' symbolic achievements. They noted the orderly division of the buildings sur-

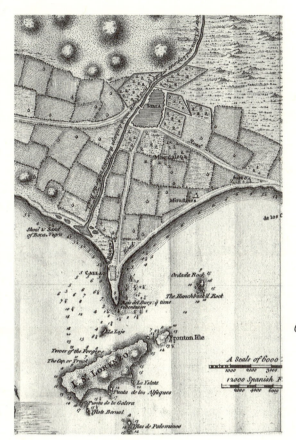

6 Map of Lima and Callao.
Credit: Anonymous English reproduction of Antonio de Ulloa, *Relación histórica del viaje a la América Meridional*, published 1784, 2: 146, "El Puerto de El Callao en el Mar Pacífico o del Sur," Spanish edition (Relación), 1784.

rounding the Plaza Mayor, with the viceregal palace to the north (what had been Pizarro's plot before being expropriated after his tumultuous death), the Archbishop's Palace and Cathedral to the east, merchants' shops to the south, and the city council to the west. They also stressed the straightness of Lima's streets. In 1630, Fray Buenaventura de Salinas y Córdova boasted that Lima "has a singular beauty in the layout and proportion of the squares and the streets, all of them the same . . . the form and layout is squared off with such order and harmony that all the streets are alike. . . . They are all extremely beautiful because of their uniformity, wideness and straightness."[2] Guillaume Raynal, a French writer who had little good to say about Peru, complimented the planners of Lima's streets for making them "wide, parallel, and crossed in right angles."[3]

The city evolved beyond this immediate center, particularly after the establishment of the High Court, or Audiencia, in 1543 and the discovery of vast silver deposits in Potosí the following year. In 1566, a quarter named El Cercado was created in the eastern part of the city for the Indian population, who were placed under the care of the Jesuits. Its name, which means "the walled city," referred to the two-meter-high wall that surrounded it. The wall had only two openings in it. Originally intended for Indian migrants who came to trade and work in the city, the neighborhood increasingly housed a more permanent population of Indians and non-Indians. Across the river, the San Pedro de los Camaroneros (shrimpers) area became San Lázaro (the saint of lepers) in 1563, as it was the site of a hospital for blacks and lepers. It included the Malambo area, where African slaves brought from ships docking in Callao were sold. Its name changed to Nueva Triana (the name of the lovely neighborhood on the other side of the Guadalquivir River from Seville), and is today the teeming working-class neighborhood of Rimac. In the colonial period, this "other side of the river" neighborhood was home to much of the poorer population, in part because of the leprosy stigma.[4] Even though these new neighborhoods initially displayed the right-angled geometry that Pizarro had imposed, changes over time corrupted this precise layout: neighbors extended their dwellings into the streets, religious buildings expanded, and the authorities inaugurated new plazas. Therefore, while travelers commented on Lima's straight lines, many areas broke that pattern, a violation that concerned eighteenth-century urban reformers.[5]

Lima became the center of the Spanish empire in South America, the equivalent of Mexico City for Meso-America. All vital decisions passed through the viceroy and the Audiencia, while the Church exercised spiritual control through its center of operations, the Lima archdiocese. Each mendicant order maintained one or more convent churches in Lima. By 1615, Lima had seven parishes and twenty convents and monasteries. The Inquisition also had headquarters in Lima. The viceroyalty's leading merchants worked out of and resided in the City of Kings. Although the colonial economy was based on the rich Andean silver mines of Potosí and Cerro de Pasco and the mercury mine of Huancavelica, coastal Lima was the economic center. As Pizarro had intended, power in colonial Peru was concentrated in and around Lima's Plaza Mayor.

In 1537, the conquistadors founded the port and presidio of Callao

where the Rimac River emptied into the Pacific. As South America's main 57
port, Callao had important warehouses and merchant houses. In fact, most
of Lima's major businessmen kept a second house there. In the seventeenth
century, Callao grew into a half circle at some distance from the shore,
with a wall surrounding it. Cannons defended it from pirate attacks and
incursions by the British and the Dutch. The road to Lima ran parallel to
the Rimac River, just south, through the rich agricultural valley.[6]

Race and Space

The city's population grew and became diverse. Three main groups, Indians, Africans, and Spaniards, populated Peru. Under the Spanish regime,
Indians constituted their own republic, divided into commoners and nobles.
This masked, however, great complexity. Indian groups included the Incas
as well as other ethnic groups that the Inca empire, which had consolidated less than two centuries before the arrival of the Spanish, could not
subjugate. These non-Inca Indians included groups on the coast and in the
Andes as well as more isolated hunter-gatherer tribes in the Amazon basin
or jungle. In the environs of Lima, Indian could refer to a resident of El
Cercado, a servant in an elite household, a fisherman and his family in the
village of Pitipiti just south of Callao, tradesmen or female merchants from
nearby Andean towns such as Huarochirí, or Indian nobles from Cuzco or
Lima itself.[7] According to the census of 1770, Indians made up 11.7 percent of the city's population; most calculations throughout the eighteenth
century put them at around 10 percent. Despite the existence of a special
Indian neighborhood, they were not segregated from the rest of the population. Indians, in fact, lived throughout the city and met members of other
ethnic groups everyday in Lima's bustling streets. Many came from nearby
Andean villages to work or buy and sell goods.[8]

Approximately 100,000 slaves were brought to Peru from Africa between
the sixteenth and nineteenth centuries, about 40 percent of them ending
up in Lima.[9] They worked on the estates up and down the coast and in
the smaller farms on the outskirts of the city. Virtually all elite households
counted on one or more domestic slaves; one household had 30. Convents
and monasteries also had large number of slaves—La Concepción monastery had an astounding 271 in 1700. A few Indians and a significant number
of poor Spaniards, mestizos, and even free blacks had slaves as well.[10] Many

58 Table 1

Population of Lima, 1535–1820

YEAR	POPULATION
1535	70
1600	14,262
1613	25,954
1700	37,000
1746	60,000
1755	54,000
1790	49,433
1791	52,627
1812	63,900
1820	64,000

Source: Pérez Cantó, Lima, 48–50.

slaves worked outside the house, handing over to their owner a large percentage of their wage. This arrangement granted the slave some independence and the opportunity to save in order to buy his or her freedom. More women than men purchased their freedom, often a familial strategy to prevent offspring from being born into slavery.[11] This helps explain not only the significant free black population, but also the impression that slaves had a relatively high level of independence in Lima.

Slaves and free blacks worked in a variety of trades that gave them an active presence in the city. They carried water and goods, sold chocolate, candles, coal, and food, and labored as carpenters, masons, wet nurses, and many other occupations. Men and women hustled for day jobs, behavior that some critics said was vagrancy and even shielded criminal activities. They joined and formed cofradías, or religious brotherhoods, some organized along the lines of their African nations. They participated actively in the city's frequent religious festivals and also manned the city's militias. It is not surprising, then, that travelers almost always commented on this massive, even frenetic African and Afro-Peruvian presence in eighteenth-century Lima. In fact, the upper classes worried that the city had become too black. The fear of the black population loomed large, as concerns about their large numbers, their seeming freedom, their potential for violence, and the breakdown of slavery intermingled. In addition, black and mulatta women were cast as highly independent and sensual, dangerous challengers of social and gender codes.[12]

Adding to the diversity of the city was a smaller number of so-called Chinese (*chinos*), actually from the Philippines, a result of the Manila Galleon trade. In addition, Spaniards continued to migrate to Peru throughout the entire colonial period. Their numbers, which included those born in Europe, creoles, and others of mixed descent who stressed their Old World background, rose slightly over the century. "Europeans" constituted 38 percent of the city's population in 1792.[13]

These sundry groups could not be kept apart, and mixed groups formed a significant and recognized sector of Lima. In this era, before the late eighteenth- and nineteenth-century invention of allegedly scientific notions of racial differences, the Spanish created a system in which collective identity was based largely on bloodlines and religion. Nonetheless, I will frequently use the term *race* here, in large part because no satisfactory alternative exists—*ethnicity* and *caste* have their own drawbacks (yet I will also use these terms).[14] As early as the sixteenth century the offspring of Spanish and Indians, mestizos, prompted much debate about how they should be categorized in the social hierarchy. While a tally in 1613 found only ninety-seven mestizos living in Lima, less than 1 percent of the city's population, by 1792 they constituted 9 percent.[15] *Castas*, a term in Lima that designated the variety of mixed-race groups (but was usually associated with free people of at least some African descent), composed the fastest growing sector of the Lima population in the eighteenth century. By 1792, they represented 19 percent of Lima's population, while slaves made up 25 percent.[16] Decades before, Viceroy Manso had emphasized the high number of mestizos, blacks, mulattos, and other castas, yet deemed the tabulating of their true number "unverifiable," as, being leery of the head tax and the labor draft, they avoided census takers.[17] The convoluted census material about castas reflects less the bad accounting and individual resistance than the breakdown of clear racial boundaries. By the eighteenth century, social terminology sought to capture this complexity, referring not only to Spaniards, Indians, and blacks but mulattos (black-white mix), mestizos (Spaniard-European), zambos (Indian-black), and then a further line of mixing such as *cuarterones* (quadroons), *quinterones* (quintroons), and *chinos*. The census of 1790 included nine groups, whereas that of 1700 had employed only four categories.[18]

The eighteenth century thus witnessed two seemingly contradictory tendencies. On one hand, the growing complexity of the Lima and Peruvian population and the parallel decline of the notion of three nations (Euro-

Table 2

Ethnic makeup of Lima's population (%)

	1700	1790	1795
Spaniards	56.5	38.1	38.0
Blacks	22.1	18.1	44.6
Mulattoes	9.7	12.1	—
Mestizos	—	9.3	9.1
Indians	11.7	7.9	8.2
Sambos	—	6.8	—
Cuarterones	—	4.8	—
Chinos	—	2.2	—
Quinterones	—	0.4	—
Total	100	99.7	99.9

Sources: Pérez Cantó, Lima, 50; Fisher, Government and Society, 251.

pean, Indians, Africans) fostered a simpler, class-based divide between elite and the lower classes. A basic division between those who were called decent people (that is, Europeans of the middle and upper classes) and the multihued lower orders took hold. This transformation reflected both the slow, halting transition from caste to class categories and the Bourbons' efforts to weaken corporate groups. Those below the category of Spaniard were seen as and presumably saw themselves as castas, often lumped together as the urban plebe. In Lima, being called a plebe or casta implied some degree of blackness.[19] On the other hand, concerned about growing social complexity and influenced by Enlightenment classification systems, the Bourbon regime created a set of pseudoscientific categories, about twenty in all, to categorize and rank the offspring of mixed groups.[20] The pinturas de castas represented virtual manuals on these genealogies, displaying the supposed physical features and material culture of these groups.[21]

Despite the algebraic specificity of the casta paintings, Lima did not have a strict, enforceable, clearly delineated racial code. In fact, ethnic identities were quite fluid. Movement between the categories was common, and an individual considered a mulatto in a parish register might be deemed a black in a judicial record. Although occasional efforts were made to reinforce racial hierarchies—throughout the eighteenth century laws to prohibit blacks from entering the university were enacted, questioned, abandoned, and reiterated—racial identities were not set in stone upon birth. Identities changed, and very different notions of what it meant to be an Indian, black, Spaniard, and so on circulated in eighteenth-century Lima. Gender identities and hierarchies were also in flux in the eighteenth century. Disagreements about both raged after the earthquake of 1746.

Race was just one component of identity. Not only class, gender, and age shaped one's idea of identity, but so also did family, neighborhood, parish, cofradía, and other institutions.[22] What is clear is that the upper classes feared the lower orders and the subversion they might incite. The precise spatial and social order Pizarro had established in 1535 continued to mark eighteenth-century Lima, but its symbolic power had eroded.

The upper classes initially established themselves around the Plaza Mayor. The lack of vacant property and the noise, smells, and bustle of the plaza, which also served as a daily market, eventually pushed the elite outward, toward the east, near the Inquisition, or the south. In June 1747, when the city council put leading property owners in charge of assuring social control and helping with the rebuilding in two- or three-block areas (usually around their property), it was able to cover almost the entire core area south of the Rimac River and west of El Cercado. Members of the elite resided throughout the core area. A single block would often have the ornate house of a distinguished member of the upper classes as well as the more simple and more crowded houses and rooms of the lower orders. In fact, an elite house would often have Indian servants, black slaves, and middle-class merchants, often mestizos, renting a storefront.[23]

The Lima aristocracy re-created itself in the eighteenth century through commerce. Most merchants had diverse portfolios that included both overseas and inland trade. Many immigrants arrived in the eighteenth century, especially Basques, who often married into high Lima society and created family networks that stretched from Europe to Lima and into the Andean hinterland. The acceptance of these immigrants and their integration into the elite tended to bridge the Spaniard–creole divide.[24] Nonetheless, increasing creole pride, or creolism, emerged in the latter half of the seventeenth century. Artists and intellectuals cast Lima as a magnificent city with public life and festivities, architecture, and intellectual developments comparable in their grandeur to those of Europe. They stressed the city's great piety, particularly its saints and the celebrations for them. These representations partially reflected the competition with Cuzco, Peru's other great city. Yet they also displayed increasing local pride vis-à-vis Europe and

7 Lima and Its Surrounding Hinterland. *Credit*: Archivo General de Indias, Seville, MP 33, "Lima y sus contornos."

Europeans, a sentiment or tension that would flavor the debates over the rebuilding of Lima.[25]

The neighborhoods of Lima demonstrated a great deal of racial mixing. By 1750, more than half of El Cercado, the neighborhood built expressly for the indigenous population, was non-Indian.[26] Although concentrated in San Lázaro and other poor neighborhoods (and found in elite residences primarily as slaves), blacks lived throughout the city.[27] By the eighteenth century, the black population included slaves, former slaves, and free descendents of slaves. Almost to a person, European travelers were struck by the freedom of this population, their loud presence in Lima's streets, and the mix of Catholic and African religious rituals they practiced. The count of St. Malo, who arrived in Lima in June 1747, eight months after the earthquake, fretted that blacks "seem not to be kept in sufficient subjection, as indulgence to uncultivated minds is often repaid with insolence. On Sundays and festivals, they are allowed to hold meetings, where they sing and play their tricks, their music being a kind of drum, of the invention of that country."[28] An anonymous account of Lima, apparently written in the 1770s, claimed that blacks and mulattos made up more than half of the

city's population and contended that "it is impossible that there is another
country in the world where these people are as licentious as here."[29] Both
the Lima elite and travelers saw mulattas as dangerously sensual and independent, a concern that would emerge in the wake of the earthquake.

Accounts and maps of eighteenth-century Lima specify few populated
centers in the surrounding area other than the port of Callao. Lima seemed
not to have a hinterland—most of the valley remained unsettled and, sig-
nificantly, the maps usually stopped at the foot of the Andes. This view
indicated as much about the social and geographical mentality of Lima's
inhabitants as it did about its settlement patterns. Months after the catastrophe, Victorino Montero del Aguila wrote, "This kingdom is powerful in
silver and gold, which enriches everyone, but it must be recognized that it
is the poorest in the world as far as the settlement [vecindad] of towns and
peoples; not one can be found within 100 leagues."[30] Agricultural centers
to the south and north, such as Ica, Pisco, and Chancay, not only had been
greatly damaged by the disaster but lay outside of Lima's highly centralized
vision. The upper classes' myopia was even more pronounced in regard to
the Indian population on the coast and the Andes. The fishing village just
to the south of Callao, Pitipiti, was rarely mentioned. Documents from the
period usually overlooked the active trading of Andean products in Lima,
yet Indian merchants brought potatoes, corn, sweet potatoes, custard
apples, pineapples, coca leaves, ice, and many other products to the city.

Upper-class observers usually failed to mention this key exchange between the Andes and Lima despite the fact that the Plaza Mayor served as
the marketplace. In 1800, Alexander von Humboldt correctly noted that
Lima lived with its back to the Andes.[31]

Architecture

The arid coastal strip of western South America did not provide Lima with
easily available stone or wood for building. In fact, the wood-burning kilns
used for making bricks led to the deforestation of the hinterlands around
Lima by the seventeenth century. Builders consequently relied on the pre-
Hispanic practice of using flexible materials such as adobes or wattle and
daub made from mud plaster and bamboo or other reeds. Because of the
absence of rain, houses had lightweight roofs, a key explanation for the
relatively low death toll in major earthquakes.[32] Ships brought stone from

64   Panama and Arica and cedar and oak from Guayaquil, Nicaragua, and Chile.
The Rimac riverbanks provided much-needed limestone, sand, and reeds.[33]
Property owners often camouflaged these rustic materials by painting the
walls with bright colors or giving them the appearance of stone. Ground
seashells provided the paste for whitewash, while indigo and red ocher
brightened walls.

Churches and the houses of Lima's affluent society counted on grandiose
facades, high walls, and wooden balconies and doors to distinguish their
structures from more humble ones that were built of the same material and
with the same techniques. The San Francisco, La Merced, and San Agustín
churches, built in the late seventeenth century and early eighteenth with
stunningly elaborate facades, exemplified baroque architecture in Peru. In
fact, historians usually date the baroque period in Peru from 1670, the construction of the San Francisco church, to 1746, the year of the earthquake-
tsunami.[34] The historian Raúl Porras Barrenechea pointed out the similarities between eighteenth-century Lima and its elite inhabitants: elaborate
and even cold on the outside yet warm and gracious inside.[35] Intricate iron
and bronze gates, windows, and inner doors gave work to the city's artisans and shielded the homes of the upper classes in the eighteenth century.
These structures concealed the upper classes from the lower orders. The
gates and grilles vividly reflected both the increasingly public and ostentatious expressions of wealth and power and the fear of social upheaval.[36]

Lima's colonial houses followed the Mediterranean courtyard style, with
the sitting room and dining room off to the side of the first patio, and the
bedrooms across from them on the far side of the patio. In the more luxurious houses, the kitchen, servants' quarters, and stables for the horses and
carriages were found in the back, off a second patio. Owners often rented
out rooms with street access to petty merchants and shopkeepers, who
lived in lofts. Where houses had two stories, stairs were in the first patio,
sometimes built into the sitting room. *Oratorios*, or prayer rooms, were also
common. Built with flexible material (usually reeds) away from large walls
and replete with images of saints, they offered a place for refuge and sup-
plication during earthquakes.[37]

Buildings in poorer areas had higher densities and used more rustic
materials. In the largely black neighborhood of Malambo in San Lázaro,
most people lived in huts made of straw and reeds.[38] The palaces of the
upper classes had more ornate facades and used more stones and wood. Yet
throughout the eighteenth century, particularly after the disaster in 1746,

quincha—a pre-Hispanic form of wattle and daub—became increasingly important in all types of houses. For the roof, more elegant houses combined wood with cane supports, while humbler ones merely used canes or banana leaves as a cover.[39] Despite the great differences between elite palaces and humble dwellings, simple telluric materials, mud and canes, were at the heart of both.

Some European travelers were unimpressed by Lima's architecture, noting the buildings' monotonous layout, particularly the prevalence of single stories, and simple materials, which they saw as an indictment of its residents' laziness or hedonism.[40] Many also believed that baroque excesses symbolized Limeños' overly zealous or even hypocritical religiosity. Others complimented this mix of baroque touches with simple layouts and materials used since before the arrival of the Spanish, adobe and wattle and daub.[41] Eighteenth-century commentators, foreign and local, understood Lima's architecture as a symbol of the city's social organization and civic maturity. Their disagreements reflected divergent notions of how Lima, a viceregal capital, should be spatially organized. These different ideas clashed whenever earthquakes forced Lima to rebuild. This would be the case in 1746.

Lima notary records dating from November 1746 through 1753 reflect significant changes in the terms of housing contracts, usually drastic reductions in the amount paid. Two hundred sixteen pertinent contracts that referred to 277 pieces of property were found, a sizeable sample, as most accounts refer to 3,000 houses in all of Lima. Most (80 percent) referred to houses (complete or partitioned), while stores (11 percent), monastery or convent rooms (4.6 percent), and rural properties (2 percent) followed. Convents and monasteries were the owners in 38 percent of the cases, individuals 25 percent, capellanias, or chaplaincies, 13 percent, cofradias 12 percent, hospitals 7 percent, and universities and secondary schools 5 percent. Because hospitals and universities/secondary schools were run by the Church, and the chaplaincies and cofradías were used to support priests and religious activities, it is safe to say that the Church owned or managed the vast majority of urban property in eighteenth-century Lima. The data also show how censos, or the complex liens put on property (88 percent), were a much more common arrangement than rent (11 percent). The censos prompted a protracted struggle involving censo payers, the Church, and the viceroy (see chapter 6).[42]

Table 3

Ownership of property under dispute in lawsuits, Lima, 1747–55

OWNERS	PERCENTAGE
Convents and monasteries	38
Individuals	25
Capellanías, or chaplaincies	13
Cofradías, or religious brotherhoods	12
Hospitals	7
Universities and secondary schools	5
Total (277)	100

Lima the Morning After

The earthquake turned the City of Kings upside down. Toppled buildings clogged Pizarro's linear vision, while chaos subverted the city's finely tuned sense of order and hierarchy. The piles of rubble and debris made maneuvering through the streets difficult. Some of the new routes were so confusing that people lost their way near their own houses. In a city known for its cacophony of sounds and penchant for aromatic flowers and perfume, terrifying noises and repulsive smells added to the survivors' distress. Moans mixed with calls for help, dogs continually howled, and birds, according to Llano Zapata, stopped singing; walls and balconies tumbled loudly to the ground, killing many people and blocking escape routes. Church bells that had not fallen rang continuously.[43] The terrible stench from the countless rotting bodies in the ruins as well as the carcasses of dogs, horses, mules, and other animals strewn throughout the city lasted for months.[44] Dazed nuns walked the streets, birds fled the city, meat was eaten on Fridays, and small altars were built throughout the city to mourn the dead and ward off another disaster. Llano Zapata noted that in other times the rags people used to cover themselves, which even in "people of distinction" barely covered their privates, would have provoked great mirth, but not in these circumstances.[45]

Observers reported great damage to buildings and monuments throughout the city. A statue of Philip V had toppled into the Rimac River, the cathedral towers had fallen into the nave, and the ceiling had crushed over fifty patients in the Santa Ana hospital for Indians. The hands and heads of executed rebels from the 1730s displayed on a great arch that graced

the Lima side of the bridge over the Rimac River fell into the debris.[46] The 67
lawyer Miguel Valdivieso y Torrejón argued that the poorer dwellings in
the areas closer to the city walls had been utterly destroyed while the more
elaborate structures of the upper classes near the Plaza Mayor had withstood the disaster better. Nonetheless, he maintained that most of these
houses needed to be rebuilt from the ground up, particularly after looters
stole the wood framing in the following weeks.[47] Among the buildings
ruined were the Mint (Casa de la Moneda), City Hall (Casa del Cabildo), the
Inquisition's jail, and the Merchant Guild (Consulado). Much of the viceregal palace on the north edge of the Plaza Mayor, which housed the high
court, the treasury, and the armory, was also ravaged, while stretches of
the wall surrounding the city had toppled over. Damage was so great to the
San Lázaro and San Bartolomé hospitals that both had to be demolished.[48]
Callao and its presidio had to be rebuilt from scratch.

An anonymous report backed up Valdivieso y Torrejón's summary and
noted that in the "most important houses" near the Plaza Mayor the wood
and bricks had saved the facades but inside "all is ruin." The author mentioned that in the areas farther from the plaza, "where such costly buildings
were not constructed," the piles of rubble made the streets indistinguish-
able.[49] Susy Sánchez found that of sixty-eight key church and municipal
buildings, forty-five were beyond repair. Previous earthquakes and Lima's
unrelenting humidity, particularly damaging to adobes, had weakened
many buildings while superior antiseismic materials and methods had
saved others.[50] Although there is less detailed information about areas outside of Lima, Llano Zapata offers some particularly eerie accounts. He described the earth ripping apart to create fissures large enough to swallow a
man on horseback; rivers spilling over onto the crops while wells dried up;
and in the mining area of Lucanas, "monstrous creepy-crawlies" spewing
out of the tunnels. In Huarua to the north of Lima, the waves had drowned
muleteers on paths near the sea.[51]

The cloistered nature of convents, with their high walls, labyrinthine
layout, and few entrances and exits as well as their relatively rustic materials, made them especially dangerous. Twelve of twenty-one nuns of the
Monasterio del Carmen Bajo perished. Father Lozano also mentioned that
two nuns had died in the Concepción convent and one in the large Carmelite convent. The Dominicans and Augustinians buried thirteen of their
brothers, and the Franciscans and Mercedarians two each. Lozano's own

68 order, the Jesuits, had lost many slaves and servants in Lima but no priest. According to Lozano, the Benedictines, Agonizantes, and San Juan de Dios orders had had similar good fortune.[52] Dozens of priests and nuns, including nine Jesuits, had been killed in Callao. A large group of Franciscans that had gone to Callao to meet their new superior, who was to arrive on the following day, the twenty-ninth, perished.[53] Dislodged from his palace and forced to sleep for months in the Plaza Mayor, the viceroy received alarming news about the state of the city, its architecture and inhabitants, and the devastation of Callao.

Counting the Dead and Controlling the Living

Estimates of the number of dead varied, and tabulators then and now face several challenges. Not only were people buried under meters of wreckage and swept to sea, but documentation on the population of Lima and Callao was lost in the catastrophe. A prominent lawyer, Manuel Silva y la Banda, put the number of dead at 16,000 to 18,000, including all but 120 of Callao's population of 6,000 (which most put at 5,000). Silva y la Banda represented property owners who sought a discount in interest rates and thus exaggerated the damage of the calamity.[54] Father Lozano estimated 7,000 dead in Callao and 5,000 in Lima, while the *True and Particular Relation* claimed that only 1,141 had died in Lima. Pedro José Bravo de Lagunas elaborated on this figure. He believed that beggars had been excluded, and thus the number was probably closer to 1,400. The epidemics that hit Lima in the following months and years added an additional 4,000 fatalities.[55] Generally, scholars put the mortality rate for Lima and Callao at 8 percent to 20 percent, higher than the 5.5 percent calculated for the catastrophic Lisbon earthquake of 1755.[56] At the center of the discrepancy is the question of when to stop counting. As contemporary testimonies indicated in gruesome detail, the death toll mounted for weeks, months, even years after the earthquake and tsunami, as illnesses took their toll. More than mortality rates, these sources tell us how people died and how the survivors responded.

People in Lima were traditionally buried inside churches, the more notable families closer to the altar and the poor grouped together in higher density in the outer areas. Not only could the churches, most of them tottering, not receive the enormous number of bodies in the aftermath of the earthquake, but people feared going into them. Instead, mass graves were dug in plazas and in fields. Many of the dead were taken just inland from Callao, where the town of Bellavista was formed a few years later.[57] By October 31, the putrid smell of decomposing flesh forced mass burials in holes in open fields, twenty or thirty bodies at a time, 1,300 in all.[58] This was seen not only as sacrilegious—burial in a church was sacred—but unsavory and unsanitary, as the smell of the shallowly buried cadavers posed, according to observers, a health problem. The viceroy put the Cofradía de la Caridad (Brotherhood of Charity) in charge of taking the dead into churches. Survivors worried that the terrible stench, above all from the many rotting dead animals, posed a health problem. One report calculated that 3,000 dead mules and horses contaminated the rubble-strewn streets.[59] Although it is now clear that epidemics occurred not because of miasma but because of infectious diseases fostered by the devastated city's terrible sanitation and, in some cases, the lack of food and acceptable water, the preoccupations about epidemics were, unfortunately, warranted.

Llano Zapata put the total number of dead at 16,000, blaming the earthquake, tsunami, and the wave of sunstroke, fevers, and other illnesses that spread because of "bad food, the unrelenting sun, and the elements." He described "many people so pale, haggard, and devastated that they looked like live cadavers, their condition inspiring fear and their dishevelment prompting pity." This keen author noted that while Lima's fifteen boticas, or pharmacies, survived, fields that grew plants to heal the ill were destroyed.[60] In another account, he called hunger "the master key of illnesses." He calculated that within four months of the disaster over 2,000 died of a variety of illnesses.[61] In his various accounts, he displayed great sensitivity to the psychological impact of the earthquake. Llano Zapata tabulated 220 aftershocks from the time of the earthquake until November 1, and a total of 430 through February 16, 1747. The panic each one prompted took its toll on the exhausted, distraught population.[62] The count of St. Malo asserted that not a house in Lima was free of "fevers, fluxes, and dysentery."[63] Summer began shortly after the earthquake, and heavy rains from El Niño worsened the epidemics.

In his memoirs, Viceroy Manso dolefully noted that the illnesses took more victims than the earthquake itself.[64] A group of doctors met to discuss how to prevent an epidemic. They blamed the misuse of bleeding, banning barbers from doing the procedure without a medical prescription. They also called for sanitary measures: cleaning up the ditches where sewage ran in the middle of the streets, dumping dead animals outside of the city limits, guaranteeing the quality of meat and bread, and burning sticks, herbs, rosemary, and several other plants to counteract bad odors.[65]

Hospitals in colonial Lima were segregated along racial lines, class and gender playing their typically important role within these definitions. All the hospitals had suffered extensive physical damage and subsequently had great difficulty in collecting the money pledged to them by individuals, the state, and the cofradías that managed them. The earthquake had destroyed San Lázaro (for lepers) and San Bartolomé (blacks and mulattoes) and greatly damaged Santa Ana (Indians), San Andrés (European/white men), La Caridad (European women), Espíritu Santo (mariners), San Pedro (priests), and Los Huérfanos (orphans). Jesuit priests had created San Bartolomé in the seventeenth century when they took pity on older black women and men—presumably slaves who had been "liberated" once they could not be exploited—who took refuge on the inhospitable cliffs of the Rimac River, often dying with no aid. This large hospital was not rebuilt until the 1770s. After the earthquake, these hospitals overflowed with victims but were owed several years of the miserly official subsidy they received.[66] The administrator of San Andrés hospital complained that all of the sixty rural properties it owned had been ruined.[67]

The fear of disease and the widespread penury made life even more difficult for the destitute. Beggars with leprosy, traditionally instructed to remain downwind of people and to clank on two pieces of wood to make their presence known, had an unusually tough time. Fearing disease and having little to offer, people skirted them, declining to aid them or to support the rebuilding of the San Lázaro hospital. For years following the earthquake, lepers lived in makeshift huts along the Rimac River.[68] They, of course, were not the only ones to be dislodged. With their homes destroyed or tottering and aftershocks continuing for months, most of Lima's population found refuge wherever they could: in plazas, courtyards, gardens and fields within the city's walls, and even outside the walls. More than two hundred people took shelter in the Marquis of Ovando's garden.[69] The viceroy continually decried the dispersion of the population and the makeshift tents or huts they formed. He believed that sleeping outside not only constituted a grave health problem—he ascribed the wave of diseases to Lima's humidity—but ruptured and imperiled the capital's sense of place and order.[70]

Speculators were busy. The shortage of wheat and working ovens meant that bakers could increase the price of bread. Llano Zapata used the terms "tyranny, cruelty, and *rateros* [thieves]" to describe this practice. Those fortunate enough to have money offered to buy gold, silver, pearls, jewelry, and other valuables at rock-bottom prices. Cash-strapped patriarchs found themselves forced to sell family heirlooms at a fraction of their value.[71] One observant historian of Lima wrote that many sinners, in between pounding their chests in religious processions, "rubbed their hands with delight" at the prospect of the acquisition of treasures and, in the longer run, property. The Church was forced to sell off many of its properties, leading one historian to label the earthquake, with eloquent exaggeration, a secularizing force.[72]

For well over a decade, people would plead in the courts that their property or its titles and other crucial documents had been lost. Sebastián Valladares, a petty merchant, claimed he had stored four dozen mirrors, boxes of cotton socks, handkerchiefs, plates, and other items with Andrés de Espinoza in the Portal de Escribano in the Plaza Mayor. Espinoza had died in the earthquake, and his executor, according to Valladares, had kept these goods.[73] In 1758, Doña Teresa Caballero Chacón Martínez went to court to confirm her identity and that of her children, as the tsunami had destroyed baptism and wedding certificates, wills, and other important papers.[74] The Treasury Tribunal located in the viceregal palace noted that their annual account book for 1740 had been ruined when the earthquake knocked it off a shelf and into the path of a ruptured water canal.[75] The earthquake also intervened in the more sacred realm. It interrupted for more than a year the investigation begun in 1743 into whether the Jesuit priest Francisco del Castillo (Lima, 1615–73) merited sainthood.[76]

The Search for Solace

In the midst of thousands of dead, incalculable property damage, and countless personal tragedies the only consolation was perhaps the belief that it could have been worse. But even this was not clear. Almost all of the key chronicles had phrases like that in the "True and Particular Relation," in which the catastrophe of 1746 was compared to centuries of earthquakes: "None ever broke out with such astonishing Violence, or hath been attended with so vast a destruction, as that which happened lately in this Capital."[77] A terrible earthquake, devastation in Callao, constant

72   aftershocks, a persistent death rate owing above all to epidemics, and widespread theft and price gouging—the disaster seemed to bring an endless set of horrors. Searching for anything positive, several chroniclers described the exemplary work of priests and nuns. The viceroy himself lauded Father Bernardo de Zubieta of the cathedral and Father Julian García of the San Marcelo parish. They "spurned fear, panic, and terror to give the holy sacraments at all hours of the day" and worked tirelessly to build chapels out of boards in order to hold mass. He noted that this work stirred some priests from their fear-induced lethargy.[78] The Buena Muerte (Good Death) or Agonizante Order, whose name embodies its focus on aiding the dying, worked tirelessly inside the city and its outskirts.

     The Marquis of Ovando called the convent of the Discalced Mercedarians a "sanctuary of angels."[79] They camped in the garden of their convent, sleeping on boards and covered by what they could drag out of the ruins. The sisters worked all day at the tasks of the convent as well as their religious duties, yet could not rest in the evenings. The threat of thieves and the constant aftershocks kept them awake, leading them to exhaustion. Ovando described their unusual reaction to aftershocks—they would take off their habits or overgarments and with their hands raised and their arms bare walk outside pleading for mercy. They would do this day or night, often spurred by false alarms, when a sister thought she felt a tremor. Ovando pitied them, worrying about exhaustion and possible illnesses from the cold nights. He helped them financially and also told them that earthquakes were caused by nature ("la misma naturaleza"), although God favored some creatures and punished others. While the nuns soon rested better and thanked Ovando, his advice reached the ears of the Inquisition.

     Ovando had already noted his misgivings about Lima's fervent religiosity and the role of the Church when he registered his doubts and "virtual indignation" about the huge number of "missionaries" who offered the wounded and dying spiritual aid but little else.[80] Ovando met with Inquisitor Inspector Pedro Antonio Arenaza, and they discussed their differing views on the causes of earthquakes. The marquis believed that the earth had certain highly inflammable areas that exuded dangerous gases. The inquisitor sustained that the earthquake was God's wrath and chastised Ovando for his observations. This conversation echoed, although at a high stratum of Lima society, discussions and reactions to the earthquake. Most of the population favored the inquisitor's views—the earthquake was

a divine message—but disagreements raged about who was to blame and
what could be done to prevent further punishment. These profound exis-
tential doubts accompanied the critical problems faced by the Lima population of assuring food, water, and shelter, protecting the goods they had
salvaged, and beginning to rebuild. For emergency aid and assistance in
rebuilding, all eyes turned to Viceroy Manso de Velasco.

Stabilizing the Unstable
and Ordering the Disorderly

[The viceroy's efforts] sapped evil's strength, which tends
to grow not from adversity but rather from disorder.
—ANONYMOUS, *Individual y verdadera*, 164

Four

Viceroy Manso de Velasco had to act quickly. Lima, the heart of Spanish South America, and Callao, the major South American port, lay in ruins with thousands dead and an unknown number wounded. The suffering of so much of the region's population weighed on him. Yet the viceroy and his confidantes rarely commented on the implications of the disaster for Madrid and even more rarely about the wounded, sick, and grieving. Instead, they constantly spoke and wrote about the physical and social upheaval unleashed in the City of Kings. Major buildings had fallen to pieces, and piles of debris had converted the city's geometric street plan into serpentine paths and confounding dead ends. Social codes and control had also deteriorated, delighting some but terrifying the viceroy and many others.

Horrified at what they saw, the viceroy and his advisors sought to rebuild the capital and port in ways that would make it less vulnerable to natural disasters and social upheaval. In doing so, they envisioned a more rational city, one with a smoother circulation of goods, people, and air. This would, in turn, help to streamline or centralize colonial administration, making tax collection, economic oversight, social control, and other state duties easier. The project in Lima would neatly reflect changing ideas of city planning in Europe.

Emboldened by new notions of circulation, space, and order, European rulers built new cities such as St. Petersburg, opened up medieval ones by straightening streets and building avenues that led to the symbolic center of power, and implemented a series of municipal codes and measures, particularly regarding sanitation. They took advantage of fires (for example, in Oslo and London) and earthquakes (in Sicily and Lisbon) to try to create an "ideal city."[1] This predilection to rebuild rather than amend or maintain irked Voltaire, who wrote in 1749, "If half of Paris burned to the ground, we would rebuild it superb and advantageous, but today we do not want to provide it, at a price a thousand times lower, with the advantages and the magnificence it requires."[2]

Manso saw the earthquake as an opportunity to rationalize Lima along the lines that the Bourbons and other enlightened absolutists in Europe were imposing in cities throughout Europe and, to a lesser extent, in the Americas. In the name of creating a more stable city, he sought to change Lima's architecture and grant his office more authority in urban affairs. To his surprise and consternation, he encountered great resistance to his plans from the Lima population. These battles afford insight into the ambiguities of and obstacles to the series of broader changes the Spanish rulers attempted to impose. The conflicts over the rebuilding of Lima, curiously, tell a great deal about why the Bourbon reformers had such difficulty implementing their military, fiscal, and social reforms in the latter half of the eighteenth century.

Manso, the Bourbon Viceroy

Born in 1689 in Torrecilla, in northern Spain's La Rioja region, José Antonio Manso de Velasco rose in the military-administrative ranks in Spain and then in the Americas. He entered the Spanish Royal Guard in 1705, participating in battles primarily against the English throughout Spain, Italy, and northern Africa. By 1735, he had reached the rank of captain of the Grena-

76   diers and brigadier of the Royal Army. He was named captain general of the Philippines in 1736 but was sent instead in the same role to the Audiencia of Chile, where he served from 1737 to 1745. In Chile, he showed particular enthusiasm for founding new towns and also oversaw the reconstruction of much of Valdivia, damaged by an earthquake in November 1737, an experience that would serve him well in Lima.[3] In 1745, Manso de Velasco was named viceroy of Peru. He was "the classic Bourbon administrative type, a man of modest hidalgo origins who rose by his own merit through a military career to the rewards of high office and ennoblement."[4]

Lima's city council, or cabildo, proved ineffectual in the earthquake crisis. It met only nine times in all of 1746 and twice after October 28.[5] In his memoirs, the viceroy hinted at the sloth of its members, particularly in regard to revenue collection. He took charge after October 28.[6] He leaned heavily, however, on an inner circle of prominent Limeños, including Pedro José Bravo de Lagunas y Castillas, Pedro José Bravo de Rivero (both powerful judges of the High Court), Diego de Hesles (his secretary), and Francisco de Herboso y Figueroa, a maestrescuela, or member of the Cathedral Chapter in charge of its school.[7] The earthquake and its aftermath showed them to be committed civic leaders, loyal to Manso and devoted to Lima. Bravo de Lagunas y Castillas, an éminence grise for four decades according to one historian, wrote several important books, including the Voto Consultivo on the wheat crisis (see below) and a history of the San Lázaro hospital.[8] Critics, however, treated them as a corrupt oligarchy that profited from a monopoly of power and shady deals, especially after the earthquake. Archbishop Pedro Antonio Barroeta wrote countless letters against this "pandilla," or gang, accusing them not only of corruption but also of immorality (including gambling, promiscuity, and in one case subtle hints of homosexuality), and, in the case of Herboso y Figueroa, of being part black or mulatto. The archbishop accused another Manso ally, the judge Juan Marín de Poveda, of having leprosy.[9] Other prominent Limeños denounced the viceroy and his inner circle in the courts for supposedly pocketing lost goods washed up on shore after the tsunami.[10]

Manso de Velasco counted on an important ally in Madrid, Don Cenón de Somodevilla, the Marquis of Ensenada. For over a decade, from 1743 to 1754, Ensenada formed part of King Fernando VI's inner circle, along with José de Carvajal y Lancaster and Father Francisco de Rávago, a Jesuit and the king's confessor. Ensenada was arguably the most powerful adminis-

8 Archbishop Pedro Antonio
Barroeta. *Source:* Cathedral
of Lima. Photograph by
Fernando López.

trator in Madrid, overseeing the reform of Spain's military, particularly its
navy, as well as the general improvement of administration through the
placement of talented and loyal officials and the dismantling of traditional
patronage networks. Both a Francophile and a fierce patriot, Ensenada
shared with Manso not only his militarism but also his background: both
were from La Rioja. In a remarkable collection of letters, the two men broke
protocol and affectionately called each other "paisano," "amigo del alma,"
"amigo de mi vida" (countryman, soul friend, lifelong friend), and other
terms of endearment.[11] In a letter of 1747 to the king, Ensenada noted his
satisfaction with Manso: "In the Americas, there are three viceroys, Eslava
[in New Granada], Manso, and Horcasitas [the count of Revillagigedo, in
New Spain], who could not be any better."[12] The marquis and Manso shared
the conviction that more power had to be granted to the viceroys in order
to improve the administration of Spain's American holdings. Their friendship did not stop Ensenada from demanding more revenue from the Peruvian coffers, but it certainly facilitated Manso's efforts to gain approval in
Madrid for his rebuilding efforts.[13]

9 José Antonio Manso de Velasco, el Conde de Superunda. *Source:* Cathedral of Lima. Photograph by Fernando López.

Manso's views on statecraft, Peru, and natural disasters stand out in a frank summary of the disaster of October 28 that he sent to Sebastián Eslava, viceroy of New Granada. He called the earthquake an "executive sentence from Heaven," which unified everyone in misery yet turned "a populous, united capital" into "many towns of unequal shelters." He decried repeatedly the dangerous "division" or dispersion of the population and thus the urgent need to "unite the *vecindario* to regain the benefits that the congregation of people offers in civil and political life." Manso found a culprit for the city's horrors: "The vanity of Lima's inhabitants, who, driven by the abundance of their treasures, had erroneously built the city, raising arrogant towers in the temples, which so ran against God's prophecies that he had sent three general destructions of the same city, that preceded the fourth that we are now facing, as well as his divine providence to make this land subject to earthquakes."[14] God had warned Lima with the 1560, 1655, and 1687 earthquakes, but the city's residents had not listened. In the eyes of the viceroy, they were paying for this lapse.

The viceroy lauded God's "beneficence" in that if the earthquake had taken place two hours later, after midnight rather than at 10:30 on a clear, moonlit evening, fifty thousand rather than five thousand would have died. This was a forthright example of the prevalent interpretation of the earthquake: a sign of God's impatience with Limeños' wanton ways. In the same sentence he criticized the city's fragile building structures, the small rooms rented to the humble, and the "errant piety" of the countless church towers and facades. To punctuate this latter point, he asserted, "Faith is what must be grand, not the temples themselves."[15] In vivid testimony, he reiterated that the City of Kings had been the victim of God's wrath owing to its ostentatious ways. He lamented that "the wretched city of the Kingdom of Peru lies converted into a Troy of dust, more pitiful than one in ashes in that fire takes from the objects that it destroys the memory of the pain while the tremors leave in the deformed churches and demolished houses a disgusting reminder of our life, showing us the delinquent barbarism with which we fade away, having erected buildings with obstinate forgetfulness of the tragedies." He ends the same paragraph by asserting, "God punishes with particular severity this arrogance opposed to his highest providences."[16] Manso sustained that if the same errors were repeated—ostentatious buildings and lifestyles—divine punishment would also recur.

In this frank letter and in some of his personal correspondence, Manso expressed his low opinion of Lima's residents, including its leading citizens. These sentiments, not surprisingly, rarely formed part of the "public transcript." In the report to Viceroy Eslava, he finished on a providential note, outlining the good that could come if God's tumultuous warning were heeded: savings might increase, women would attract husbands with their humble habits rather than their costly accoutrements, and wise men would spend on houses and buildings rather than on coaches and clothing. This appears to be wishful thinking that did not convince even Manso himself—he seemed to doubt that Limeños' ways would actually change.[17] In 1747, when reporting to Ensenada on the progress of the rebuilding, he promised to be a "vigilant sentinel" in order to "stimulate these somewhat pusillanimous and indolent people."[18]

Viceroy Manso de Velasco's views on the earthquake epitomize the mentality of many eighteenth-century Bourbon authorities: disdain for the luxury (and, in some cases, debauchery) of the upper classes, both men and women, and for the supposed excesses of the Church, its buildings, fes-

80   tivities, and the behavior of some members. An interventionist state composed of competent, independent authorities was required to solve this
grave situation. This attitude captures the spirit of enlightened despotism
or absolutism, which envisioned the state shepherding Spain and its possessions to prosperity while discouraging baroque practices. These concepts would guide Manso's long-term plan to rebuild Lima. Yet in the hours
and days following the catastrophe, he had more immediate concerns. He
had to aid survivors, assure supplies of food and water, and survey the
damage.

The Fate of Marble and Dust

Miguel Valdivieso y Torrejón, a lawyer representing property owners in one
of the disputes following the earthquake, left a bleak summary of Lima's
woes. He noted that while the finer houses near the Plaza ("those modern
works") that had been rebuilt or reinforced after the large earthquake of
1687 had been damaged but had withstood the calamity, "in the rest of
the city and in the Montserrate [the poor neighborhood west of the plaza
along the Rimac River] not a house was left standing." He claimed that only
twenty of the city's three thousand residences had withstood the calamity
("A True and Particular Relation," cited 25). Reviewing the damage to buildings such as the Audiencia, the Cathedral, and the shattered Inquisition
building, he pondered the fate of more ordinary buildings: "If this is the
fate of marble, what will have happened to the dust? What shape will the
miserable works be in, if those of magnificence and power suffered so"?[19]

Viceroy Manso de Velasco received contradictory reports about the
physical damage. Wildly divergent estimates would continue for years, as
legal battles about property ownership, debts, and rebuilding costs continued. Representatives from the Merchant Guild, lobbying for a tax break,
wrote, "Ships, some lost at sea and others destroyed on land, were ravaged,
making the sea as clean of ships as land was of buildings. This city's houses
have been reduced to piles of useless debris, as the few that are still standing only serve to show their former shape and to cost the owners the price
of demolition."[20] In another document, they described the destruction of
merchants' houses, buildings, and warehouses and declared that Lima had
been "completely abandoned." Despite the hyperbole, they were unsuccessful in their efforts to lower the excise tax.[21] Individuals also exaggerated

the damage to further their own interests. Father Ignacio Meaza of the San Francisco de Paula order had returned to Spain without permission after the earthquake and contended, falsely, that all of his order's hospices and convents had been ruined. He requested that he thus be allowed to enter the San Benito de Salinas or Celestine order and return to live in Lima with his two sisters, who the courts believed did not exist. He was prohibited from returning to Peru.[22] Controversies over debts continued for decades. Many individuals exaggerated their losses, hid resources, or simply took advantage of the chaos to not pay.[23]

Notary records highlight the extensive damage. For example, the overseer of the San Andrés hospital claimed that sixty properties whose rents financed the hospital had been destroyed; Madre Teresa de San Joseph, the abbess of the Santa Rosa monastery, and María Leonor Fausto Gallegos, the abbess of the Nuestra Señora de la Peña de Francia monastery (Santa Claristas), grieved that all of their orders' property had been ruined.[24] Virtually all of the 277 cases reviewed focused on changing the terms of the contract in light of the damage wrought by the earthquake. The results varied. Some renters no longer paid the rent but instead promised to rebuild the house; others sought reductions in the rent or *enfiteusis* (an ancient form of rental agreement) or an extended delay in reinitiating payment. The renters or occupants of the house were placed in charge of rebuilding in 90 percent of the cases.

Callao left no documentary record and experienced less controversy—all real estate had been toppled and dragged into the sea. A document from 1747 attempted to tabulate the losses. It divided the population into three classes or estates and also included the Church and the State. It listed 75 "first-class families," claiming they had lost 273,000 pesos in furnishings and 1,137,000 pesos in capital. It cited 6 individuals as examples of the "second class" and used them to calculate the total losses for the more than 150 families in this category. All 6 were administrators of the port's warehouses, and they were reported to have lost 24,000 pesos in furnishings and 166,000 in capital. The document recognized that they were more affluent than most and calculated that the other 144 second-class families lost an average of 4,000 pesos. The third class was composed of "shipwrights [calafates], carpenters, boatswains [contramaestres de navios], and free blacks." Three individuals were listed, (including the master carpenter Bernardo el Chuncho, a nickname for people from the jungle), with

14,000 pesos in furnishings and 62,000 in capital. The other 97 members were calculated to have a net worth of 500 pesos and thus totaled 48,500 pesos. The Church was deemed to have lost 555,000 pesos in jewels and silver and gold. The document tabulated much greater losses for the king. These totaled 3,815,000 pesos, including warehouses, stores, and a variety of other property.

Touring on horseback and meeting with his aides and scouts, Manso de Velasco learned about the destruction in Lima, Callao, and the surrounding areas. The months he spent sleeping in a tent in the Plaza Mayor no doubt increased his sense of urgency. What most disturbed him was the dispersion of the population, the rupture of the orderly arrangement of where people worked, ate, slept, and resided. Accounts of the earthquake describe with astonishment and fear these disruptions. In a petition to the Crown to act on the two central issues concerning reconstruction, the possible demolition of two-story buildings and an adjustment of interest rates on the loans and obligations owed to the Church, Manso de Velasco lamented that the city was "defenseless" or "vulnerable" (desamparado) and that people were "taking shelter in the gardens and other unpopulated areas around the city, in straw or wooden shacks that necessity made highly desirable. . . . miserably spread throughout the fields and poor quarters."[25] People had taken refuge in any available open space—gardens, plazas, Church property, schoolyards, the Alameda de Descalzos in San Lázaro, the bastions of the murals, and the fields outside of the city.[26] The haphazard reed and wood huts that housed much of the city's population constituted such a fire hazard that in November the sale of gunpowder for fireworks, a central part of all celebrations, was banned.[27]

The Plaza Mayor became even more disorderly than usual. Joseph Guillermo, who had the concession to rent vendors' stalls, complained that "the plaza was filled with many people (mucho vecindario), and it was necessary to build rooms for the viceroy and his family as well as for the different courts." Although the city paid him for his efforts, he claimed the money did not compensate for his expenses and the lost revenue from his usual business of renting out spaces to market women. Worsening his problems, thieves had stolen all the wood from the stalls.[28] The viceroy himself joined in a chorus of complaints about the noise and bad smells of the Plaza Mayor caused by the multitudes living there and the goods that were still sold there, claiming at one point that they were damaging

Table 4

Estimates of property damage in Callao (in pesos)

OWNERS	NUMBERS/NAMES	FURNISHINGS	WEALTH	SUBTOTAL	TOTAL
First-Class Families	75 families	273,000	1,137,000	1,410,000	1,410,000
Second-Class Families	Agustín Ayala	4,000	16,000	20,000	
	Diego Muños	3,000	20,000	23,000	
	Orejuelas	8,000	100,000	108,000	
	Pedro Jimenes	4,000	12,000	16,000	
	Pablo Reyna	4,000	12,000	16,000	
	Joseph Menfeguria	1,000	6,000	7,000	
	144 other families, 4,000 each	—	—	576,000	766,000
Third-Class Families	Bernardo el Chuncho	4,000	30,000	34,000	
	Pedro Boller	4,000	20,000	24,000	
	Juan de Villarreal	6,000	12,000	18,000	
	97 other families, 500 each	—	—	48,500	124,500
Church and Monasteries	Iglesia Mayor	—	—	60,000	
	La Compañía (Jesuits)	—	—	200,000	
	San Francisco	—	—	75,000	
	La Merced	—	—	60,000	
	San Agustín	—	—	50,000	
	San Juan de Dios	—	—	30,000	
	La Cofradía de los Soldados	—	—	30,000	
	Santo Domingo	—	—	50,000	555,000
King	68 Warehouses (10,000 each)	—	—	680,000	
	Convents, Houses, and Farms	—	—	150,000	
	Viceregal Palace, Royal Storehouse, Large Houses	—	—	1,690,000	
	Small Houses and Stores (41 pulperías, 8 tiendas de mercancía y maderas)	—	—	1,295,000	3,815,000
Total					6,670,500

Source: "Razón de las familias y caudales que se perdieron en la ruina del año 1746 en la irrupción del presidio y puerto del Callao en precios, muebles, fincas, alaja de templos y Real Hazienda hecha por la más infima estima y rebajada a lo sumo" AGI, Lima, Leg. 787, pp. 282–84.

84 the Cathedral's jewels and adornments, many of them temporarily housed in the plaza.[29] Referring to the chapel that was constructed in the plaza, he complained of the "tightness and indecency of such a humble structure."[30]

The dispersion of people outside the city walls and in the plazas and alamedas concerned Manso de Velasco greatly. It upset both the original sense of place so precisely set in stone in the 1530s and Manso's Bourbon sensibilities. In his memoirs he observed, "It was impossible to govern the republic unless the *vecinos* were united, and there were many motives for me to attend to this all-important task."[31] The situation not only nettled the sensibilities of leaders like Manso (even as it caused him months of uncomfortable sleep), but also threatened to disrupt the economic and social codes that sustained Spanish urbanism. The fact that much of the population was living in fields and plazas while others made do inside of what was left of their residences was much more than a temporary inconvenience; it was a dangerous disruption of colonial order. Viceroy Manso frequently expressed his concerns to Madrid that people would refuse to rebuild because of their lack of money or fear and that the city's venerable checkerboard order would thus be lost. He presented this as an argument for aid from Spain—usually in the form of reducing what Lima sent to Spain—and for the measures he took to foster rebuilding. In his efforts to return people to their houses, economic and social issues intertwined.[32]

The viceroy took immediate steps to guarantee food, water, and security for the city. "Before the dust had settled" (according to one account), Manso secured the Mint and surveyed the city on horseback. He ordered that water canals and mills be fixed and that bread and other foodstuffs be sold in the plaza, even if they had to be requisitioned from nearby towns. Guaranteeing the supply of food was the foremost obligation of eighteenth-century rulers in Europe and the Americas, and bread was a vitally important product, in both caloric and symbolic terms. In this period, bread shortages or price increases caused a surprising number of regime-threatening riots and disturbances.[33] The situation was serious in Lima, as the earthquake had destroyed several ships hauling Chilean wheat and damaged bakeries and silos in Lima. Manso proudly stressed that after recognizing the shortage of wheat and thus of bread and the alarming price increases, he had quickly taken measures to assure the supply of this staple. Llano Zapata, however, described hunger, skyrocketing prices, and the tasteless dirt- and sand-filled bread that was produced in the days after the earthquake.[34]

These efforts took place in the context of a decades-long struggle between Chilean and Peruvian wheat producers. According to many historians, the earthquake of 1687 had devastated Peruvian production, ruining
or "sterilizing" fields and perhaps prompting a plague, thus opening the
door to producers from Chile. Recent interpretations have downplayed the
impact of the earthquake and focused instead on the battle between Lima
producers, aided by authorities such as Manso de Velasco, and the ultimate
victors, Chilean producers aligned with Lima merchants.[35] Because of his
physiocratic beliefs in the need for rural production as well as his concern about dependence on distant Chile, accentuated by the earthquake
and tsunami, Manso de Velasco attempted to overturn this trend and favor
Peruvian producers. One of his major ideologues, Bravo de Lagunas y Castillas, published a long treatise on the need to foster Peruvian agriculture,
particularly wheat.[36]

The viceroy required suppliers to provide this product. He ordered that
all ovens and bakeries be repaired as soon as possible, and he sent soldiers
to nearby rural towns to seize wheat reserves.[37] He also maintained price
controls. Merchants pleaded in the courts for either a price increase or a
decrease in the minimum weight of the bread, a common solution to avoid
the unsavory measure of increasing the time-honored price. They emphasized their own losses in the earthquake as well as the high price of wheat.[38]
The viceroy's adversary, Archbishop Barroeta, excoriated him years later for
his wheat policy. He claimed the viceroy forced Limeños to eat inferior,
more expensive bread, putting their health in danger. He demanded that
what he considered favoritism toward Peruvian wheat be stopped.[39] While
the controversy formed part of an enduring struggle over supremacy in the
South American west coast economy, for the viceroy it constituted an immediate crisis that had to be confronted. A ruler had to provide bread for
his people.

Economic Obstacles

The viceroy faced many impediments to rebuilding Lima, including, of
course, financial constraints. Three months before the earthquake, in late
July, he noted that the Lima treasury was "so in arrears, with its sources
exterminated, that it doesn't provide enough to pay even the established
annual salaries."[40] A month later he tabulated debts totaling 2,673,357
pesos. These were overwhelmingly military in nature as the incursions by

the British naval commander Edward Vernon and George Anson in the early 1740s had prompted navy expenditures to more than double and left many officials unpaid.[41] He acknowledged additional deficits in Potosí as well as in the Concepción and Valdivia presidios and predicted little improvement unless the war with England ended.[42] The earthquake made the situation much more difficult. Rebuilding Lima and Callao required a huge investment at the very time when production and distribution centers had been destroyed. On November 1, he complained that everyone pressured him for money, "putting me in the tightest bind."[43]

Despite the earthquake, Manso turned Peruvian finances around: the large deficit when he took office in 1745 became a surplus by the late 1740s. He achieved this while remitting large amounts to Spain and rebuilding Lima's and Callao's defenses and primary buildings. He turned to some emergency sources but relied much more on traditional ones. The increase resulted from his efforts to boost collection rates and find new revenue sources. In other words, he accelerated mid-eighteenth-century efforts masterminded by the Marquis of Ensenada in Madrid to rationalize and increase tax collection.

Immediately after the earthquake he gathered an emergency council, the Junta de Tribunales, and pushed through a series of measures. Emphasizing the wreckage of the earthquake and the urgent need for funds, the junta assigned the next two years' income derived from the *corregidores*—rural authorities who purchased their positions and were in charge of a variety of taxes, above all the Indian head tax,—for rebuilding Lima; demanded more money from the Huancavelica mercury mine; and tapped 100,000 pesos from the Santa Cruzada, or Holy Crusade, funds assigned to fight infidels. Manso justified this latter emergency measure on the grounds that the English as well as the Indians fighting with Juan Santos in the Peruvian jungle were "as dangerous as the infidels of Africa." The Church disagreed, and Manso never received the 100,000 pesos.[44] Manso improved the collection of the *alcabala*, or excise tax, almost doubling revenues, and successfully reinstated the tobacco monopoly. In addition, in a practice that began in 1745, before the earthquake, the viceroy sold six titles of count and three of marquis to status-seeking members of the Lima elite, who supplied much-needed money.[45]

The earthquake accelerated efforts to streamline the tax system and grant the viceroy more authority in fiscal matters. These efforts were crowned in

1751, when viceroys were put in charge of the Superintendencia General de Real Hacienda, incorporating "under one person the authority to collect, administer, and farm out the royal revenues."[46] Aided by the Treaty of Aix-la-Chapelle of 1748, which halted the threat of English incursions, and by increased silver mining in the all-important Potosí mines, Manso improved Peruvian finances. Lewis Mumford and Charles Tilly have shown how warfare strengthens the state. The case of Lima indicates that warfare combined with a natural disaster can accelerate this process. The viceregal office had much greater powers by midcentury.[47]

The correspondence between Manso and Ensenada sheds light on these changes. In hundreds of pages, few words of sympathy from Madrid for Manso and the people of Peru can be found. Even more glaring is the lack of monetary aid from Madrid. In fact, the Marquis of Ensenada kept up his friendly but persistent requests for more money from Peru to swell the Madrid coffers. In November 1745, Ensenada asked for "frequent support" as the war "endures and could last for years." In 1748, he pleaded, "Help me with as much as you can in order to put blood into this body [Spain], that's become a cadaver."[48] He objected to the use of the corregidor funds for Lima and demanded that payment to Spain not be hindered. Pablo Emilio Pérez-Mallaína Bueno uses an anecdote to capture this situation. Lima's hospitals had suffered greatly in the earthquake. Not only were they tottering and overflowing with victims, but their properties were damaged and they were owed several years' of the miserly official subsidy they received. Nonetheless, Madrid requested that Peru, specifically its Indians, send money to expand the Court's General Hospital of Madrid. At the very time Lima lay in tatters, its wounded unable to find succor in hospitals, the court demanded that Peru help finance a Madrid hospital.[49]

Manso's fiscal success derived not only from his abilities to increase taxes, but also from his cautious expenditures. The vast majority of state rebuilding expenditures focused on the new Real Felipe fort in Callao, the center of Peru's maritime defenses, as well as on the Royal Palace, the Mint, and the Cathedral. The account books indicate minimal expenditures on first aid or other emergency measures. This was deemed part of the Church's duties and not that of the viceroyalty, a sentiment that hindered secularization efforts. The viceregal state sought to decrease the physical presence and spiritual and economic power of the Church at the same time that it recognized its central role in health and charity. Pérez-Mallaína

Bueno tabulates 1.3 million pesos spent on the rebuilding of the presidio and these three key buildings from 1747 until 1761, a sum far greater than Ensenada thought necessary but less, for example, than the defense expenditures prompted by the conflict with the British in the early 1740s.[50]

The earthquake not only shattered Manso de Velasco's efforts to balance the budget, but also disrupted all aspects of the economy. While importers, bakers, and wheat producers sparred about the causes and solutions to shortages and price increases, the viceroy worried about bread riots, and the people about hunger. In January the viceroy reacted to reports about skyrocketing prices for laborers, building materials (especially wood), and transportation by exonerating products from certain taxes, opening up imports, and establishing price controls. Property owners as well as the city council complained bitterly, however, that in this case as in previous periods of shortages, supply and demand trumped official prices—people charged what they could get. These complaints did not call for market freedom or the invisible hand but rather for the viceroy to enforce the prices he had imposed. The viceroy's efforts after the earthquake confirmed the central role that early modern rulers had in provisioning goods, an important component of the effort to maintain order.[51]

In early 1747, property owners claimed that wood, unlike wheat, which had returned to its normal price after a few months, was still impossibly expensive. As noted, looters targeted wooden door frames, often causing ravaged homes to topple over. People fought on the beaches for washed up beams, and some original owners attempted to claim them or request the right to gather wood floating near the shore.[52] The overseer of the Santa Ana hospital lamented that two of the institution's buildings were uninhabitable because all the wood used in their doors and windows had been taken to build huts for people outside of the city walls.[53] Property owners contended that because people wanted to rebuild with this strong material, even if every ship "in this ocean came loaded with it, it would never be enough."[54] They presented the lowering of the price of wood as an essential step in moving people from temporary housing, where they were exposed to diseases and disorder, to their customary houses. Suppliers, however, contended that the price had increased in the port of Guayaquil and that the deaths of mariners and others in Callao meant that labor was scarce, expensive, and shoddy. Furthermore, they had to pay for guards to avoid looting.[55]

The city could not count on the usual supply of coerced labor. In the early 1740s, the war with England had reduced the number of slave ships reaching Callao. Indians forced to work in Lima often slipped back to their towns. One account claimed that laborers brought to rebuild Callao left because of their concerns over the coming crop.[56] Authorities frequently decried the lack of workers.[57]

The economic controversies that raged for years, however, were not so much about budgets and expenditures as about property and credit. The struggles highlighted how deeply entailed urban property was. Beyond the battle between owner and renter or user were layers of debts and liens to third and fourth parties: convents, religious brotherhoods, chaplaincies. The courts not only had to decide when rent should be resumed for a damaged building, who should pay for rebuilding, or who "owned" the land where a house had stood until the earthquake, but also had to disentangle multiple economic obligations, usually to different realms of the Church, that went back centuries. The loss of titles and other documents in the earthquake and tsunami made the problem that much worse. In the end, while many individuals and corporate groups reached agreements and the courts intervened in other cases, the viceroy had to forge a policy that accelerated resettlement and rebuilding. In doing so, he tangled with the upper classes and the Church as well as with deep-rooted notions about property, capital, and order.

Contending Notions of Lima: Obstacles to Urban Reform in the Aftermath

Five

After the initial measures taken to assure adequate supplies of food and water and to restore social control, Viceroy Manso de Velasco and city council officials turned to the question of how to rebuild Lima. They surveyed the area east of Lima and discussed the possibility of moving the city.[1] Recalling the devastation of the earthquake of 1687 and many others, those in favor of relocating emphasized that the present site would never be free of the danger of tremors.[2] The viceroy rejected this plan, however, primarily because of its cost. He calculated that rebuilding elsewhere would require at least 300 million pesos, an enormous sum. Estimates of building a new cathedral alone came to at least 7.5 million pesos, while repairing it cost little more than 1 million (they had actually spent only a third of that by 1761). He also mentioned the high cost of constructing walls around the city and the expense of a presidio to protect it.[3]

The city council presented other arguments against a move. They began with the legalistic point that the viceroy did not have the king's permission and thus could not make such a decision. They then emphasized the population's opposition to the move. Among many disadvantages, the authors stressed that the empty fields and buildings of the abandoned city would become a haven for thieves and vagrants. They worried that giving runaways such a prime place to relocate would further swell the ranks of maroons and weaken the institution of slavery. This image of blacks and other lower-class groups operating independently from a devastated Lima represented one of the primary fears of the city's elite: the ultimate dissolution of urban order. Finally, they pointed out that the move would invalidate the existing financial obligations between religious orders and property owners. Not only would this ruin the orders economically but it would be the "seed of endless conflicts and lawsuits."[4] By early 1747, authorities no longer considered moving Lima.[5]

Instead, the viceregal regime created an elaborate plan to rebuild the city in such a way as to minimize future damage from earthquakes. The French astronomer, mathematician, and architect Louis Godin oversaw the rebuilding efforts. A member of the Paris Academy of Sciences since 1725, Godin led, with Charles Marie de La Condamine and Pierre Bouguer, the scientific expedition in 1735 to determine whether the earth flattened at the equator, as Jean Dominique Cassini contended, or at its poles, as Isaac Newton and his followers believed. While successful in scientific terms— they confirmed the Newtonian view—the expedition was beset by internal squabbles, harsh conditions, and economic problems.[6] In 1744, Godin took the chair in mathematics at San Marcos University in Lima, where he stayed until 1751. In his efforts to rebuild Lima, Godin proved himself to be a technically sophisticated, forthright supporter of strict building codes, traits that would earn him the enmity of many of the city's leading families. Many saw him as an intruder arrogantly attempting to impose order on an unruly city, a view that paralleled the broader reaction in much of Spanish America to the Enlightenment and the Bourbon Reforms.[7]

Godin worked very quickly and presented his report on November 10, 1746, less than two weeks after the earthquake. He recommended widening streets, limiting the height of buildings, prohibiting arched towers, replacing stone structures with wattle and daub (quincha), and assuring adequate plazas and public space to serve as refuge in case of disasters. He called for streets at least twelve *varas* wide (a vara is .84 meters, or a bit less than a yard) and outer walls no higher than four varas (which was increased to five varas). The walls would count on wide bases for support and taper as they rose. The plan prohibited tall, heavy structures and sought to assure ample space in the streets even if buildings fell. Because the plan prohibited second stories and thus decreased living space, he lobbied unsuccessfully for demolishing the walls that surrounded the city in order for it to expand. Godin warned against the dangers of high buildings and church towers, contending that rebuilding the towers was "to dig graves again." These reforms were strikingly similar to the measures taken in Europe after the earthquakes in Sicily in 1693 and in Lisbon in 1755, where urban reformers also sought to widen streets and plazas in order to assure escape routes, hinder looting, and provide camping space. The disasters in Europe served as opportunity and pretext to implement the Renaissance ideal of wide, straight streets, in sharp contrast to the medieval pattern of narrow, twisted corridors.[8]

Unlike Europe, where palaces such as Versailles and entire cities such as St. Petersburg were built to flaunt the magnificence of absolutist kings and where majestic avenues were opening up congested medieval cities, urban design in eighteenth-century Spanish America was characterized by more humble efforts, primarily the creation of bare-bones military settlements in frontier areas and administrative changes in the cities. The promoters and beneficiaries of absolutist urban reform in Europe, royal families, with their grandiose palaces and respective courts, did not reside in Spanish America.[9] Furthermore, in contrast to Muslim-influenced Mediterranean and Balkan cities, the colonial cities had been designed in checkerboard fashion and thus did not need to be straightened. With its right angles and seemingly neat spatial hierarchy, Lima and other cities founded in the sixteenth century embodied the Renaissance notion of an ideal city: ordered and symmetrical. The Spanish, who saw the Americas as a source of revenue rather than as a site for investment, saw no need to build grandiose monuments or transform the city's precise blueprint. In fact, while pressing Madrid for aid that would not come, Manso sought to create a more humble Lima. He and the court in Madrid never contemplated a grandiose homage to absolutist order along the lines of Versailles or St. Petersburg. Instead, they envisioned a less ostentatious, more orderly site, a reflection of midcentury Spanish absolutism.[10] Their plan, however, faced great opposition from the city's upper classes, who defended their right to stand out and loom above the common people.

Upper Classes and Upper Stories

Godin's guidelines called for all walls higher than 4.5 varas to be demolished and for streets to be at least twelve varas wide. In fact, he wanted to reduce heights to four varas or lower if streets were less than twelve varas. He sought to guarantee that even if the walls toppled into the streets, a clear path remained in the middle. While Godin quickly conceded that buildings could be up to five varas high, he argued that if convents and monasteries needed walls higher than this, they could place them inside their property line and have smaller rooms. This constituted a skirmish in the brewing battle between the State and the Church (see chapter 6). He initially justified these measures on the need for "private rights" to cede to "public rights," criticizing the "vain elevation" of many of Lima's buildings. Here, Godin reiterated his countryman Amedée Frezier and other travelers' condescending view of the Lima upper classes as ostentatious and self-indulgent. While recognizing the sacrifice that his plan required, Godin promoted it assertively. He noted that "cures rarely come without pain, at times worse even than the sickness itself."[11] The viceroy backed Godin's prohibition of two-story structures, asserting that they endangered "the poor who live in storefronts and narrow homes."[12] The Junta de Tribunales, an emergency council, also supported the plan to prohibit second stories and limit church towers and balconies but opposed demolishing the walls surrounding the city (a measure that would not take place until 1870). Godin's plan can be interpreted as part of the Bourbons' efforts to assert their power over the Church and secular society.

On January 16, 1747, workers placed posters in four busy plazas, (Mayor, La Merced, San Juan de Dios, and La Encarnación), and town criers walked the streets to publicize a decree ordering that all "second stories [altos], towers, and walls of convents that appear to be in danger of falling" be torn down. The initial objections to this proposal centered on the demolition and rebuilding costs. Property owners emphasized the inflated cost of materials and laborers, noting, for example, that reeds used in quincha cost ten *reales* rather than the customary two and that reliable workers, even if well remunerated, were difficult to find. Their complaints prompted Manso

94   to request a report on price increases since the October calamity. As discussed above, he subsequently established official prices, at the same rate or only slightly above previous ones. Corregidores in outlying areas were asked to encourage Indians to come to work "voluntarily" in Lima.[13]

Owners of houses that had second stories designated for demolition quickly protested Godin's reforms. On January 21, 1747, two sisters, Doña Inés and Doña Catalina Ayessa, both nuns, and Doña Isidora de Arandia, the widow of Don Diego de Orbea, contended that their houses were in good shape and that the demolition would impoverish them and force members of their family into the streets.[14] The prosecutor turned down their petitions, but the Junta de Tribunales granted them eight days to present their case. By the end of January, dozens of prominent homeowners, many of them titled nobility, joined together to fight the measures. Thus began an extended battle over the viceroy's efforts to clip the architectural prerogatives of the upper classes. While Manso and Godin presented the reforms as questions of public safety, the upper classes tenaciously defended their right to own imposing houses and facades. They believed they had not only the right but the obligation to demonstrate their prominence in their architecture as well as in their public attire and other forms of ostentation.

Salvador Gerónimo de Portalanza represented them in the courts, presenting highly detailed challenges to the ban on *altos* on January 24 and, following rebuttals by the cabildo, in February and May.[15] Twenty-four people signed the document, but Portalanza frequently referred to his efforts as a defense of three hundred families. Among those signing were the Marquesa de Torre Tagle, the Conde de Torreblanca, and other matriarchs and patriarchs of Lima's leading families.[16] They initially concentrated on four points. First, Portalanza argued at length that many of the altos were already made of quincha and not only withstood earthquakes but also actually stabilized the entire building. Tearing down the second story would weaken the house. He provided several examples and demanded a "certification" or inspection of the condition of two-story houses. Second, he questioned the viceroy's right to condemn "respectable houses." Citing the medieval *Siete Partidas* (1251–65), Portalanza claimed that the viceroy could only do so if the land was required for "public works, defense, extension of monasteries, or to build a magnificent building," if the owner were found guilty of treason, or if the building had been placed on public property.[17] Portalanza and his associates therefore strongly questioned the viceroy's

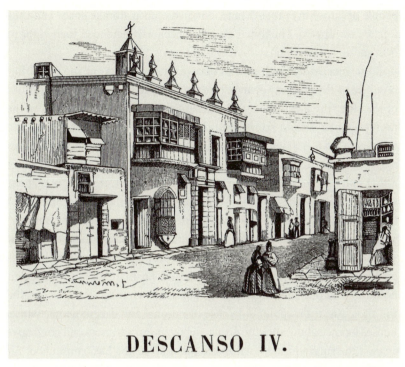

DESCANSO IV.

10 Colonial Lima with Balconies and Tapadas. *Source:* Simón Yanque (Esteban de Terralla y Landa) *Lima por dentro y fuera,* illustration by Ignacio Merino, "Calle de Lima" (Paris, 1854).

prerogative to carry out his plan. Furthermore, he contended that property owners should be compensated for any buildings torn down or not rebuilt. He did not provide figures, but he clearly sought to make the reforms exorbitantly expensive for the Crown. This constituted a small battle within the larger, incipient struggle over the implementation of the Bourbon Reforms, by which the viceregal state attempted to decrease the autonomy of the upper classes.

Third, the property owners asserted that they had a social right and even an obligation to build grand residences and that their houses followed the Crown's mandate to improve cities: "the kingdom's laws uniformly support the construction of magnificent monuments in the cities, especially capitals, because decorum, splendor and luster depend on them."[18] They elaborated this position in subsequent petitions. Fourth, Portalanza pointed out the lack of space to build within the walls surrounding the city. In a city so constricted, the destruction of second stories would not only deprive people of a roof over their heads, but also reduce storage space and thus weaken commerce. The upper classes tenaciously defended their right to own socially prestigious two-story buildings.

Portalanza ended with several statements pointing out the social importance of the property owners he defended. He reiterated that one-third of the city, "the most noble and distinguished," had been affected by the decree against second stories and therefore "not all of the people share this desire" to tear down second stories. He contended that the "barbarous masses" (el bárbaro bulgo) should not be taken into consideration, but rather only "the rational people" (el pueblo racional), who know that the second stories are the only thing that has protected them in earthquakes." In other words, although the majority of the population might want the second stories torn down, their insignificance removed them from consideration. He repeatedly distinguished the property owners from the mass of the population, contrasting the generous Spaniards and their elegant homes to the pusillanimous Indians and their wretched huts. Defending the altos was at this point a defense of rational and decent people whose houses loomed above the city, displaying technical advances and good taste against the vulgar masses, who were ignorant of the basic notions of architecture and lived in primitive eyesores. Portalanza closed by noting that shipwrecks had not meant the end of sailing and thus earthquakes should not doom second stories.[19]

The city council responded in early February that Portalanza represented only three hundred people and that the majority of the city's population clamored for the demolition of altos. The council members pointed out that even after three months, people had not returned to sleep in the second stories because of their well-founded fear. According to the cabildo's response, these people, presumably including many of the property owners behind Portalanza, knew these structures posed a danger. The cabildo's response then revisited the essence of the viceroy's arguments: that Lima's architecture could not withstand the region's periodic earthquakes and that the destruction not only took many lives and destroyed property, but also prompted chaos. If building methods were not changed, the misery, looting, and turmoil witnessed in Lima would recur. At this point, the writer left the usual level of abstraction and descended rhetorically to the streets. He described vile living quarters and rampant diseases, so horrifying that many survivors envied those who had perished in the earthquake. The author insisted that private rights must cede to public rights. On February 23, Viceroy Manso de Velasco upheld the prohibition of second stories.[20]

The author of the cabildo response, Godin, and Viceroy Manso were not social egalitarians. While attacking the property owners' vanity, which they deemed reckless, they did not pretend to banish social distinctions or question the elite's right to predominate. They merely sought, in terms of urban planning, to assure wider streets and lower buildings and, in political terms, to reduce the clout of Lima's upper echelon. In a parallel discussion on rebuilding the Cathedral and the difficult balance between the need for safety and the architectural requirements or expectations of an eminent city such as Lima, Viceroy Manso used the term "moderate ostentation." This epitomizes their view of limited, state-regulated architectural grandeur.[21]

Portalanza appealed the viceroy's decision, gaining some time. In April, the cabildo presented another detailed defense of the reforms and criticism of the property owners, focusing on the danger of second stories, even built with quincha, and on whether the owners had the right to build hazardous structures, no matter how magnificent. The technical arguments included such points as how quincha fell, whether it had crushed people in October, and whether it deteriorated over time. The document's author also reached back, citing the *Recopilación de Indias* (1681) to show that no compensation was necessary. He countered the argument presented frequently by Portalanza that classical civilizations had allowed grandiose buildings, maintaining that the enduring grandeur of Rome, Venice, Sicily, and Naples merely demonstrated their use of superior building materials. The author used Constantinople as an example of architectural splendor and egalitarianism: "The learned had the same size house as a plebe." Finally, he argued that beauty was not acceptable if it came at the cost of dangerous structures and that "cities are made for citizens and not citizens for the city."[22] In a separate document written in the same period, in April 1747, the viceroy complained bitterly about the property owners' preference for the "vain ostentation of their sumptuous buildings" over the population's safety.[23]

In a brilliantly crafted rebuttal, Portalanza and Manuel Silva y la Banda responded with over one hundred points justifying the maintenance of the altos.[24] They developed the arguments made in the previous rebuttal, breaking them up into dozens of points and presenting many examples and citations. Although they insisted less on the question of whether the viceroy had the right to condemn and prohibit second stores, they developed in exquisite detail, clarity, and style their other three key contentions: that in light of the lack of land within the walls and the high price of goods and labor, they could not afford to give up (the upper) half of their property; that altos did not endanger the city but actually made buildings stronger; and that their clients had the right to loom above the city. This last social justification sustained the legal, economic, and technical arguments.

Moreover, Portalanza and Silva y la Banda emphasized that the ban on second stories could not come at a more inappropriate time, with an economy devastated by inflation and shortages and a city with no space to expand within its walls. They detailed the high price of bricks, adobe, and workers and the reduced state of the owners' personal finances. They argued that even if the money were available, there was little empty space to build within the walls of Lima. Churches and public institutions such as the Mint and the Inquisition had been expanding into plazas and adjacent plots, people continued to camp out in makeshift huts and tents on church grounds, plazas, and the few empty fields, and real estate prices had escalated. They noted that if they were to rebuild single-story houses, they would need considerably larger plots, forty by eighty varas rather than twenty by sixty. For these reasons (and others), property owners had to remain where their houses were or had been. The two petitioners provided several explanations of why owners could not simply move into the first floor. They argued that the high cost of building materials and laborers made converting two-story houses into a single story impossibly expensive. Furthermore, the loss of the second stories would dramatically reduce the size of elite residences. It was not merely a matter of squeezing into the first floor, they contended, as these were used for servants, for carriages, as stores and rental property. In terms of both design and status, therefore, single-story edifices were not appropriate for the elite's standard of living. Not only would they have had to make do with less space or endeavor to purchase additional property, they also be faced with the loss of income from renting parts of both the first and second stories. Sixty years earlier, in fact, in the wake of the earthquake of 1687, property owners had opposed bans on second stories because of the threat to rental income.[25] Unable to rebuild elsewhere or relocate into their first floor, the property owners contended that they needed to maintain or rebuild their second stories. Several times they invoked the horrors three hundred leading families would have to endure if forced to move out of Lima.

In addition, Portalanza and Silva y la Banda insisted that the altos were safe. They pointed out that low walls had killed many people, giving the example of Pablo de Olavide, who lost his parents and sister when a one-story house they were visiting collapsed.[26] They countered the cabildo's arguments about the durability of quincha and time after time demanded an inspection in order to show that altos built of this material had stood up well in the earthquake. They noted that the area within three or four blocks of the Plaza Mayor, where the two-story houses were located, was the center of rebuilding activities while the more distant areas, which had only single-story houses, were ruined and largely deserted. The activity around the plaza showed that the altos had endured and that the owners were not fearful.[27] They dismissed people's fear of tall structures, labeling it several times "superstitious."

While Portalanza and Silva y la Banda demonstrated in detail and with verve the lack of alternatives to two-story houses and the safety they represented for the owners and others, they never strayed far from the argument that the upper classes had the social right and perhaps even obligation to rise above the city's lower orders. They repeated in various forms that the three hundred families they represented were not of the "vulgar classes" but rather "the foremost in the city." They also ridiculed the idea that Lima should be rebuilt "with reed huts, reducing the capital of the Peruvian kingdom to a town of barbarous Indians . . . rather than magnificent houses." They noted that low houses with small rooms fostered diseases. Just as Godin envisioned wide streets facilitating the circulation of air, they stressed their need to rise above the unhealthy, humid, and crowded streets. At one point they suggested in passing that all houses should be two stories. They therefore did not address the question of how the majority of the city's residents were to avoid the hazards of low buildings. To confront the cabildo and Godin's argument for more consistent or harmonious housing, they summoned the grandeur of classical architecture and its use of heavy materials and celebration of social hierarchies.

The property owners made clear their concern about losing a key marker of their respectability. The two-story houses as well as the heavy facades and elaborate grillwork that characterized them distinguished their residences from those of the middle and lower orders. The cabildo response itself had stressed that even houses that cost over 100,000 pesos "were held up just by an adobe wall." In other words, behind the intricate exteriors, the houses of the elite and of the lower orders were essentially the same.[28]

The property owners thus stressed the need to distinguish their houses with elaborate fronts and second stories. They did not attempt to mask this concern but instead touted the taller houses as a social right, one that differentiated them from the lower classes.

The argument of the property owners ultimately centered on the convergence of their right to have tall buildings and the social benefits of these structures for an eminent city such as Lima: "The grandeur of the city and the magnificence of its buildings are the true common good that links everyone." In essence, they expressed the Renaissance notion that a city's nobility or grandeur depended on the splendor of its buildings. Richard Kagan summarizes these ideas and their debt to Leon Battista Alberti: "As Alberti understood, *civitas* resided in architecture: a monumental church, a spacious square, a sumptuous palace, an imposing perimeter wall, even the city's physical fabric, especially one organized in accordance with an ordered, symmetrical plan of the kind that Alberti, together with other Renaissance architectural theorists, considered the epitome of urban design."[29]

Portalanza and Silva y la Banda argued that rebuilding the second-story houses (and presumably the ornate facades and balconies) benefited not just the owners but the city of Lima as a whole, which as a viceregal capital required distinguished architecture. They were not self-centered patriarchs putting their comfort and finances ahead of the city's safety, but rather leading citizens who sought to resurrect Lima's magnificence and glory.

The petition of the two men refuted specific points by the cabildo. For example, they ridiculed the use of Constantinople as a model, noting that it had different, inferior customs, laws, and religion than Spain and Peru. The authors also at one point discounted the argument that they were a small minority, as the Church's buildings (convents, monasteries, *cofradías*, and congregations) and hospitals also needed to rise above a single story. They did not press this point, however, instead stressing their small numbers but social significance and the value or benefits that grandiose buildings would bring devastated Lima.

The property owners clearly thought the viceroy and his French advisor were taking matters too much into their own hands. They did not believe that the viceroy and the cabildo should have free rein in redesigning the city. In this controversy, the upper classes voiced their opposition to strong, interventionist policies of the Bourbon state. They did this in the courts, presenting a profound critique of the project while also gaining time by dragging the case into the legal system. Their economic, social, and political concerns coalesced into a cohesive defense of the prerogatives of the upper classes. Visible here is one of the first of many skirmishes between Peru's elite and the viceregal state over the implementation of the Bourbon absolutist project.

Viceroy Manso de Velasco and the members of the cabildo, after enduring months of pressure, ultimately relented. The cabildo members came from Lima's finest families, and many of them, having two-story houses themselves, no doubt sympathized with the owners. The decision also probably reflected the impressive technical arguments by the property owners. Their insistence that the altos had withstood the earthquake, a claim that was verifiable by a short stroll from the Plaza Mayor, seemed convincing. In November 1747 Manso de Velasco ordered a house-by-house inspection to review which upper floors could besalvaged. He instructed that whereas all of those made of adobe had to be torn down, those of wattle and daub that appeared sturdy could remain. In effect, the inspectors called for many tall walls and arches to be torn down or at least reduced in height but rarely condemned the second stories.[30] In his memoirs, the Conde de Superunda justified his policy reversal by recognizing the lack of plots on which to build new houses in the city and the fact that adobe houses with wood-framed second stories had, in fact, survived the earthquake.[31] Yet in a letter of 1748, he recognized with clear bitterness the "very efficient" legal struggle against the reforms.[32] The property owners had succeeded in defending their second stories in the face of Godin's reforms.

Conclusion: Over the Waves

Manso de Velasco successfully rebuilt Lima. The chaos and disorder in the days, weeks, and months following the earthquake that so petrified Lima's population, the scattering of the population, and the crime wave did not last. The viceroy boasted in his memoirs that order had largely returned in time for the royal funeral of King Felipe V, delayed in Lima until August 7, 1747. He acknowledged that "poor people" had resisted leaving their make-shift lodging in the plazas and public places where they had found refuge, yet leaving them there would have left "the capital of the kingdom in great disorder, ugliness, and discomfort, taking away the land designated for recreation [desahogo] and beauty." He waited until houses were rebuilt in the city center and then encouraged the humble to rent rooms and stores at low rates. He allowed some to stay in Acho, Los Naranjos, Cocharcas, and other peripheral areas because the low rents they paid benefited them as well as the landowners. All in all, however, his plan to rebuild from within had worked.[33] Within a decade, many of the city's main buildings had been rebuilt, at least sufficiently for them to reopen, and Lima's spatial order had survived.[34] In early 1747, builders started work on the new Real Felipe fort as well as a new town just inland from Callao, Bellavista. Although the initial plan to leave the destroyed area uninhabited never worked—people rebuilt in the old area next to the beach—Real Felipe, with its precise pentagonal layout and impressive walls and cannons, consolidated in highly symbolic fashion the viceroyalty's defenses, and Bellavista attracted a growing population.[35]

The inauguration in 1758 of the San Lázaro hospital for lepers prompted poetic celebrations of Manso's efforts. The Jesuit father Juan Sánchez extolled the viceroy's "generous piety," deeming him the magical force, architect, and designer of Lima's resurgence. He lauded the new town of Bellavista for "laughing in the face of the sea's insults." Referring to the Mint, rebuilt in neoclassical style, he posed the question, "Shouldn't citizens and foreigners take note, when strength, beauty, art, majesty, order, and ingenuity all vie for the triumph?" After complimenting the Cathedral and the Royal Palace, Father Sánchez praised the viceroy's "military genius, civil providence, governing prudence, political vigilance, rectitude, fidelity, budgetary caution, religious zeal, and Christian piety."[36] A decade before, Manso de Velasco had earned greater honors. In recognition of his rebuilding efforts, in 1748 he was granted the title Conde de Superunda, or "Over the Waves."

Rebuilding changed Lima's architecture, accelerating the transition from the baroque to the neoclassical. The catastrophe destroyed many classic churrigueresque buildings, and urban reformers wreaked more damage in the following decades. Altars, facades, and buildings were demolished, often replaced by neoclassical structures. In ordinary private houses, the increased use of flat roofs and of quincha and adobe stood out. Paradoxically, in their efforts to create a viceregal capital that might reflect their increasingly centralized power in their colonies, the Bourbons relied on the building techniques of quincha and adobe, derived from pre-Hispanic societies. Less elaborate arches and facades, if any, would grace new or re-built churches and the dwellings of distinguished residents. French styles became increasingly popular. Although Godin and Viceroy Superunda eventually relented in their struggle with the upper classes and their higher buildings, lower walls and, in general, lower buildings were more common after 1746. Not only did style and techniques shift but the kind of building changed as well. In the late eighteenth century's more secular world, new construction centered on civic rather than ecclesiastical buildings. These included, by century's end, a theater, a coliseum, a bullring, a poorhouse, and a botanical garden.[37] Secularization and *afrancesamiento*, or Frenchifi-cation, took place even within houses, as some owners converted prayer rooms or *oratorios* into salons.[38]

Nonetheless, the rebuilding had not been as triumphant and smooth as the official accounts and the subsequent celebrations indicate. On the one hand, the various projects had been beset by financial problems, personal squabbles, delays, and conflicts. The case of the Cathedral demonstrated all of these. Although the aptly named *Pompa Funeral* for King Fernando VI in 1760 sustained that "once he [the King] understood the extent of the damage, desirous of promoting God's glory, he ordered the temple re-paired at his expense," all involved complained about the lack of financial support.[39] Problems in the rebuilding of the Cathedral increased when the brother of the archbishop, José Barroeta y Angel, became the director of the project and Pedro Bravo de Rivero assumed the position of overseer (*juez*). Archbishop Barroeta and Bravo de Rivero were bitter enemies and fought over expenses and other issues. Disagreements surged over how high the Cathedral towers could extend as well as over finances, forced Indian labor, and deadlines. The archbishop made numerous complaints, including one charging that a painting of the shield of the (Madrid) Royal Arms had been inappropriately placed above the archbishop's chair. Leaders of the Cathe-dral Chapter, bitter rivals of Barroeta, claimed it had previously been there but in a larger sculpture. The painting remained.[40]

Of course, disagreements and delays are part of any project, and in eighteenth-century Lima many if not most authorities fought frequent and bitter turf battles over space and protocol. Archbishop Barroeta was particularly obsessed, deluging Madrid with complaints about the viceroy, his advisors, the Cathedral Chapter, and others. My discussion has shown, however, that beyond these battles, which were whitewashed from official accounts, the viceroy faced great opposition to his plans. The upper classes fought him arduously in court, defending their prerogative to stand above the majority. They opposed all attempts to weaken or mask their social dominance, in battles that ranged from architecture to sumptuary laws about what they could wear. This previewed the difficulties the Bourbons would face in attempting to reform the administration of their American colonies.

William Biek's observation that absolutist "French monarchs had to make peace with a preexisting society that they had increasingly infiltrated but never explicitly conquered" offers an interesting perspective on mid-eighteenth-century Lima.[41] The Lima upper classes were not an entrenched aristocracy with special rights but nonetheless proved to be spirited opponents of the viceroy's reforms. They had enormous social and economic power within Peru and no doubt lobbied vigorously against the reforms in ways invisible in the historical record. Their legal efforts are quite visible, and in the courts they managed to impede the full-scale implementation of Godin's plan. Although the viceroy claimed victory, a more correct appraisal might see the conflict a tie or a stalemate. Some of the Lima elite supported the measures—although their unity should not be exaggerated—but a sizable, potent group battled them. They backed other measures taken by Manso and subsequent viceroys and constituted the bulwark of local support for the Bourbons. Nonetheless, they proved themselves very capable of challenging reforms they did not like.

This legal battle was not the only, or even the greatest, controversy surrounding Viceroy Manso de Velasco's efforts. Destitute landowners besieged the colonial state, claiming that the damage or destruction of their property made it impossible for them to make interest payments on their obligations and debts to the Church, *censos*. The Church, in turn, contended that its various elements had lost considerable property and desperately needed money to rebuild churches, monasteries, and convents and to aid those in need. Manso de Velasco crafted a delicate compromise, one that satisfied neither lenders nor borrowers. Curiously, in these lawsuits, property owners, who in the discussion about altos stressed the buildings' stability, emphasized and probably exaggerated their losses. The Church, on the other hand, contended that the devastation was much less than initially believed. In rebuilding Lima, Viceroy Conde de Superunda found himself in the middle of a battle between the Church and property owners, a confrontation complicated by the fact that all of the elite families had members in the Church and others held appointments in the audiencia. Yet Superunda was not merely an unfortunate administrator stuck between two powers. As was the case with the battle between elite property owners and the viceroy, he also had a project in mind, hoping to use the earthquake to weaken the presence of the Church or, more probably, to improve its internal order. The Church–State conflict foreshadowed an enduring standoff.

Licentious Friars, Wandering Nuns, and Tangled *Censos*: A Shakeup of the Church?

The convent is the institution that represents and incarnates the colonial spirit. True in all the Spanish holdings in the Americas, this is even more so in Peru, especially Lima. The soul of our city is the cloistered soul. It still lives, although hidden and forgotten.

—JOSÉ DE LA RIVA AGÜERO, *La Historia en el Perú, 213*

Six

The earthquake and tsunami provoked tensions between the Catholic Church and the viceregal authorities, prompting discussion and changes regarding the place of the Church in colonial Peru. The calamity struck churches, convents, monasteries, and urban and rural properties owned by the Church in and around Lima, destroying some and damaging most. It ruptured the elaborate network of credit that flowed to and from property owners through the Church, particularly the convents. As noted, the analysis of notary records found that convents and monasteries owned 38 percent of urban property. If other realms of the Church are added such as hospitals, chaplaincies, religious brotherhoods, and schools, the number approaches 75 percent. The previously reliable flow of income from a variety of sources dwindled as individuals claimed they no longer had the property, funds, or moral obligation to pay. The destruction of property and contraction of income came at the very time when demand for the Church's services, such as aiding the destitute, caring for the moribund, and attending to the dead, escalated. The viceroy and the courts had to address this financial crisis. Not only did the dispute reach the courts rapidly, but the economic importance of the Church made the credit issue fundamental in financing the rebuilding of Lima.

The crisis, however, went far beyond these very serious property and credit losses. Viceroy Manso de Velasco's vision of a rebuilt Lima harmonized with Spain's secularization efforts, which foresaw a smaller role for the Church under the supervision of the Crown. Reformers viewed the earthquake as an opportunity to pare down the Church's presence in Lima and in the viceroyalty, above all, to remove the mendicant orders from the city's public life and rural parishes and return them to a monastic existence and to the missions. In coordination with the Marques de la Ensenada and the Madrid court, Viceroy Manso de Velasco took various, generally moderate measures to weaken the presence of the Church. The mendicant orders fought back, contending that the Church had been devastated by the earthquake and that its pious work and moral presence were more necessary than ever. The archbishop of Lima, the representative of the secular church, also bristled at the viceroy's efforts. Like the architectural reforms targeting the upper classes, the measures that aimed to reduce the Church's physical presence and its financial predominance sparked an enduring controversy. They also highlighted diverse groups' fears as well as their visions of a rebuilt Lima.

Discussions about the role of the Church after the earthquake were not limited to these financial and administrative issues. Instead, they often focused on the moral state of the Church, particularly the orders. Building on critiques and scandals dating from the beginning of the century and earlier, many proponents of reform emphasized the wanton ways of priests, the decadence of Lima's teeming convents, and the greed of archdiocesan authorities. They cast their efforts as solutions to the questionable state of the Church through the rectification of the behavior of some of its members, to be accomplished by returning them to monastic life and removing them from the temptations of the secular world. This was not a simple two-sided battle—many of the most startling condemnations of the Church came from its own members. Both secular and regular clergy provided ammunition to the reformers, detailing extensive excesses and *relajación*, or relaxation, two key terms in the polemic. Many Church members agreed with the interpretation of the earthquake as a severe sign of God's wrath at the immoral ways of the city, including those of the religious communities. Discussions about what to do with the Church brought together property and financial issues with beliefs about the causes for the disaster and the moral decadence of the city.

The City of Kings (and Bishops, Priests, Nuns, Doncellas, and the Pious)

The Catholic Church had a monumental and ubiquitous presence in eighteenth-century Lima. At the time of the earthquake, the city had twenty-six monasteries for men, fourteen convents, and approximately ten *beaterios*, another form of female religious community. In 1700 one-fifth of the city's female population lived in convents: the inhabitants included nuns, various types of spiritual women who had not taken vows, and the considerable servant population that waited on these two groups.[1] Religious orders, particularly San Juan de Dios and the Bethlehemites, managed many of the city's ten hospitals. Secular clergy were in charge of the city's seven parishes, with the exception of El Cercado, the Indian neighborhood, which was bestowed on the Jesuits. As all of the maps from the period testify, churches constituted the spine of Lima.

In the eighteenth century, it was impossible to walk in Lima (El Cercado excepted) more than two blocks without finding a church, convent, monastery, or beaterio. Directions were almost invariably given in terms of proximity to a religious building, even after the placing of block-by-block signs and the implementation of a more rational numbering system in the 1780s.[2] Notary records from the period usually designated locations with such terms as "behind San Francisco" or "one block up from Santa Clara."

Ermitas, or small chapels, were also found inside the city's walls. In San Lázaro, people venerated a large cross in the Baratillo market, Santa Cruz de Baratillo, while the Malambo neighborhood counted on the chapel of Nuestra Señora del Socorro until it was destroyed in the earthquake. The earthquake also ruined a small chapel in Cocharcas, in the Indian neighborhood. The presence of the Church did not diminish outside of the city walls. Ermitas graced the San Cristóbal hill just east of the city and the hills of Amancaes to the north, while two religious houses, the Montserrat and San Francisco de Paula *hospederías*, aided those on the road between Lima and Callao.[3]

The Church dominated Lima's aural and temporal landscape as well. Bells rang constantly, calling people to mass, announcing a festival or important funeral, marking the proximity of the viceroy, warning of fire, pirates, or earthquake.[4] Saints' days were more commonly used than the secular day and month to denote a date. Members of the religious community participated in or led all of life's key rituals and rites of passage—birth, baptism, first communion, marriage, and death—and were the main providers of social services such as education, health, and charity. They were also prominent in civic rituals such as processions marking the arrival of a new viceroy or a birth or death in the Spanish royal family.

Lima's extensive religious population, its elaborate and omnipresent churches, convents, monasteries, and chapels, and its exuberant, corporal public devotion defined the city's baroque essence. Frequent religious processions (the Chilean historian Benjamín Vicuña Mackenna referred to Lima's double fog, the infamous *garúa* mist and the cloud of incense that hung above the city), and ornate facades like that of La Merced church embodied the city's spirituality.[5] As eighteenth-century reformers attempted to rein in the independent, multivocal, heterogeneous nature of the baroque, the church was a central battleground, presenting seemingly infinite fronts.

Taming the Church

Postearthquake reformers sought to halt new convents and monasteries, police the behavior of irresolute priests (particularly regulars), drive nuns back into the convents (closing the door firmly behind them), reinforce the primacy of the viceregal state over Church authorities, and discipline the lower classes. In light of the omnipresence of the Church and the region's severe financial woes, even these moderate reforms constituted a considerable challenge.

Motivations for these changes came from several fronts. Secularization, a mainstay of the Enlightenment, is best understood by moving back and forth to and from Protestant Europe, Bourbon Spain, the viceregal palace and the adjoining Cathedral, the streets of Lima, and the parishes and missions of Peru. The more radical secular or anticlerical strands of the Enlightenment did not flourish in Spain. While intellectuals elsewhere in Europe questioned the existence of spirits and magic and, in some cases, the significance of religion and the predominance of the Church or churches, Spanish vanguard intellectuals by and large sought to dislodge scholasticism without challenging the Catholic Church.[6] The Bourbon rulers themselves were deeply religious and envisioned Spain as a firmly Catholic kingdom, despite Pope Clemente XI's support for the Habsburgs in 1709 in the midst of the War of Succession. The Bourbons promoted, however, an active regalist campaign that sought the creation of a "national Church" dependent not on the Vatican but on Madrid. They stressed reforming or "improving" the Church itself, limiting its numbers, controlling its property, and channeling its efforts to aid in the absolutist project and the improvement of the country, what some have deemed the creation of an "enlightened" or "illustrated" clergy. The Crown also targeted baroque religious practices, particularly lower-class customs, fostering a more austere and homogeneous religiosity.[7] Throughout the eighteenth century, the Bourbons emphasized their rights over the Church and sought to reform it in order to put it to good use in the remaking of Spain.

The Crown already counted on the Real Patronato in the Americas, granting them control over Church finances and personnel, and thus did not have to confront the papacy on this front. Instead, it promoted such reforms as the limitation in 1716 on the ecclesiastical *fuero*, or privilege, and a series of decrees (in 1703, 1708, 1727, 1731, and 1739) that established a minimum number of members for convents, measures that increased the power of the Crown and weakened the independence of the orders.[8] While these reforms paled next to those of Spain itself, let alone other parts of Europe, the place of the Church in Spanish America was changing. The Bourbons sought to clarify the ambivalent divisions of power characteristic of the Habsburgs, placing the Church and religion firmly under the Crown's increasingly centralist rule.[9]

The midcentury reforms in Lima embodied Bourbon regalism, particularly concerns over the independence and unruliness of the mendicant orders. They also brought into focus and public discussion decades of scandalous reports and deep misgivings about the religious communities' conduct. Many of the postearthquake reforms targeted this behavior. Beyond the sensational accounts of wayward priests and nuns, what stands out in these reports is how intertwined the administrative problems of excessive ecclesiastical numbers and financial difficulties are with the moral denunciations. In the eyes of many, the excesses and poverty prompted moral laxity, which only furthered the problems. In fact, the excessive numbers, economic problems, and immorality cannot easily be separated or divided into cause and effect; in the denunciatory language of the era, they amalgamated into a single cry for change. Calling for controls on the religious communities' presence and behavior for their own good, these denunciations buttressed regalist policies in Spain and the Americas.

It would be incorrect, however, to dismiss this as official discourse, tendentious allegations orchestrated to support regalist policies. The denunciations, which became an important stimulus to the postearthquake reforms, often came from members of the Church itself as well as from pious people who had little interest in or knowledge of Crown and viceregal policies. The reports expressed a deep-rooted preoccupation over the state of the Church and Lima's sinful ways, a preoccupation that shaped discussions about the causes or meaning of the earthquake itself. God's wrath was deeply feared; much of Lima desperately desired the correction of errant behavior by members of the Church. They felt that something was gravely wrong and that the consequences, if things did not change, would be apocalyptic.

Excesses and *Relajación*

In the late seventeenth century, both the Viceroy Duque de la Palata and the archbishop encouraged the king to limit the number of convents in Lima to the five largest ones: La Encarnación, La Concepción, Santa Clara, Trinidad, and Santa Catalina. These five *conventos grandes* (as well as Descalzas on the other side of the river, in San Lázaro) had a massive physical, spiritual, and economic presence in colonial Lima yet were not alone. From the late sixteenth century through the seventeenth, smaller convents, or *recoletos*, had been built. These included the Mercedarian Nuestra Señora de Belén (1604), the Dominican Venturosa Magdalena (1606), and the Franciscan Nuestra Señora de Guadalupe (1611), characterized not only by their smaller populations, but also by the greater asceticism of their residents.[10]

The proposals by Viceroy Duque de la Palata and the archbishop supported a papal letter by Pope Urban VIII and a number of royal decrees that

11 "Procession of Religious judges (foreground) and prisoners (centre) entering
the Cathedral, where the sentences of the prisoners will be read."
Source: Durret, *Voyage de Marseille a Lima* (Paris, 1720).

12 An *Auto de Fe* in the Plaza Mayor, Lima.
Source: Museo de la Inquisición y del Congreso, Lima.

limited the number of convents by closing down those with fewer than eight residing nuns. The large number of convents was seen as an impediment to "regular observation" and to "discipline."[11] These efforts resurfaced periodically in the first half of the eighteenth century and kindled discussions in Lima and Madrid after the earthquake. While some called for limiting the number of convents, others focused on the excessive numbers of residents in the large convents. They contended that the smaller ones, the *recoletos*, embodied the austere monastic life, while the large ones fostered disorder and even rowdy behavior, thus discouraging spiritual life and embarrassing Lima. In 1700, La Concepción had over 1,000 residents: 271 nuns, 47 *donadas*, or servants, who had taken vows and provided a small dowry, 162 seculars (ladies, schoolgirls, babies), 290 servants and maids, and 271 slaves.[12] An official visit by the archbishop to several convents in 1725 found a shockingly high number of servants of assorted races: black slaves, mulattas, Indians, and mestizas. The report's author noted that many of the slaves were married, implying that the husbands might have opportunities to enter the convent, and that other men were all too often allowed in to bring gifts or to run an errand. He complained about the high number of secular women who had entered the cloistered world to escape from their husbands. In this and many other cases, the denunciation of "excess numbers" in the convents emphasized servants and secular women (and men), who usually outnumbered the nuns themselves.[13]

A few years later, in 1729, elections for the abbess in the Encarnación convent prompted a scandal that spilled over the walls. Founded in 1558, and thus often referred to as the first South American convent (it was demolished in the 1920s to make room for the northeast part of the Plaza San Martín), this Augustinian convent had traditionally housed the daughters of the elite. In 1700, it had a population of 817 women: 229 nuns, 29 donadas, 280 servants, 144 slaves, and 135 lay girls, or *seglares*, who studied there.[14] In 1729, María de las Nieves defeated Rosa de la Cueva in elections for abbess. De la Cueva contested the elections, and some nuns supported her by leaving the convent. Priests sent to put out the flames of the growing controversy blamed black and mulatta servants as well as the nuns' relatives, who jockeyed for their candidate. Accusations, threats, and clashes continued until the mid-1730s, accentuating the belief that the convents were overpopulated and that divisions between the monastic and secular worlds were eroding dangerously.[15]

A scandalous report sent to the pope in 1722 detailed the questionable behavior of priests and nuns and the institutional causes for the decline of the Peruvian Church. It made these discussions quite public, influencing policies in the ensuing decades. As Alfredo Moreno Cebrián has shown in his analysis, the report emerged from a struggle among viceroys, archbishops, and pretenders to both positions. It was actually written by José María Barberí, a Roman secular priest, advisor to Viceroy Príncipe de Santo Buono (Cármine Nicolás Caraccioli, viceroy from 1716 to 1720), and confidante of Archbishop Soloaga (in office 1714–22) who died the year the report was written. The three of them battled with the former viceroy of Lima and bishop of Quito, Diego Ladrón de Guevara (viceroy from 1710 to 1716) and Diego Morcillo (archbishop of Lima in 1723–30, viceroy in 1720–24). Incensed by Ladrón de Guevara's seeming favoritism regarding chaplaincies and positions in the Lima Cathedral, the excesses in the city's convents and monasteries, abuses by district authorities, *corregidores*, and priests, particularly against Indians, the "indecent" dress of the clergy, and priests' public encounters with women, especially the *tapadas*, Archbishop Soloaga wrote indignant reports and implemented changes.[16] The Relación, written in 1722, developed these points.

The Relación contended that regular priests were no longer concentrated in the distant missions and conventual life but instead were dispersed in rural parishes. This undermined the missions, prompted disarray in conventual life, heightened the exploitation of the Indian inhabitants of the Peruvian countryside, and in general demoralized the Church and thus Peru. The author noted that mission work was limited to the Franciscans in the central jungle, Cerro de la Sal, and to the Jesuits in Mojos and in Charcas, or Upper Peru; other orders had abandoned this obligation. Instead, the orders held "almost 1,000" rural parishes, many of them sold to third persons. In an argument that can be found in virtually all of the era's denunciations of the orders, Barberí sustained that this state of affairs drew friars away from mission work and prompted debilitating struggles over control of the parishes. The author describes the scandalous flow of money and lobbying for positions in order to gain control of the parishes, a complaint reiterated throughout the eighteenth century. Regalist reformers sought to uproot the expensive and contentious elections, which they believed accelerated the materialist drift of church members and empowered the orders' authorities, commissaries, and vicar-generals.[17] The Relación also denounced the exploitation of Indians and other rural residents, deeming it harmful not only for the mistreated rural people but also for the friars themselves, as their materialist pursuits led them astray. The denunciation centered on the necessity of removing regular priests from rural parishes.[18]

The report also describes sensual celebrations after elections for abbess. Led by musicians and "many mulattas," the flag-carrying victors visited the viceroy and archbishop and then returned to the convent. Days of festivities would ensue, with the mulattas scandalously entering the convent and participating in dances, plays, and even bullfights. Among many lurid observations the author refers to priests' concubines and the much less common critique of "the so abominable vice of juntas of women with women." He portrays "secular" Lima as unapologetically lascivious and sinful, noting that "la putería no quita Hidalguía" (whoring does not take away nobility). For example, women and men appeared in public with their concubines. The author underlines this moral decay, a vision repeated in *Noticias secretas* by the Spanish naval officers and scientists Jorge Juan and Antonio de Ulloa and other mid-eighteenth-century denunciations of Lima's sinful ways, with the Latin-rooted term *concupiscence*.[19]

In the same section, Barberí described the collusion of authorities, landowners, and priests in the exploitation of Indians in the countryside. He contended that divisions between the secular and the ecclesiastical had collapsed and desperately needed to be restored. Profits from rural estates and virtual putting out systems (in which authorities provided the wool and Indians were forced to produce textiles) financed scandalous elections in Lima, while priests and nuns had been seduced by the wayward behavior of Lima's residents, from the dissolute members of the elite to the sensual mulattas who played such a large role in gender preoccupations (and fantasies) of the eighteenth century. He decries how "monastic priests wander around the city alone, young, some on foot and others on mule with indecent saddles, which in light of their cost run against their vows, many with silver spurs, publicly entering prostitutes' houses, strolling in front of them. . . . and many take their concubines with them on the same mule in public strolls."[20] Barberí believed that the first steps in restoring the barriers between the regulars and the temptations of daily life was removing them from rural parishes, reducing the number of convents and monasteries in Lima, and placing minimums and maximums on the number of nuns and priests allowed.

In another notable precedent to the earthquake of 1746, the report stressed that the decadence of the Peruvian Church had provoked God's ire. In his introduction, Barberí blamed Lima's earthquakes, the sterility of the land, and the pan-Andean epidemic that had spread from La Plata to Peru since 1719 on "the very gravity of these sins, overlooked by superiors and judges."[21] In 1730, Viceroy Castelfuerte labeled the "sinister operations" of the Prelates Generals and related behavior 'the principal cause why calamities and adverse events persist with such stubborn determination, sent by God to punish this afflicted kingdom." He called for "paternal providence from His Majesty" in order to "suspend or lighten divine anger, the very just lash of the Lord's wrath."[22]

These scandalous reports concurred with European travelers' accounts of Lima's lax moral standards and public debauchery. Amedée Frezier, a French naval captain and engineer who visited Lima (although for a week only) in 1713, ridiculed Lima's supposed religiosity, deeming it an illusion. He decried the contradiction between the facade of so many clergy and church buildings and the reality of so little pious behavior.[23] Juan and Ulloa, while more respectful of Lima society than non-Spanish Europeans, provided the most well-known descriptions of the excesses and sinful customs of members of the Church.[24]

These sensational descriptions of Lima, examined at length in the following two chapters, reflect a variety of attitudes and preoccupations. They demonstrate imperial yearnings, a desire necessarily grounded in denigrating the Spanish, and echo eighteenth-century denunciations of luxury, a key theme of intellectual currents in Europe.[25] At the same time, they convey Lima's well-developed public forms of flirtation and barely concealed obsession with concubines and lovers. The examination of Lima's debates about the Church indicates, however, that Europeans were not the only participants in discussions (or denunciations) of Lima's morality. Concerned about what Europeans were saying but much more worried about the implications of this behavior for the city itself, city authorities and others addressed this matter also. The Lima population believed that something was terribly wrong and that the earthquake had been an ominous warning. These discussions and fears helped shape the rebuilding of Lima and the reform of the Church, particularly the secularization campaign.[26]

Secularization

The earthquake occurred in the midst of renewed debate in Madrid about the size and strength of the regular orders in the Americas. As noted, a number of royal decrees from 1703 to 1739 had established a minimum number of eight members for convents and monasteries. In July 1746 the Crown revoked the permission that had been granted to the Discalced Carmelites to build three new convents in Mexico and ordered governors not to authorize new monasteries and convents unless the Council of the Indies granted permission. In 1749 the first of a series of decrees was dispatched that called for regular priests in parishes to be replaced by seculars.[27] David Brading has noted that the Crown was "impelled to action by a strong letter from the current viceroy of Peru, the Count of Superunda, who complained of the excessive number of nuns resident in Lima and sharply condemned the frequently licentious behaviour of the religious who administered rural parishes."[28] In the months and even years after the earthquake, the viceroy provided Madrid with distressing accounts that bolstered their efforts to limit the orders. Putting these reforms into effect in Peru, however, proved more difficult.

In December 1746 Viceroy Manso sent the first of several reports about the state of Lima, stressing the pitiful state of the religious community and the difficulties this posed for rebuilding. He noted that the six oldest convents in the City of Kings were severely overcrowded, to the point that they "looked more like labyrinths than religious houses, facilitating their ruin."[29] He blamed overcrowding for the high number of fatalities and extensive damage from the earthquake as well as the predicament of nuns who were forced to seek refuge in the secular world beyond the crumbled walls of the convents. Manso described the appalling scenes of nuns in tattered habits or makeshift clothes searching for family members. He noted, however, that some good could come from this situation, if strict limitations on the number of nuns residing in each convent were set and their finances put in order. In fact, he postulated that perhaps Divine Providence had devised this "tremendous blow" to improve the convents.[30] In the coming years, Manso emphasized that overcrowding undermined monastic discipline and increased the devastation of earthquakes, arguments accepted and reiterated in Madrid. He understood the earthquake as an opportunity to fortify the distinction between secular and sacred spaces.

Although Manso's denunciations of the overpopulated religious houses focused on convents, he also decried the surplus of priests, particularly regulars, and called for change. He lobbied for reducing the number of Dominicans, Franciscans, Augustinians, and Mercedarians, noting that they had become "a target of criticism by foreigners and Spaniards who pass through these kingdoms, surprised by the licentious freedom with which the priests live."[31] He referred to the disparaging reports mentioned above by French and other Europeans, including Spaniards, on the moral state of Lima.

In December 1748, Manso developed these ideas, initially sketched out in his correspondence following the earthquake. He adamantly called for the removal of regulars from rural parishes, what he presented as the central cause for a viceregal-wide decline of religiosity and economic stagnation. As was the case with his comments on the overflowing convents, Manso repeated well-known arguments for secularization, providing ammunition for the reformers in Madrid. In this communication of 1748, he noted that allowing regulars into the parishes (doctrinas) over the centuries had been a temporary remedy that had gone on for too long. He deemed it "damaging and prejudicial."[32] Manso described the wealth accumulated by the orders and the related poverty of the seculars. This prompted growing ambitions among the regulars, leading them away from a dignified monastic life and sparking scandals regarding their economic accumulation and the election of leaders. Manso also pointed out the difficulties for the regulars to return to their observant ways once they had become accustomed to the "freedom of the outside world."[33]

The viceroy then referred to the difficulties for the parishes and their humble members. He claimed that regulars, concerned only about funding the urban convents and monasteries, left the dioceses in a ruined, bankrupt state. Frequent visits by their prelates — cast as the ultimate culprits — encouraged priests to funnel money toward the cities. Secular priests, on the other hand, did not have these demands and thus worried more about the well-being of their parishes. This was not necessarily out of the goodness of their hearts: the seculars' ascension in the hierarchy depended on their leaving their diocese in good order rather than channeling money to the higher-ups and the religious houses of Lima.[34] This critique of the regulars' intrusion into the doctrinas constituted a familiar centerpiece of the secularization efforts. Manso's report would be widely discussed and repeated in Madrid.

Three principal advisors to King Fernando VI pushed for reform. His confessor, Francisco Rávago, a Jesuit, called for a reduction in the number of priests within each order to a level that could be supported by the order's income. Rávago cited numerous papal bulls to this effect and noted "the King, as a good son of the Church, in executing these is doing nothing other than helping fulfill what they ordered."[35] The two core members of the king's inner circle, Secretary of State José de Carvajal and the Marquis de la Ensenada, urged rapid ecclesiastical reform.[36] Ensenada was a staunch regalist who sought to extend the Crown's *patronato real* (an agreement between the Catholic Church and the Crown that granted the latter extensive power in church affairs in the Americas). As the king's right-hand man, he stressed improving finances as the means to shore up Spain's position in Europe, which was weakened by the War of Jenkins' Ear (1739–48). Multiple interests converged in the efforts to rein in the Church, specifically the orders: a fear of its autonomy in the Americas, battles with Rome, and the search for greater revenues.

In 1748, Ensenada and Carvajal brought the archbishops of Mexico and Lima, Manuel Rubio y Salinas and Pedro Antonio de Barroeta, respectively, to the court in the Escorial. The prelates agreed about the excess number of the orders and their possessions and supported the call for change. With this endorsement in hand, Carvajal and Ensenada convinced the king to create a special junta consisting of the two archbishops, four members of the Consejo de Castilla, and five from the Consejo de Indias to debate the necessary reforms.[37] This would bypass the normally slow and conservative channel in which American policy was implemented, the Consejo de Indias. The junta was the recipient of Manso's detailed reports.[38]

The junta justified its efforts through the argument that the economic activities of the Church, particularly the accumulation of land, not only distorted the economy and thus harmed individuals, the State, and the monarchy, but also led priests astray. Their accumulation of goods impelled them away from moderation, purity, and their spiritual duties and toward ostentation and, even worse, sin. This overlapping of economics, politics, and morals meant that the three topics examined by the junta—the reduction of the number of convents and monasteries in Lima and Callao, the transfer of rural parishes from regulars to seculars, and the consolidation of convents—were much more intertwined than might seem apparent at first glance.

The junta met at Carvajal's country home outside of Madrid from

120   November 29, 1748, until March 1749. After reviewing historical anteced-
ents, they examined various reports from the viceroys. The first Count of
Revillagigedo, viceroy of New Spain from 1745 to 1755, described the controversy surrounding the plan for Carmelite expansion, noting that if it
were not for the economic malaise caused by the religious orders "that
Kingdom [Mexico] could be the most opulent in the world, owing to its
incomparable riches and dilated extension." They also discussed the fiscal
impact of the order's economic strength, citing letters from Lima in the
1730s about the difficulty of collecting sales taxes. The junta then reviewed
Manso de Velasco's somber reports on the state of Lima.[39] He had criticized prelates for accepting excessive numbers of novices in order to gain
their dowries and a share in their "stockpile of interests" in the parishes.
Families, particularly the poor, had no alternative but to offer their children
to the orders. The junta repeated some of Manso's key points, such as the
impediments to the observance of monastic life caused by overcrowded
convents.[40]

The junta debated at length what to do with Lima's convents and monasteries. The discussion rambled in part because the members were reviewing
several issues simultaneously: not only the rebuilding of the convents but
the reduction of their population and the need for greater internal order.
They made many recommendations in regard to the "new" convents and
monasteries in Lima and Callao: only allow those with legitimate licenses
to rebuild, limit each order to one for each gender, prohibit those which
had lost their estates to rebuild, and, above all, wait for further information
from the viceroy, who would consult with Archbishop Barroeta when he arrived in Lima. No agreement was reached on the controversy over whether
to allow convents and monasteries in the new town of Bellavista, created
to replace the port of Callao, or the more general issue of the consolidation
of convents and monasteries and the limitations placed on their numbers.
The king's resolution vaguely agreed with many of the points made by the
junta and called for *cédulas* (decrees) that followed the (contradictory) reports of Rávago, Carvajal, and other members. A *sumario*, or summary, was
written and rewritten, passing through several hands. Viceroy Manso and
Archbishop Barroeta were instructed to follow the guidelines of the junta
and in 1751 received numerous decrees.

The viceroy received contradictory instructions five years after he had
made his initial proposals. Geography (the distance between Lima and

Madrid) and bureaucracy conspired against his reforms.[41] Moreover, the
orders fought the proposals tooth and nail. They contended that they had
the right to regroup and rebuild and that the City of Kings needed their
services and guidance. Thus with only a few exceptions (the Augustinian
Recoleta de Guia, for example), the monasteries, convents, beaterios, and
parishes were rebuilt, albeit slowly, in some cases in the 1770s or 1780s.[42]
The problems over the size of large convents simmered for years. The issue
resurfaced in the late 1780s, when the junta's documentation was taken
into account in order to impose a minimum number of priests in each monastery and to shut down the smaller ones. After several years, the disposition was revoked, what Ismael Sánchez Bella calls "another instance of the
vacillations of the rulers' ecclesiastical policy."[43]

Separation of Rural Parishes

The junta noted that they had not taken specific action on the issue of the
number of convents because the question of removing the regulars from
the doctrinas took precedence. This would be the focus of their discussions.
As summarized above, Manso de Velasco provided insights on the state of
Lima. He tallied the damage prompted by allowing regulars into the rural
parishes over the centuries: the wealth accumulated by the orders, which
fueled ambitions, debased lifestyles, and prompted scandalous elections,
and the related poverty of the secular priests and rural inhabitants. The viceroy added his voice to the widespread accusation that the orders exploited
the rural parishes to subsidize their urban enterprises.[44] The junta also believed that the regulars' economic activities set off a number of unfortunate consequences. The friars' need to make money for monasteries and
convents as well as for their superiors corrupted election practices within
the orders, led many of the priests astray, and hurt the Indians who resided
in the doctrinas. The anonymous narrator of the "Colección Histórica" referred to the Indians' "continual humiliation" as the friars forced them to
spend what little they had in festivities and to work as domestic laborers.[45]
To discuss this issue, the junta began by reviewing historical precedents,
specifically seventeenth-century efforts.[46]

The junta worked decisively on this issue. The king agreed with their
report. which called for the removal of regulars from doctrinas of Mexico
and Lima. This reform weakened the financial base of the orders and "re-

centralized" them, moving them back to the cities. With supportive papal bulls, by 1753 the reforms were extended beyond Peru and Mexico. Vacant parishes, many of them managed by regulars since the sixteenth century, had to be turned over to seculars. David Brading's study of secularization in Michoacán examines how the orders reacted and some of the curious consequences. For example, the lack of priests who spoke indigenous languages hastened the entry of indigenous people into the Mexican church.[47] In contrast to the debate about the size and number of convents and monasteries, the junta made precise recommendations on secularizing doctrinas, advice implemented by the Crown.

Yet the changes in Lima did not seem to be either immediate or drastic. Secularization did not break the chain depicted by midcentury reformers of regular priests funneling resources taken from rural areas into Lima in order to finance election campaigns and to subsidize boisterous convent life. Regulars continued to hold many rural parishes, and accusations of rural exploitation and urban decadence surfaced for decades. Implementing the junta's plans proved difficult.

Censos

The debris from the earthquake had not even been cleared nor had discussions about rebuilding convents and controlling mendicants begun when rancorous controversies about what was to be done with liens on property, *censos*, ensued. The earthquake uncovered the depth and complexity of the entailment of property in colonial Peru, including obligations destined for "pious works" (obras pías), chaplaincies (an endowment for a cleric), and the censos themselves, the focus of the Lima controversies. The term denoted a number of types of arrangements in which a property owner pledged an annual payment to an institution, usually a convent or the Inquisition, in return for what was usually but not always a loan of money. Monasteries, in order to avoid the abominable sin of usury, "did not enter into loans, but rather contracts of purchase and sale in which the nuns purchased the right to collect an annuity."[48] Centuries of euphemistic sidestepping, however, had largely subsided, and in the eighteenth century the terms *principal* (the same term, frequently plural, in Spanish) and *interest* (*rédito*) were often employed. In the aftermath of the earthquake, the battles focused on the redeemable (*redimibles*) and irredeemable (*irredimibles*) censos (limited in time or perpetual) owed overwhelmingly to the city's convents.⁴⁹ The *censo* was the financial foundation of colonial Lima. Of the 277 cases I reviewed in the notary records regarding property disputes or contractual changes from 1746 to 1753, 243 (88 percent) involved censos. Renting was much less common, making up the remaining 12 percent.⁵⁰

The term thus referred to a variety of arrangements in which individuals or institutions owed money to the Church, usually to convents. Not only was the terminology vague, but the cases often stretched back over centuries, during which time the proprietors and the terms changed. The records expressed how deeply entailed property in colonial Lima was. For example, Doña Luisa de Masilla had ceded the rental from a house behind the Copacabana church in the Cercado neighborhood to a chaplaincy. The property also had two censos for different *cofradías*, one of which was managed by the Jesuits. The chaplaincy was years behind in payment to the cofradías, and the Jesuits demanded that they be granted all future rental income. In addition, the Jesuits claimed to have invested in rebuilding the house after the earthquake. In early 1747, Juan de Murga de Villavicencio sought to rent the property from the chaplaincy, offering to pay off much of the debt to the Jesuits. He would be exonerated from years of rent for the payments to both cofradias as well as the cost of making the house habitable.⁵¹ Most of these cases involved multiple parties and numerous liens on the damaged property. After October 1746, the accumulated debts often exceeded the value of the damaged property. Both the complexity and the indebtedness bothered the Bourbons.

Viceroy Manso de Velasco believed that measures had to be taken quickly because uncertainty and lengthy lawsuits would prevent rapid rebuilding. Three weeks after the earthquake, he had posters placed in key plazas requesting testimony about the state of the city's residences.⁵² He would justify his initial measures as emergency palliatives against the dispersal of Lima's population outside the city's walls and in plazas and other open spaces, the antithesis of Spanish urbanism. The viceroy contended that, because most of Lima's were houses ruined, "no good reason could be found for the owners to sacrifice their savings and use it for repairing them, to revive an extinct censo, when it would be cheaper to buy an empty plot of land."⁵³ Years later he claimed that his efforts brought people back from the "surrounding areas, the squatter camps [rancherías] and huts [chozas]."⁵⁴ He knew that property owners needed relief in order to return to

124 the city. On the other hand, he also realized how much the Church relied on the censo money. For example, he recognized that one of the terrible consequences of moving the city of Lima would have been the termination of the censos and *obras pías* that the Church depended on for its upkeep and spiritual work. Individuals could not be expected to pay back censos on property they no longer used. In the gloomy aftermath of the earthquake, the viceroy sought a solution that would satisfy both sides, property owners and the convents, and hasten Lima's reconstruction.

With the support of the Audiencia and the Cabildo and presumably of property owners, the viceroy took drastic measures in January 1747. He cut the principal in half, reduced the interest rate from its customary 5 percent to 2 percent for *redimibles* and 1 percent for *irredimibles* and granted a two-year moratorium. Supporters noted that these reforms reflected the widespread de facto renegotiation of censos, as property owners successfully demanded extensions and reductions. Discounts were already going into effect.[55] The Church, however, rapidly denounced these measures as unfair and untenable—they could not survive with this drastic reduction. They highlighted the math, showing that the annual rate paid for a redeemable censo worth 1,000 pesos fell from 50 pesos (5 percent) to 10 pesos (2 percent of 500).[56] This controversy began nearly a decade of wrangling over the censo reforms and of debates over the terms of the modifications, the state of Lima's houses, and the comparative economic importance of property owners versus the Church. The discussions, most visible in extended court cases that stretched from Lima to Madrid and in numerous publications defending either property owners or the convents, constituted an important round in the Church and state tussle.

The Church convinced the viceroy to reconsider his measures. Cabildo and Audiencia members immediately tried to block this reexamination of the credit issue, probably a reflection of the fact that most of the members—Lima's upper crust—had extensive censo obligations and thus stood to lose in any alteration to the measures of 1747. The viceroy therefore convoked a three-person special junta to hear the ecclesiastics' claims. Defenders of the Church insisted that not all buildings in Lima had been uniformly destroyed and that the clerics required the income in order to fulfill their spiritual and humanitarian obligations. They charged that "it seems that only fairness for the property owners [censuatarios] was considered, as though the *censualistas* did not deserve it, running hospitals that use their

income in healing the sick, so important for charity and the public bene-
fit."[57] In March 1748, the viceroy modified the initial reforms. The principal
was not automatically cut in half but was to be reviewed on a case-by-case
basis. In addition, the interest rates were to increase to 3 and 2 percent
(from 2 and 1). The viceroy sent this proposal to the king in June 1748, in
the midst of a pitched and fascinating struggle over these censo modifications.

Property owners rallied around Manuel de Silva y la Banda, a lawyer,
member of the Cabildo, and the procurador general. Claiming it was not
the viceroy's prerogative to amend the initial steps and invoking precedents
such as Chilean earthquakes and Panamanian fires, the property owners
in mid-1748 demanded a town meeting to discuss the revisions to the reforms. In unusually direct language they accused the viceroy of overstepping his office and overlooking their needs and rights. Silva was initially
more cautious, lauding the viceroy's virtue and intelligence but ascribing
the flawed measures to his religiosity and above all to the influence of the
clerics around him, such as Andrés de Munive, the vicar-general of the
archbishopric.[58] The viceroy responded angrily to the criticism and the call
for a town meeting, investigating whether the instigators could be charged
with sedition. He suspended the publication of Silva's manifesto on the
situation, although a bit late. The first sixteen pages made it out of the
printer's shop, ending, however, in midsentence.[59]

In 1747 Antonio Joseph Alvarez de Ron published Representación jurídica, a
forty-nine-page denunciation of the initial measures taken by Manso that
summarized the Church's position. A member of the Audiencia, Alvarez
de Ron was a lawyer for the Church, a close ally of Archbishop Barroeta,
and an enemy of Viceroy Manso. The structure of the Representación jurídica
is similar to that of the published arguments about the two-story controversy summarized in chapter 5. In seven sections with a total of ninety-one
subsections, the author uses impressive rhetorical skills (including many
nice turns of phrase as well as classical allusions) to refute the decree of
January 1747 and the general arguments presented by property owners. He
first notes that the measures sought "equity" but failed—the Church suffered a huge decrease in its income and was forced to "beg" (mendigar). Its
multiple spiritual activities, encapsulated in the term culto, would decline
if the decree were not amended. Alvarez de Ron pits it as a battle between
buildings and the people, who faced moral and economic calamity if the

126   Church languished. He mocked the situation: "In order to restore buildings, the inhabitants are destroyed."[60]

Alvarez de Ron questions whether the viceroy has the right to take such radical measures and at what point or under what circumstances censos could be terminated. He claims that previous viceroys had not reduced censos to the same degree in the three "general ruins" of Lima (1581, 1655, 1687), after other earthquakes in Chile (1647) and the Philippines (1648), and after the fire of 1737 that destroyed Panama City. Alvarez de Ron does not merely weigh the spiritual role of the Church against the economics of the secular world, but instead makes a forthright defense of the economic importance of the Church. He points out that many people had made fortunes from the censos. Although not explicitly, he is contrasting their customary 5 percent rate with the much higher interest normally demanded for commercial loans.[61]

The author then argues that the world of the Church and that of seculars cannot be easily separated in economic terms and that most people relied on the Church for economic aid, from alms for the poor to the request for credit by "patricians." Alvarez de Ron ventures that three-fourths of the Lima population depended economically on the Church, thus making it a more important economic institution than the property owners who demanded a discount on their censos.[62] The measures taken by the viceroy were not only unjust but also misguided—they would endanger Lima's spiritual and economic worlds.[63]

Property owners, too, produced an erudite and detailed defense of their position. In 1748 the Audiencia lawyer, Cabildo member, and San Marcos University professor Miguel de Valdivieso y Torrejón published a refutation of the censualistas' arguments and also lobbied the viceroy not only to restore the measures of 1747 but to take them further. He begins by countering what he perceives to be the two pivotal arguments presented by Alvarez de Ron and his allies: that the Church had not gained a fair hearing and that censos were not part of the viceroy's jurisdiction. Valdivieso cites various classical theories of property and medieval Spanish laws, but he never strays far from the basic argument that if the censos are permanent obligations despite what happens to the property, they constitute usury.

The final section of the tract describes the vast destruction of the city, emphasizing the large number of shattered, uninhabitable houses. Valdivieso details the enormous cost of rebuilding in light of labor and supply shortages. Because of Lima's dire economic situation, property owners could not expect to recover their rebuilding costs. He calculates that houses that require twenty thousand pesos' worth of repairs are worth only ten thousand pesos. Valdivieso urges consideration of all of these factors when he calls for censos to be forgiven if the property is ruined and to be reduced to the extent of its damage. He argues that cutting the principal in half did not cover the damage by the earthquake and that the percentage rates needed to be reduced even more.[64]

Valdivieso clearly exaggerated the earthquake's damage. He deemed most of the city uninhabitable, yet people quickly moved back into their residences and most of the monumental churches, convents, and monasteries remained standing. This report contradicted the position of property owners in defending their two-story houses, which stressed how well their houses had withstood the earthquake. Although Valdivieso's report and the hundreds of pages of legal procedures do not specify names, it is probable that many of the same people who defended their elegant homes with the argument that they were strong enough to withstand future calamity at the same time demanded a vast reduction in the censos because of the damage.

The viceroy forged a compromise that irritated all sides yet managed to prompt rebuilding without bankrupting monasteries. However, the viceroy confronted his own challenge on this issue: the demands the monasteries made after the earthquake that they be paid back their considerable loans to the viceregal state at the stipulated 5 percent. Emphasizing the sorry state of their convents and of the nuns themselves, the abbesses of the convents charged that the viceroy had not only reduced the interest rate but had also stopped payment, despite the fact that these censos were not for destroyed property but had actually been de facto emergency loans.[65]

The abbess of Nra. Señora Del Prado "grieved and worried about the bankruptcy of her convent" owing to the shortfall of 4,026 pesos they had previously received from the Lima treasury in annual loan repayment. The abbess made graphic arguments about the state of the convents. She cited the threat of thieves jumping over the crumbled walls of the convents while the abbess of the Santa Catalina de Sena convent mentioned nuns dying from exposure. Most of them gave detailed accounts of the amounts loaned to the Royal Treasury and their absolute dependence on these funds.[66] Pablo Emilio Pérez-Mallaina Bueno tabulated that Lima's Royal Treasury owed ten convents over 800,000 pesos, a formidable part of its debt in 1745 of 1,560,756 pesos.[67] The tone of the abbesses' arguments varied, as did their intransigence: some accepted partial payments, while others, like the abbess of La Concepción convent, continued to insist in 1758 that they be paid back in full.[68] The viceroy did not make his reasoning public, but no doubt the sorry state of the Lima treasury as well as the fact that some of these loans dated from the 1640s made him reluctant to pay.[69]

In July 1748, he sent his proposal and the bulky paperwork that chronicled the debates and controversies to Madrid. He did not address what to do with the Lima treasury's debt to the convent. It moved slowly through different echelons of the Madrid court and a final resolution approved by the king was returned to the viceroy in 1754.[70] It largely validated his measures of 1748 but instructed him to pay back the convents in full. They were excluded from the now-official reduction in interest rates. The fact that La Concepción convent registered a complaint four years later, in 1758, indicated that payment was not immediate.[71]

In terms of the struggle between property owners and the Church, Valdivieso as well as Silva hint that these transatlantic debates and investigations lagged behind what was happening on the ground: a reduction in the censos. They claimed that in light of Lima's difficult economic situation, censuatarios and censualistas were bargaining and that the interest rates had been reduced. Notary records confirm that occupants or potential buyers or renters were negotiating with monasteries, convents, and other religious corporations for vastly improved terms. For example, the Purísima Concepción brotherhood sold a house in San Lázaro "demolished by the earthquake, stripped of windows and doors by thieves" to Francisco Campos for 817 pesos. He was to pay a censo of 3 percent a year, that is, 24 pesos and 4 reales. The contract stipulated that he was to rebuild the house and that if there were another earthquake the censo rate would not be reduced.[72] Property owners wanted these reductions to be confirmed by a viceregal or Crown decree; the Church sought a return to prior conditions, particularly as time passed and the economy returned to its pre-earthquake pace. From Manso's perspective, the censo issue had prompted unfortunate bickering and earned him enemies among both property owners and the clergy. Nonetheless, he had succeeded in avoiding a flood of lawsuits and in hastening the rebuilding of Lima.

Discussions about limiting the Church's presence in eighteenth-century Spanish America were thus not reduced to the Madrid court, its viceregal representatives, a few prescient reformers, and religious representatives. Because of the central physical, quotidian, and financial presence of the Church, debates emerged immediately after the earthquake and continued for more than a decade. The discussions moved far beyond policy makers and key institutional representatives, involving much of Peruvian society. On the one hand, the breadth and intensity of these discussions reflected the importance of the censos and the centrality of the mendicant orders in urban and rural society. The discussions could not be limited to a small circle of reformers and representatives of the interested parties—they affected far too many people.

On the other hand, the arguments moved beyond policy-maker and lobbyist circles because they involved so much more than jurisdictional squabbles, credit, and property rights. The discussions, particularly those about the convents, focused on the perceived moral disorder or disarray in Peru and the search for a remedy. Reformers within the Church and the State saw priests and nuns, above all the increasingly materialist mendicants who had abandoned the rigors of monastic life, as the culprits and thus strove to control and, in some cases, limit their numbers. Others blamed immoral women and the unruly lower orders for Lima's moral imbalance, whereas many nuns blamed themselves. The discussions about seemingly staid institutional questions such as censos and the rural parishes involved not only the broad theme of the role of the Church in viceregal society, but also the widely perceived moral malaise in Peru and the prevention of divine wrath.

The viceroy's timid efforts to weaken the physical and economic presence of the Church and improve its moral order accurately preview the following century or so of State (colonial and republican)-Church relations. Throughout the latter half of the eighteenth century and into the nineteenth, reformers posited different motivations for change: the excessive dominance of the Church in financial and real estate markets, its moral decline, and the concomitant need to strengthen the state. The viceregal state slowly moved to replace the Church in its "health, education, and welfare" role, building or supporting orphanages and hospitals. In 1769, Viceroy Manuel de Amat expelled the Jesuits from Peru, taking control of their considerable real estate and wealth.[73] A review of this process, however, demonstrates its slow, incomplete course. Besides the expulsion of the Jesuits and the removal of the regulars from rural parishes, phenomena

130   that emanated from Spain itself, the challenge to the Church was halting and contradictory. The State was not certain that it wanted to assume many of the Church's administrative and economic responsibilities, just as Viceroy Manso de Velasco ceded the care of the sick and wounded after the earthquake to the Agonizantes and other orders.

In fact, the rhetoric that decried this institution's omnipresence underlined at the same time the obstacles to replacing it. Reformers called for an "improvement" of the Church, backing regalist efforts to increase the State's control over the Church rather than a more radical secularization policy. Peruvians could not fathom life (and death) without priests, nuns, and religious processions. Lima was unimaginable without its dozens of churches, monasteries, convents, and shrines. Finally, the Church itself put up a good fight, defending its presence in Lima and beyond. Although many other factors need to be considered in order to understand secularization in Peru from 1750 to 1850, the decade from 1745 to 1755 highlighted the motivations and obstacles to reform. Ultimately, it was much easier to criticize wayward priests than to uproot an entire institution.

Controlling Women's Bodies and Placating God's Wrath: Moral Reform

Lima cannot be understood without its women.
—VENTURA GARCIA CALDERÓN,
"Para una antología de la limeña," 7

Seven

The Franciscan friar Mariano Badia sent a gruesome, exaggerated testimony of the October 28, 1746, earthquake/tsunami in central Peru to his Catalan monastery, the Escornalbou, which had provided many of the recent wave of evangelizers to Peru. He claimed incorrectly that one hundred thousand persons had died in the earthquake, tsunami, and the year-long aftershocks. In describing burials in hastily dug ditches in the days following the catastrophe, he observed, "The majority of women died with broken legs. Undoubtedly, God wanted to show that it was punishment for their vanity and the legs they did not cover." The friar contended that God often warned of impending punishment through a variety of signs, but if the bad customs were not amended, he fulfilled divine justice. The friar cited the fire in Panama in 1737 as well as the earthquake.[1]

Badia's observation about women's broken legs has

132   a perverse undertone. From the grim perspective of the aftermath of the catastrophe, he seemed to interpret the devastation not only as inevitable, because of the Lima population's disregard of multiple warnings, but also justifiable. A certain amount of satisfaction can be discerned in his comments. His letter depicts a distraught man of God who, wandering among the cadavers and wreckage, mourns the dead but also recognizes and even celebrates the power of God and the justice of punishing sinners, particularly women, who had died in very symbolic (and painful) fashion. Although more stern and misogynist than others, Friar Badia was not alone. Most of Lima interpreted the earthquake as a sign of God's wrath and believed that rebuilding and preventive measures needed to focus as much on improving the city's morals as on reforming financial and architectural practices.

Most blamed the catastrophe on the questionable practices of the Church and the profanity of Lima's social life, particularly that of women. Authorities and Church officials spent an extraordinary amount of energy in attempting to regulate the behavior and dress of women. Badia himself summarized some of the measures taken to modify the profanity of women's dress in Lima before and after the earthquake. In 1734, "to guard against horrible punishment, to incite divine mercy, and to extirpate profanity in women's dress," Cathedral authorities had stipulated stiff penalties for women who displayed their legs and arms or who showed any cleavage. After the earthquake, these campaigns intensified. In January 1747, the Cathedral Chapter took measures against all women who wore immodest clothing. Days later, Viceroy Manso de Velasco backed up this measure with fines, imprisonment, and public humiliation for those who disobeyed.[2] The campaigns sought not only to put women in their place, but also to reorder and fortify gender, class, and race hierarchies. Gender, class, and race could not be easily separated in eighteenth-century Lima; yet in the anxious months and years following the earthquake, authorities put women's dress codes first. They wanted to make sure that the women of Lima were properly dressed.

In light of the widespread panic prompted by nuns' premonitions about the imminent destruction of Lima due to its sinful ways and the great concern about women's dress and profanity, it seems that most of the city's inhabitants believed the earthquake was not the final act of divine justice but merely a severe warning. If the city's profane dress and lax social mores were not reformed, more devastation was sure to come. The reformers thus expressed a sense of urgency—strict dress codes were imperative. In fact, in 1744, two years before the earthquake, at the behest of the Franciscans Lima's archbishop had published a selection of texts compiled by a Spanish priest about the need to reform women's dress. "Soli Deo Honor, Et Gloria [Honor and Glory only for God]. . . . To Persuade Women to Be Proper in Their Dress and Neckline" belittled the excuses men and women made to justify their wearing of risqué clothing and gave dozens of examples of divine wrath for this sin. Distributed for free in exchange for the promise to pray for souls in purgatory, this book no doubt fortified the interpretation of the earthquake as divine wrathful retribution.[3]

Concerns about controlling women in Lima, however, had not emerged only after the earthquake and other signs of God's anger that nuns and others described and lamented. Throughout the eighteenth century visitors and authorities fretted over the wanton ways and independence of women and sought to tighten control of public life. Therefore, in order to understand the obsession with women's dress a longer time frame and broader set of explanations or motivations than those that focus on the earthquake and God's wrath need to be employed. For many, the reform was not solely an effort to placate God but also an opportunity to increase control over women and their bodies. This impulse was deeply embedded in discussions about luxury and decadence, essential themes in the Enlightenment generally and in the widely discussed published reports of European travelers to Peru.

In Vain against Vanity: Centuries of Campaigns against Limeñas

Eighteenth-century Lima conforms to the definition of a baroque city as a "stage set."[4] Descriptions and paintings from the period demonstrate that Lima epitomized the baroque emphasis on lavish public festivals and processions and ostentatious urban life. It also displayed the characteristic confluence of extreme piety and sensuality. Raúl Porras Barrenechea, paraphrasing the urban historian Lewis Mumford, noted the dual and seemingly contradictory tendencies of baroque cities, particularly Lima: "On one side, an inflexible code, mathematic uniformity, regularity and order, that translates into the rigid layout of the streets and the geometric design of the countryside, and on the other side, a rebellious core, anticlassical,

134 antimechanical, sensuous, that is expressed in the clothing, in the sexual life, in the religious, and the political." Processions and festivals brought out this seeming contradiction, as teeming, multicolored, sensual, and undisciplined throngs of people converged in the precise geometry of Lima's streets.[5] Processions and public rituals, however, did not seek to unify or homogenize. Accounts such as the Eliseo Peruano (1725), the "El Dia de Lima" (1748), and the "Júbilos de Lima" (1755) by Francisco Ruiz Cano of celebrations for the rebuilding of the Cathedral emphasize the heterogeneity of Lima's population. Various social groups and estates participated in diverse ways. The city's Indian nobles, for example, re-created (or invented) Inca rituals. As we will see in the next chapter, these festivities could bring simmering tensions to the surface.[6]

European travelers commented, usually disparagingly, on the active social life and women's apparent freedom in Lima's streets. The Irish sea captain William Betagh noted that "gallantry and intrigue are here brought to perfection; for they [men] devote so much of their time to the service of the fair sex, that it is unmannerly not to have a mistress, and scandalous not to keep her well." He described women's beauty and the rules by which both sexes disguise themselves in order to mask public gallivanting. He portrayed the *tapadas*, the women who used shawls to cover half their faces, and the measures taken to avoid stumbling upon philanderers, such as never peering into coaches or retrieving a dropped handkerchief. Betagh condemned these practices and their cost, contending that the chasing of women ultimately enervated and even feminized Lima's men, stifling reform.[7] As Octavio Paz noted about Mexico City in Sor Juana's time, "The violent contrast between asceticism and dissoluteness appears throughout the Baroque Age, in all countries and classes."[8]

European denunciations of Lima's sensuous ways demonstrated a mix of mind-sets and motivations, including imperial yearnings (the English contemplated controlling the Pacific coast) and varying levels (depending on the traveler and his nationality) of disdain for women, mixed races, the Spanish, and the Americans. European debates about luxury and consumption weighed heavily in the condemnations. European travelers to Peru constitute an important chapter in Old World characterizations of the Americas as hypersensual, impossibly heterogeneous, and corrupt, judgments that could prompt disdain, guilty pleasure, and calls for intervention.[9] The study of Lima indicates that the Peruvian population was conscious of these discussions, occasionally responding directly to those critics whose opinions reached Madrid and Lima. More important, Peruvians participated in similar discussions. The view of the City of Kings as a lush, sensual wasteland was not merely a European construction. The Lima population was anxious about the seeming freedom of women and the city's libertinage, major themes in the debates about the causes of the earthquake and other forms of God's wrath.

Starting in the sixteenth century, viceregal and church authorities rebuked Lima's women for their independence and implemented policies to limit their public freedom and to dictate the type of clothing they could wear. The tapadas had been the favored subject of clerical fury, sumptuary laws, and foreign fascination. They wore a blue or black shawl around their faces, revealing a single eye and thus concealing their identity. As critics and enthusiasts noted, the custom facilitated female public coquetry and independence. They wore a second shawl (*manto*) around their shoulders. A long, floor-length skirt, or *saya*, was drawn tightly around their hips, emphasizing the feminine form but restricting movement. The skirt could be drawn up to display the ankles. Writers noted the paradox of the tapada garb: its concealment of identity gave women great freedom yet the tight skirt restrained walking, to the point that many slipped or fell when stepping over the small streams of foul water that ran down the middle of most streets.[10] The social ambiguities of the tapadas both amused and intrigued writers and authorities. Most tapadas were from the city's white or European population and consequently enjoyed that sector's social prestige and domestic workers (slaves and servants), which allowed them to promenade. Yet covering their face and concealing their identity allowed for transgression.

Mulatta women could wear the sayas, mantos, and silk gloves and even be accompanied by their elite lovers without detection. This piqued the interest of many travelers, who cast mulattas as the embodiment of sinful sexuality. Tapada garb could also conceal age. Young men could find to their embarrassment that the woman they were flirting with was much their elder. To cite Manuel Fuentes, "An elegant body, a white, shapely arm, a light, small foot, a sliver of a black, expressive eye, these could pertain to a toothless grandmother whose exposed eye was her only [functioning] eye."[11] The independence the veil offered to Lima's women and the concealment of such social hierarchies as race and age that it afforded worried the authorities.

A seventeenth-century Spanish intellectual, Antonio de León Pinelo,

13 Tapada. This is unusual, as tapadas
normally concealed one eye. *Source:*
Simón Yanque (Esteban de Terralla
y Landa), *Lima por dentro y fuera,*
illustration by Ignacio Merino
(Paris, 1854).

LA TAPADA
(de noche)

14 La Tapada (at night). *Source:*
Bonnaffé, *Recuerdos de Lima*
(Lima, 1856).

LA TAPADA
(Saya y Manto)

15 La Tapada (saya y manto).
Source: Bonnaffé, Recuerdos de Lima
(Lima, 1856)

who spent years in Peru, wrote a book entitled *Veils on Women's Faces: Their Consequences and Damage*. He sustained that the tapada fashion originated in the late fifteenth-century suppression of Muslims and Islamic practices in Spain. The Crown repeatedly prohibited the veil so that the *moriscas*, or women of Moorish descent, grudgingly adjusted their dress, using a shawl to conceal just one eye.[12] Leon Pinelo summarized four major inconveniences of veils: confusion by family members; the freedom afforded to women; men's lack of respect for veiled women; and the "crimes and sacrileges" committed by men dressed as tapadas.[13] The fashion passed from Seville to Lima, as did the preoccupation and frequent efforts to prohibit or limit it. The frequency of such attempts itself indicates the difficulty of controlling women and their dress. Guillermo Lohmann Villena found that measures to manage or even prohibit the tapadas were instituted in Lima in 1564, 1583, 1609, 1610 (two), and 1613. In this last case, the Crown's lawyer noted the number of laws, decrees, and orders against the tapadas "due to the great sins committed by their concealing clothing and the ensuing scandals and damage to the Republic. The excess freedom and dishonesty in the streets, temples, and plazas in Lima has reached the point that preachers are hoarse from condemning them in the pulpit."[14]

Further strictures were adopted in the seventeenth century, particularly after the earthquake of 1687.[15] Ventura García Calderón, an early twentieth-century enthusiast of the tapadas and part of a generation that provided important studies of colonial Lima while also romanticizing it in contrast to the gritty, industrial city that was emerging, joyfully summarized these failed policies: "In vain the austere holy men threatened them in their sermons with divine wrath and excommunication, taking angry verses from Isaiah 'against all women who adorn their body with superfluous and vain apparel of dresses, jewels, curls, and the rest.' No, they won't suppress the saya and manto until they, the women, decide so."[16] A few pages earlier, he had testified to their sensuality: "A gleaming and dangerous eye where flirtatiousness and holiness made a dangerous pact under the ringlets of their hair, the high and concise chest, low hips."[17] Observers placed the brazen but respectable tapadas between the polar extremes of devout nun-like women and unruly, grossly sensual mulatto women, "between piety and Afro-Peruvian sensuality."[18] Almost all observers commented on tapadas' seemingly incongruous blend of piety and sensuality, in many ways the essence of the baroque.

In the long history of sumptuary law, the late medieval and early modern periods, from the fourteenth century through the seventeenth, were high points in governmental control of consumption. Within this period, the laws increasingly focused on clothing. By the eighteenth century, the number of laws emitted in Europe was declining, while the campaigns increasingly intertwined with debates about the social and economic impact of luxury and extravagant consumption.[19] Yet the campaigns in Peru indicated the persistence of "the moral contagion" perspective, in which moralists harangued that vices flaunted publicly had catastrophic consequences.[20]

Mid-eighteenth-century concerns about sumptuary practices thus had behind them centuries of historical precedent on both sides of the Atlantic. Why did the Church and civil authorities react as they did to changing fashions in the eighteenth century? Lima had been struck by a series of misfortunes beginning in the late seventeenth century, and these heightened anxieties; much of the population, as noted, believed that the disasters were punishments for the city's sinful ways and that the worst was still to come. Moreover, European travelers' well-publicized fascination with Lima women brought to the fore issues of decency, opulence, luxury, and profanity, the fundamental elements in the rhetoric and policies in Bourbon Peru referring to women. For critics, Lima seemed to be the worst of two worlds. Habsburg delegation of power and the consequent inability to rule the streets as well as baroque piety and extravagance continued to mark daily life. At the same time, increasing French influence under the Bourbons ushered in more risqué clothing and a more active court life. A strange alliance thus emerged between Franciscan moralists and midcentury absolutists who attempted to "take back the streets," with uneven results.

With the transition from Habsburg to Bourbon rule, livelier colors and racier cuts replaced the dour, dark suits favored by the Habsburgs. Black, ruffled collars, long sleeves, and high necks went out of style, replaced by brighter-colored fabrics, including silk and linen, that revealed much more of women's arms, ankles, and breasts. Shawls covered these enticing bodily attributes but never to the satisfaction of clerical critics, while corsets accentuated women's figures. Jewelry and other accessories became increasingly ostentatious.[21]

The tapadas and Lima's women in general fascinated European visitors, who left a treasure trove of descriptions. They disagreed about the tastefulness—what for some was alluring for others was vulgar. Accounts from the first part of the eighteenth century were descriptive, whereas criticism became much more marked toward the second half of the century. In fact, tensions between Creole defenders and European critics emerged. Despite these differences, almost all European travelers commented on the appealing sight of the tapadas as well as on the jewelry, dainty feet, and aromatic perfume of Limeñas. All stressed the vanity and flirtatiousness of public life in Lima, some with a tone of respect, others with ringing condemnation. These accounts offer rich detail about Lima's women and gender relations. Furthermore, they echoed in Lima, influencing campaigns against women and contributing to transatlantic debates.

Lima: The Center of Luxury

The advent of Bourbon rule in the early eighteenth century opened up Spanish America to French travelers. In fact, hundreds of travel accounts on colonial Peru counter the notion that Spain maintained a closed and backward empire. The aforementioned French engineer and naval captain Amedée Frezier visited Lima in 1713 and wrote an influential report of his journey. Although he spent only a week in Lima, his guide to the City of Kings was read widely in both French and English. He had little good to say of the city's inhabitants, deriding criollos for their dirty habits and wasteful luxury. He noted, "Both Men and Women are equally inclined to be costly in their Dress. . . . We saw Ladies who had about them above the Value of 60,000 Pieces of eight in Jewels: They are generally beautiful enough, of a sprightly Mien, and more engaging than in other Places; and perhaps one part of their Beauty is owing to the Toils of the Mulattas, Blacks, Indians, and other hideous Faces, which are the most numerous throughout the Country."[22] Throughout his report, Frezier repeated this description of the extravagant expenditures made for dress and other vanities as well as the contrast between the European population and the multicolored lower classes. He criticized the proximity of diverse social groups in Lima, noting that well-dressed black servants often accompanied elite women. Not surprisingly, he condemned Lima's apparent piety as a mask for widespread licentious behavior, describing an undisciplined religious life, superstitious practices, slothful habits, and extensive concubinage.[23]

Several other French travelers contributed to this vision of a city with certain charms yet disturbingly fluid social divisions. They agreed that the city ultimately was decadent and superficial. In 1716, De la Barbinais Le Gentil wrote that "women in this country have unbridled freedom and they boast about this liberty." He added, "Everything is tolerated and fear of condemnation, a limitation on passions imposed by practice or the law in the rest of the world, is unknown or scorned there."[24] Le Sieur Bachelier published his account in 1720, in the wake of Frezier and the also influential Louis Feuillé. He stressed the wealth of the Jesuits, Lima's precise layout but rustic architecture, and the abundance of the poor. He described the odd sight of the sizable population of well-dressed beggars.[25]

Betagh left a lively account of his escapades in Peru. He was arrested and imprisoned for plundering in the port of Paita in 1720 but, perhaps because he was Catholic, was transferred to Lima and treated well. He claimed that the population grew because of the high number of deserters who, attracted by the abundance and charms of Peru and the "encouragement all white faces meet with," left their ships when they landed in Paita and Callao. He continued,

Of all parts of the world, the people here are most expensive in their habit. The men dress as they do in England, their coats being either of silk, or fine English cloth, and hair camlets, embroidered, or laced with gold and silver; and their waistcoats commonly the best brocades. The women never wear hoops or stays, only a stitched Holland jacket near their shifts. . . . Then as to pearls and precious stones, which they wear in rings, and bracelets for the neck and arms, they are very extravagant, though the value is hardly equal to the shew [sic] they make.[26]

He carefully describes the ornate rules and customs of public flirtation, as "the forepart of the night is a masquerade all the year round." In the evening, men tucked their hair under a cap and wore a handkerchief around their neck "so that it is an universal fashion to be disguised some way or other; for those who have no mistress are ashamed to be thought virtuous, and must be in some mask or other to countenance the way of the world."[27] Strolling couples kept a good distance from other people, "twelve yards at least," and, in order to avoid making impertinent or embarrassing discoveries, were in no circumstance to acknowledge an acquaintance or approach another couple. He noted that the siesta was also a time for romance. Betagh pointed out that although this strict protocol generally kept the peace, jealous violence occasionally broke out. He described the case of a woman who had learned that her lover was seeing another woman. She ran him through with his own dagger. The judge surprised everyone by letting her off, claiming that it was an excess of love rather than malice that caused her actions.[28]

Betagh seemed to admire this energetic gallantry and its complex etiquette, yet he also condemned its cost:

How agreeable soever these practices are to the Creole Spaniards, yet they cause an inconvenience to society; for the men are so seriously taken up with these sorts of matters, that the women engross most of their time, and spoil public conversation. For this reason, there are no taverns or coffee-houses; so that men are only to be met with at their offices, or at church. The same inconvenience, in a greater or less degree, attends this propensity to gallantry, wherever it prevails; and may be justly considered as the bane of industry, corrupting the minds of both sexes, and instilling the basest principles of indolence and debauchery.[29]

For Betagh, the focus on mistresses and gallivanting showed Lima's men to be enervated and even effeminized. He criticized the viceroy's opposition to a boxing match that sailors attempted to organize, evidence, in his eyes, of Peruvians' unmanly squeamishness. He recognized that "if gallantry prevailed here [England] as much as in Peru, we should soon grow as much out of love with prize-fighting, and with whatever else had any affinity with labour or danger, as they: so natural it is, for the love of pleasure to dastardize the very bravest people." Betagh used what he saw as the vast, unsettled areas of Spanish America as further proof of the inhabitants' indolence.[30]

Published in English, Betagh's account did not resonate in Spain and Lima nearly as much as those of the French travelers. The accounts by the Spanish naval officers Jorge Juan and Antonio de Ulloa, however, made a huge impact in political circles on both sides of the continent. In their portrayal of widespread corruption and indolence, the wanton ways of the Lima population played a big role. Ulloa writes, "And although Lima is the capital of the country, it will appear that it is not a model to other places, with regard to dress, customs, and manner of living."[31] In Ulloa's travel account, *Viaje a la América meridional*, he began his review of Lima's dress by noting that the cloth used was quite common and inexpensive and thus it was "not uncommon to see a mulatto, or any other mechanic, dressed in a tissue equal to any thing that can be worn by a more opulent person."[32] As we will see, this deterioration of caste barriers concerned authorities in the aftermath of the earthquake. He then stated, "They all greatly affect fine cloaths, and it may be said without exaggeration, that the finest stuffs made in countries, where industry is always inventing something new, are more generally seen at Lima than in any other place; vanity and ostentation not being restrained by custom or law. Thus the great quantities brought in the galleons and register ships notwithstanding they sell here prodigiously above their prime cost in Europe. . . . the men are greatly exceeded by the women, whose passion for dress is such as to deserve more particular account."[33] This report, published in 1748, encapsulated the different preoccupations with Lima women's dress: the social egalitarianism, high expenditures for foreign imports, and vain ostentation. This is not a coincidence—Juan's and Ulloa's writings influenced debates in Madrid and Lima.

The theme of women's attire made up more than half of the chapter "Of the inhabitants of Lima." Ulloa reiterates the concerns about social passing, extravagant clothing, and vanity. He described how the use of lace had "spread through all ranks, except the lowest class of negroes." He observed that the "lower classes of women, even to the very negroes, affect, according to their abilities, to imitate their betters, not only in the fashion of their dress, but also in the richness of it."[34] Ulloa noted that Spaniards find Peruvian clothing "extremely indecent," stressing the short petticoat overloaded with jewels and other ornaments, including pearls, diamonds, and gold and silver jewelry. Velvet and silk constituted the much sought after finer materials. He proclaimed, "A lady covered with the most expensive lace instead of linen, and glittering from head to foot with jewels, is supposed to be dressed at the expence of not less than thirty or forty thousand crowns; a splendour still the more astonishing, as it is so very common."[35] This widely read account contributed to the image of Lima as the center of astounding expenditure on clothing and public celebrations. Juan and Ulloa depicted the smuggling of European imports as one of the causes of the viceroyalty's seeming decline. Nonetheless, protection of the Spanish Peruvian monopoly was not the main reason for this depiction of Lima. It seems more likely that Ulloa was truly struck by the city's luxury, a well-developed trope in contemporary discussions in Europe. Although troubled by women's "haughtiness" and independence from their husbands, Ulloa complimented Limeñas' intelligence and charm.[36]

The Count of St. Malo, Courte de la Blanchardiére, arrived in Lima in early 1747, months after the earthquake. He noted Lima women's sartorial splendor and expense as well as the subversion of racial hierarchies: "The women here are so richly dressed, that one of no high station would make a very brilliant appearance at a French theatre. Their hair is twisted and tufted with diamonds, pearls, and artificial flowers: they wear a black hat, embroidered with large earrings of diamonds and pearls. Some of the better sort of the mulatto and negro women, also aim at this extravagance."[37] The count describes the widespread use of diamond bracelets to cover women's arms, "naked up to their very shoulders," and the extravagant use of diamonds, gold, and jewels. He observes with horror women's habit of chewing tobacco. After describing the drinking, dancing, slovenly eating habits ("their fingers, which are almost covered with diamond rings, are their only forks, which they call tenedor natural, or natural fork"), and the practice of a group sharing a glass of pisco, or "strong waters," he exclaimed, "Peru seems to me the very centre of luxury and debauchery; whereas before, I thought the Europeans could not be exceeded." He also disparaged the "excess freedom" of slaves and mulattoes, decrying their

144   insolence and parties on Sundays when they drank *guarape*, sugarcane alcohol, and "sing and play their tricks."[38] In 1751, a German, Wolfgang Bayer, referred to Lima as Sodom and Gomorrah, contending, "There is no type of sin against the sixth commandment that this bad and shameless people have not given in to, which is why in all areas of this country the repugnant venereal disease predominates."[39]

Writers, particularly Spaniards, continued to condemn Lima's social disorder and moral codes in the latter half of the eighteenth century and early nineteenth. In fact, Gregorio Cangas, Hipólito Ruíz, Esteban Terralla y Landa, and others escalated the attacks, casting Lima as a decadent, dangerous wasteland. Throughout the eighteenth century, European criticism of vain Lima women went hand in hand with denunciations of the city's multicolored spectrum and imprecise social boundaries.[40]

These reports by travelers as well as the literary representations of the extravagant lifestyle of Lima women influenced discussions and policies in Peru. In the early 1750s, Viceroy Manso de Velasco referred to French accounts of Lima as the "derision of foreigners." He made a similar comment about "foreign and Spanish detractors" who criticized priests' "licentious freedom." He used this criticism to justify the reforms he sought to impose after the earthquake.[41] The impact, of course, varied. Juan and Ulloa represented the Crown and reported their findings in Madrid. Their widely read publications converted them into powerful authorities on the Americas, and their interpretations of mass corruption and exploitation became important texts in the decades leading up to the wars of independence.[42] Betagh, on the other hand, published in English, and only in the twentieth century did scholars discover his revelatory tales of Lima.

These accounts reflected or helped shape rather than prompted discussions in Lima on the issues of vanity, luxury, and social freedom. Their themes or tropes can be found in seventeenth- and eighteenth-century Peruvian texts criticizing or lauding Lima.[43] In the 1650s, Francisco Antonio de Montalvo noted that because of the fine attire of both the nobility and the common people, differences between them could barely be discerned on festival days. He described the silk coats used by mulattos and the jewels and silver and gold found in the houses of common people. The text "La Estrella de Lima" (1688) boasted of Lima's splendor, citing its consumption of products from Milan, Seville, France, Flanders, Cairo, China, etc.[44] The travelers witnessed this posh public life but also read about it and discussed it with Limeños. In no sense did this representation begin as a European construction. For state and church authorities in Peru, these often sensational reports constituted an additional incentive to take measures to regulate the behavior of women, but they were not the primary one.

Vanity and Ostentation

Why were the state and the church so concerned about women's dress, particularly after the earthquake? Three related factors stand out in the historical record before and immediately after the earthquake: social and racial emulation, luxury and vanity, and divine wrath. The role of clothing in social emulation had long worried the colonial state. The veils of the tapadas could be used to mask identities, allowing, as we have seen, for mulattas to be confused with ladies and spinsters with young courtesans. Almost all of the travelers noted the ability of dark-skinned women, usually deemed mulattas, to imitate the apparel of the upper crust. They also decried Lima's multiracial households, which included not only white patriarchs and matriarchs and Indian servants and black slaves, but individuals somewhere in between these social polarities. In the middle of the eighteenth century, many Lima women dressed their slaves well—at least those that accompanied them in public—often in clothing similar to their own, an act that in Lima was a sign of prestige. For many foreigners this constituted appalling social proximity.[45]

Throughout the seventeenth and eighteenth centuries, decrees and laws were enacted to fortify dress-based racial distinctions. In 1691 and 1716 "royal ordinances against the abuse of dress and other superfluous expenditures" limited the use of gold, silver, satin, silk, and other luxury items. In 1725, the Peruvian viceroy emitted an edict that sought to "moderate the excess in the clothing worn by blacks, mulattos, Indians and mestizos." Several years later, Viceroy José de Armendáriz, Marqués de Castelfuerte, reinstated these dress codes, promising enforcement.[46]

Rebecca Earle has linked the preoccupation with social emulation to changing notions about race. Before the late eighteenth century, race was seen as an attribute of culture and was manifested, among other ways, in what one consumed. Thus, the use of Spanish clothing could make one, presumably, a European. She contends, "The transformative potential of emulation was thus an integral part of colonial South American racial clas-

146 sifications."[47] The happenstance and rarely enforced legislation indicated concern over "excessive" social mobility but did not effectively tighten the porous boundaries between social groups. Earle argues that an increasingly physical (blood and skin color) understanding of race and the division of Spanish American society into "decent people" and the lowly plebe in the early nineteenth century ended this sartorial flexibility, at the very time when Europe was abandoning strict dress codes. Elite groups increasingly ridiculed the lower classes' efforts to dress as equals, and portraits and other depictions stressed class differences. At a time when sumptuary laws were in decline worldwide, they resurfaced in Spanish America because of concern about race.[48] Earle provides an enlightening hypothesis that illuminates changes in dress and the dress code. As the review of travelers' accounts above indicates, race almost invariably entered depictions of eighteenth-century Lima. Yet other factors need to be considered. The discussions in Lima indicate the importance of broad discussions about luxury and the deep-seated fear of divine punishment.

As in all of Europe, Spain was the site of pitched debates about luxury throughout the early modern period. Although discussions about luxury and excess had raged for centuries, the polemic in eighteenth-century Europe was moving away from condemnation of wasteful extravagance and its ties to vice and corruption. Instead, the social and economic impact of ever-widening trading circuits and the rising consumption of new goods became the focus. Authors like Voltaire, Adam Smith, and David Hume defended the role of consumption in contributing to refinement and the economy. On the other hand, Montesquieu, Jean-Jacques Rousseau, and other critics noted the cost that increased consumption exacted on traditional society and criticized excessive splendor.[49] In eighteenth-century France, the term luxury encapsulated broad, diffuse uneasiness about changes related to the blurring of clear social and gender divisions and to the breakdown of traditional society. The "confusion of rank" permitted by new consumption patterns and wealth was the principal apprehension.[50]

In Spain, the debates took place in the context of broad discussions about the causes of Spanish decline. In 1788, Juan Sempere y Guariños published Historia del Luxo, y de las leyes suntuarias, which stressed the economic benefits of consumption and debunked moralist counterattacks.[51] Sempere formed part of a generation of enlightened intellectuals who emerged under Carlos III, a group that incorporated leading voices from France, England, and Scotland.[52]

Two quite divergent groups led the charge against luxury in Spain. On the one hand, moralists backed by the Inquisition stressed the decadent consequences of modern thought and social practices, particularly for women. They battled the changing social mores of the eighteenth century, invoking the threat of divine wrath and social decay. On the other hand, another group of critics emphasized growing social and economic inequalities with the rise of the bourgeoisie and their superfluous expenditures. For example, one radical critic, León de Arroyal, wrote a poem that depicted his disgust with the pomp of the upper classes and ended with the following lines: "I'm justly horrified, as I know that all of this is from the blood of the poor."[53] In Peru, the moralists led the campaigns, but tones of the social criticism can also be heard. As we will see, the European debates about luxury echo in the controversy over women's dress and public life in eighteenth-century Lima.

Reformers, however, saw the need to "moderate" women's clothing for reasons that went beyond fortifying racial and gender hierarchies and discouraging wasteful pomp. In Lima, they saw it also as an urgent response to repeated divine warnings about the profanity of the city's ways. Women's lewd dress was sinful—an indicator and possible promoter of broader transgressions—and thus needed to be amended. While travelers might have stressed lax social boundaries and Spanish ideologues condemned luxury, advocates for change in Lima, mostly but not solely church members, stressed the impropriety of women's dress and the divine wrath it prompted. The earthquake of 1746 had been a severe warning. While reformers expressed some anxiety about racial passing and luxury, they focused on the dangers of profanity and the control of women's bodies. The clergy were at the forefront of the campaign.

"Husbands, Books, and Sermons Were Not Enough"

On September 11, 1734, the vicar-general of the Cathedral, Andrés de Munive, presented an edict "against women who use profane and scandalous dress." Its first sentence underlined the enduring nature of the problem, judging women's immodest dress "the source of scandals in Christian republics, due to the harm they cause, fostering mortal sins and constituting an offensive object to correctly modest people. Thus in every period ecclesiastics have fulminated against them, with the zealous goal of correcting such detestable abuses." He decried, however, that the situation

148   had deteriorated in Lima and was dire: "In recent years this unfortunate disorder has spread in this city and its hinterlands, with women wearing their skirts so high as to show their legs, uncovering their arms or with short sleeves and folds exposing their intimate parts, and showing off their breasts." He finished the paragraph by recognizing the energetic but unsuccessful efforts by "apostolic missionaries" to stem this trend and thus the need to take new measures.[54]

Father Munive therefore prohibited women "of all classes and conditions" from dressing in a way that displayed their legs, arms, or breasts and from carrying their dress's train in such a way as to reveal "the interior." He again referred to the need to cover the parts of the body that can "serve as an incentive or trap [tropiezo] to the eye." Those who disobeyed would be punished with excommunication and their names publicly listed (tablilla), while those who were caught in inappropriate dress would be immediately expelled from church. Exhorting priests and other church authorities to enforce these orders, Munive had the edict posted in all of Lima and Callao's churches so no one could "feign ignorance."[55]

The viceroy at this time, the Marqués de Castelfuerte, also took measures. A royal decree of 1725 approved his edict to "moderate the scandalous excess in the clothing worn by blacks, mulattos, Indians, and mestizos of both sexes, which resulted in frequent robberies committed to pay for this costly gala." The viceroy contended that his previous measures had not been fulfilled, citing the case of two female slaves of the Conde de las Torres, a member of the Audiencia, who flaunted the decree less than a day after its emission. The Consejo de Indias agreed with his efforts and stipulated fines for tailors who contravened it.[56] Viceroy Castelfuerte directed authorities in 1734 to fine "Spanish women" one thousand pesos for indecent dress, the money to be used for hospitals and poor prisoners, while "lower-class" women were subject to jail and banishment from Peru. Blacks, mulattas, cuarteronas, zambas, Indians, and mestizas caught in such attire were publicly humiliated for half a day, after their hair and eyebrows were shaved. Women with profane sayas that exposed their feet had their clothing destroyed in the Plaza Mayor and could be imprisoned in the city's hospitals, ordered to serve the poor, or exiled to Valdivia, Chile.[57] In his memoirs, Viceroy Castelfuerte underlined his efforts to reform the city's customs, particularly its profane dress.[58]

In 1734, the bishop of Arequipa, Juan Cavera de Toledo, issued a decree against women's profane dress, particularly in the coastal village of Moquegua. He decried the inattention to the sermons of evangelizing priests evident in the "scandalous dress. . . . even among the leading ladies." Citing the "pernicious consequences and spiritual ruin" that women's indecent dress prompted, he set clear standards about what parts of the body should be covered and the punishments for transgressors.[59] In 1744, a subsequent bishop of Arequipa imposed a series of equally strict guidelines and punishments, noting that divine justice in the form of plagues and earthquakes had not been enough to curtail rampant sensuality and immorality.[60]

Interpreting the earthquake in 1746 as a sign of divine wrath, particularly at women's indecency, the authorities took measures to amend and appease. On January 27, 1747, the Cathedral Chapter decreed the following:

> The recent earthquake that took place last year was an act of divine wrath, and the inhabitants, instead of making amends, have continued in their old customs, with women, in the most part not having moderated their indecent and immodest attire, now more noticeable because of the lack of shelter in which they had hidden themselves, particularly when they ride a mule, when more than their feet are exposed, with offense to their and others' modesty. In light of this, the members solemnly order all women, of any state or condition, to use clothing that covers their feet and to cover themselves when they ride mules, and at all times their arms, at least to their elbows, and that their breasts not be visible, and, with the threat of the same punishment, their servants also not be allowed to vary their clothing.[61]

On February 1, town criers announced the decree, posting it on churches and chapels. It demanded compliance based on both "conscience and threat of censure."[62]

This blunt decree stressed that the destruction of houses as well as convents and other buildings had forced women into the streets and plazas, making them much more visible. The loss of personal items, including clothing, perhaps initially justified the unusual and perhaps less modest attire worn by most of Lima's population in the immediate aftermath. In the eyes of the church, however, it had now become a dangerous vice rather than a temporary necessity; women needed to cover up. The final sentence about servants expressed concern not about social emulation—dark-skinned, lower-class women trying to imitate fashions—but about the practice of elite Limeños of dressing their servants and slaves in similarly fine and profane clothing.

On February 3, the viceroy stipulated fines for those who disobeyed the decree of January 27. Like Viceroy Castelfuerte in the 1730s, the viceroy backed up the Church's measures with penalties according to the social standing of the guilty party. Women faced fines of fifty pesos, fifteen days in jail, and the loss of the clothing. Those who did not have the means to pay faced thirty days in jail and either hard labor in a bakery or personal service in a hospital.[63] Archbishop Barroeta, not to be outdone by the Cathedral Chapter, also decreed against women's dress, demanding in 1751 that they make sure to cover their ankles and to wear dresses with sleeves that reached their elbows.[64]

A valuable study of clothing in colonial Chile points out that in the preoccupation with women's clothing, the Church worried more about profanity and indecency while the Crown and the viceregal state stressed the dangers of luxury and vanity.[65] Yet in times of catastrophe and the belief in divine wrath, these preoccupations meshed. The November 1746 account of the earthquake sent to the viceroy of New Granada, Sebastián de Eslava, written by Viceroy Manso de Velasco (or perhaps by his principal advisor, Victorino Montero del Aguila), indicates how these notions had become entangled. The report contended that the terrible damage inflicted on Lima could have positive consequences if it resulted in the curtailment of vain ostentation and thus in an improvement in the city's economic and moral life. The writer wove together these aspects in a biting denunciation of the city's errant ways, underlining the inevitability of God's wrath in such a wicked city. At the same time, he stressed the multiple benefits the city might enjoy if its inhabitants amended their customs.

The author decried Lima as a "coliseum of vanity," describing its ornate buildings, luxurious coaches, and indomitable and frivolous women. He linked these disparate features in a portrait of a corrupt, wasteful system that could, however, be amended. The writer provides numerous examples of lavish excess and the more productive uses, in social, economic, and moral terms, to which these resources could be put: the amount that women spent on flowers and perfume could provide a daughter's dowry or build a house, while the expenditures of "crazy vanity" on lace, diamonds, and braids could finance the decoration of the new houses in silver. In this paragraph on wasteful ostentation, the author noted that other nations "laugh at us."[66] He welcomed the prospect that the pitted, rubble-strewn streets might not be able to accommodate coaches for years, contending that this would save millions of pesos and discourage affairs. He deemed that the realization of this forecast—which proved to be false, as coaches returned to the streets within months—would be a blow to "the enemy, profanity." He also described and tabulated the great expense for social gatherings and funerals.

The author countered those who might question his logic and his calculations of the enormous savings to be gained by practicing a less ostentatious public life by pointing out that it was God who had acted; further actions must be taken to appease him. He wrote, "The Kingdom will not be destroyed by keeping among its inhabitants and in newly erected houses the two million pesos, minimum, spent in this city every year on coaches and the flippant clothing [ligereza del adorno] of women. . . . We should consider that this reduction in expenditures, which should be the subject of human laws, was initiated by God in the form of ruins, because husbands, books, and sermons were not enough to contain the prevailing will of women."[67] In other words, God had been forced to act because of the failure of mortals. Although the ornate residences and coaches are usually ascribed to men and the extravagant clothing to women, in this passage Lima's female population is cast as the ultimate cause of the city's extravagance. The author argues that decreasing expenditures on coaches, clothing, and ornate buildings would not only appease God but also improve the city and the viceroyalty's economic situation—including tax revenues—and moral order.

The Franciscans

While the diatribes against women's extravagance reiterated preponderant eighteenth-century tropes, the Franciscans led the charge against profane dress. As noted in chapter 2, this order had taken a particularly important role in the missions in Europe and the Americas since the Council of Trent (1545–63) and the creation of the congregation for propagating the faith, De Propaganda Fide. The wave of Franciscans who arrived in Peru after the succession wars in Spain brought new (or revived) forms of evangelization, targeting in many cases women's profane behavior and dress in their spectacle-like masses and campaigns. Women's dress obsessed them. For example, in the 1730s, Friar Eugenio Lanuza y Sotelo observed that Lima had "an infinite multitude of miserably poor, caused in part by the vanity that locals have in spending for festivities. Women's dress is unique here in that it is overwhelmingly indecent and horrifying."[68]

In the 1750s, the viceroy and a number of institutions sent a testimony on the Franciscans' efforts to Spain. Manso de Velasco lauded their success in reforming "customs, vices, and abuses" in all the cities, towns, and places where they had evangelized. They had not only reformed "corrupt customs and scandalous practices that vice had introduced," but also "planted the seed of virtue in their devout confessions and public penitence."[69] The Cathedral Chapter described the Franciscans' heroic efforts after the earthquake, noting the multiplication of blood processions and spiritual sermons that resulted from their example. It noted that the people sought out Father Joseph San Antonio, who had helped rid the city of "obscene friendships, hatred, and rancor" and thus reconciled many married couples.[70]

In what was undoubtedly later understood as awe-inspiring prescience, in 1744 the Franciscans convinced Joseph de Zevallos, Lima's archbishop, to reprint a book of essays and treatises on women's dress collected and published in Spain by Father Juan Agustín Ramírez. Its title page declared, "Reprinted in Lima through the diligence of the Apostolic Missionaries of San Francisco." The text itself began by noting that the Franciscans, not satisfied with twenty-two days' of evangelization "in the streets, plazas, their Church, and in the school of Guadalupe," recognized the need to propagate their ideas not only through public activities but also through "written text."[71] In his introduction, Archbishop Zevallos stressed the benefits of good morals and confronted the excuses used by men and women to justify their profane dress. In support of this introduction as well as of the text itself are numerous examples of God's punishment of women who did not heed such warnings.

The archbishop proclaimed that "ladies and leading women [Señoras y Principales]" could distinguish themselves from ordinary women by wearing proper dress and observing social mores. At the same, they would save money otherwise spent on elaborate dress. Because lower-class women mimicked the fine fabrics and low cuts, distinguished women would stand out if they wore more subtle clothing. Prefacing Ramírez's argument, Zevallos challenged three excuses for such dress: that men themselves increasingly dressed in fine cloth ("black silk") and new designs; that fathers and husbands encouraged women to dress profanely; and that the women had excused themselves by gaining the permission of "learned doctors" and confessors. He dismissed men's fashion as equally sinful and called on men not to set a bad example. On the second point, he instructed men to teach "Christian doctrine" in their households and to "impose the holy fear of God."[72] He noted that priests could not go to houses and thus it was the "father of the family's" obligation to foster Christian doctrine and to watch over women, both family and servants. He discounted the argument that the dress might not be intended "to provoke," noting its sinful nature whatever the user's intention. In this section he encouraged a separation of the sexes in the domestic sphere and pointed out the dangers of "dishonest and profane dances and songs." Finally, the archbishop reiterated the need for confessors to teach the "holy fear of God," dismissing inattention to this matter as a possible justification or excuse for questionable attire.

Father Ramírez begins his text by recognizing the difficulties in convincing women, who are often either "ignorant" or stubborn in their profane ways. He cited the patience and *fatigatus* of Christ with a Samaritan woman at a well in Sychar (John 4). He focused on women who wear "profane, provocative, and lascivious clothing for those who look at them." He emphasized how God punishes women who claim ignorance; "they only cover their flesh when they experience God's wrath, and no matter how much they are persuaded, they will not do it beforehand." He lamented the exposure of "the neck, shoulders, throat, and much of their breasts and back," stressing the damage done not only to the sinners' own family and servants, but to everyone who looked at them, including the young, the old, and religious people. He cited Jeremiah 5:26, which calls women's exposed shoulders and back "the trap" that ensnared many souls.[73]

The author then provides examples, such as a woman in Spain who fell dead after declaring in church "Father, no matter how much you preach, I don't have to amend my dress." He also presents detailed revelations, particularly from Saint Bridget (1303–73). In these accounts, the bloodied Jesus appeared to a woman announcing that he was paying for her sins or, in another instance, threatened a woman that he would send balls of fire to "burn and consume this vanity." They described a woman who, because of her sinful ways and use of cosmetics, was punished by being condemned to an afterlife in ash-colored rags.

The bulk of the booklet consists of examples of women and men punished for their profane dress. These stories included the usual early modern horrors: devils in mirrors, cauldrons of burning liquids, dragons using nets to prevent souls from entering heaven, angels predicting death, and the constant threat of eternal damnation in hell. One story argued that women

154   with profane clothes and indecent necklines were worse than whores ("rameras"): "Demons prefer them because they harvest more for hell than prostitutes themselves." Father Ramírez vehemently condemned women inappropriately dressed in church, threatening them with the wrath of angels and seraphs. The author finishes by addressing the three excuses used by women discussed by Archbishop Ramírez.

The Franciscans themselves also summarized their efforts to reform Peru and to offer aid following the earthquake/tsunami. The representative of the Twelve Apostles Province, their Peruvian congregation, wrote that among their achievements, "the modification of profane clothing, scandalous songs, and indecent dances had decreased crime and adultery while sparking marriages, penitent processions, and blood processions [procesiones de sangre] in the streets and Plazas."[74] Their efforts focused on "placating the very just wrath of God, who had stood up to his creatures who had provoked him with their vices and relaxed customs." They described Friar Tomás de Cañas, named the provincial head of the Franciscans days after the earthquake, walking barefoot through the rubble-strewn streets wearing a thorn crown and a noose around his neck and beseeching survivors to seek penitence.[75]

Father José de San Antonio, whose evangelizing zeal is summarized in chapter 2, petitioned Spain in the late 1740s for more Franciscans for Peru. He cast women's dress as the core reason for the moral problems that plagued Peru and had prompted the earthquake. He wrote,

> One of the more scandalous vices that the writer and his brothers have tried to uproot in these extended kingdoms of Peru, Santa Fe, Quito, Tierra Firme, and Chile . . . , the origin and beginning of the perdition of countless souls, large amounts of money, homes, and families, is that of provocative and scandalous clothing worn by women of all states and colors, with the principal ladies the most involved in this utterly infernal abuse, and only if they reform their clothing and dress with the desired decency for several years. . . . Their servants and slaves, as well as the rest of the Spanish, Black, Mulatta, Indian, and Mestiza women of the city will follow suit, and then all the rest from the mentioned kingdoms.[76]

For Friar San Antonio, the city's dreadful moral state derived from or was rooted in women's improper clothing. He lamented that the divine warning in the form of the earthquake and the actions taken by the viceroy and

the Cathedral Chapter had not succeeded in suppressing profane dress, a crucial step in restoring order and placating God. The Franciscans worked diligently to make these changes, garnering the explicit support of the viceroy, archbishop, and other authorities.

Much of Lima saw the earthquake/tsunami as an act of divine wrath and presumably supported the measures described above. Tapadas themselves might have agreed with the need to moderate public behavior. Nonetheless, subsequent campaigns against women's clothing and behavior as well as the depictions by foreign travelers indicate that the effects, if any, were temporary. French fashion continued to be the rage, foreigners described Lima's licentious ways, and sporadic campaigns returned. For example, in the 1780s the Capuchin friar Mariano de Junqueras condemned Lima's "relaxed customs." His report, which reached the Consejo de Indias in Spain, put much of the blame on "the monstrous profanity in the clothing of European women born in the Kingdom of Peru, the most indecent ever seen, which impedes the uniformity of the King's subjects and gives incentive to foreign contraband."[77] The Consejo, however, recognized the futility of legislating changes to women's dress, contending that only commerce and enlightenment, not edicts, could change "the peculiar habits and customs of pueblos."[78]

In 1791, the *Mercurio Peruano* published an article condemning the extravagant expenditures of a tapada, a grave threat to the domestic budget of "an honorable man."[79] Such anecdotes indicate that the campaign against women and their inappropriate dress in the decade following the 1746 earthquake/tsunami did not succeed. Tapadas continued to stroll, public flirtation and rampant concubinage marked social life, and men and women of differing social groups spent a great deal of money on clothing and jewelry. In 1835, Flora Tristan stated that "there is no place on earth where women are so free and exercise so much power as in Lima."[80] A Chilean intellectual who visited Lima in 1850 contended that the *saya* and the *manta*, the clothing of the tapada, "are the tools for women's independence, having done more for their elevation and social influence than the books and congresses with which French women have tried to attain them."[81] Although these quotes need to be considered cautiously, they indicate that the efforts to placate God's wrath by controlling what women wore and how they acted by and large failed.

"All These Indian and Black People Bear Us No Good Will": The Lima and Huarochirí Rebellions of 1750

[Lima] is a bloody city, woe to this bloody city, which boasts by spilling the blood of many people and all of the Indians, only because they are Christians and not Spaniards. —FRAY ISIDORO DE CALA (?), [José María Navarro, ed.], Planctus Indorum, 417–18

Eight

The proliferation of racial categories and the fluidity of racial identities in eighteenth-century Lima did not mean, of course, that race was not an issue; power was divided largely along racial lines. In his study *Aristocracia y plebe* (Aristocracy and plebe), Flores Galindo contended that the fear of the lower orders shaped the elites' behavior throughout the eighteenth century and that internal divisions among the lower classes, primarily along racial lines, impeded or crippled rebellions and revolutions until the wars of Independence in the first quarter of the nineteenth century. In other words, at the same time that a horizontal line was being etched between the elite and the plebe, divisions between the lower orders hampered collective action.[1] Other scholars have questioned the significance of racism among the lower classes, showing the prevalence of "mixed marriages" and the daily interaction among blacks, mulattos, Indians, and other members of Lima's heterogeneous lower classes.[2]

In fact, the same evidence can support both views. Countless criminal trials describe Indians, *zambos*, mestizos, and others working and living together. All of Lima's neighborhoods were racially mixed. Yet when a conflict emerged—often over a small debt or minor affront—racial insults escalated tensions, and violence often ensued. Whereas racial insults were uncommon in midcolonial Mexico City, criminal records in Lima frequently mention them, often as the spark of violence among members of the plebe.[3] Although always present, the issue of race and social control took on a heightened urgency in the earthquake's aftermath when the lower classes used or seemed to be on the verge of using violence to take matters into their own hands. A crime wave, a conspiracy, and an Andean uprising brought to the fore lower-class, particularly black and Indian, discontent and alternative visions for Lima, prompting elite fear and retrenchment.

The accounts of the disaster uniformly decried the crime wave that followed, blaming it on the lower-class population, particularly blacks. After jewelry and clothing had been taken from abandoned houses as well as from survivors and the dead, thieves began to pry wood, doors, and windows from the frames of the costly homes. The treasurer of the Purísima Concepción *cofradía* bitterly noted that a house it owned had been destroyed, with the remains "ransacked by thieves." In 1749, the administrators of a chaplaincy, Pablo and Agustín Vásquez de Velasco, sold an "empty plot of land, without doors, windows, or any wood, because they have stolen everything."[4] The *Desolation of Lima* claimed that "Blacks and the slaves dedicated themselves to looting the deserted ruins."[5] Llano Zapata described the theft of a silver rosary from an image of the Holy Virgin in the Santa Catalina plaza. Noting that this was not an isolated case, he condemned "the insolence of the plebe and lower-class people of this court [corte], who even with the fear of the punishing earth or of God offended, would not exclude the sacred from their looting or the human from their robbery." In another passage, he denounced Lima's multicolored lower classes: "People of this type abound in the large courts, especially here where the different nations have become a miscellany of colors, and those less exposed to blush are more inclined to larceny and insults."[6] Another account referred to the "incorrigible horde of the plebe," and several described horrific scenes of the poor robbing the wounded or stripping jewelry off the dead.[7] The viceroy himself fretted that slaves no longer obeyed their masters.[8] He set up gallows in Callao and Lima and increased patrols. Elite commentators cast blacks and the mixed-race plebe as opportunistic criminals. They deemed slaves even less trustworthy and potentially more dangerous.

The robbers seemed to have organized their efforts a couple of days after the earthquake, when these measures were taking effect. On October 30, a black man on horseback screamed that another, even larger wave would soon strike, this time reaching Lima. He and others called for people to flee east, toward the hills. The viceroy, Ovando, and several priests could not dissuade people, and a swarm of panicked survivors left the city. Ovando described the shocked and exhausted faces of the desperate people who fled. One woman threatened to hit him with a rock and screamed that she preferred to die there rather than return and be confronted "every second by such terrible fears."[9] Everyone suffered from shock and panic: "children's sobs, women's cries and shrieks, men's sighs, and old people's moans and groans became a sea of tears." People ran to the hills "shouting out their sins."[10] The rumor had apparently been a ruse by thieves to facilitate the ransacking of Lima.

The viceroy related the looting and disorder to the dispersion of the population. For example, in January 1747, when he doubled the number of district mayors (alcaldes ordinarios) from two to four, he justified this act as a measure to "assure order and public peace throughout the city and to avoid the robberies, homicides and other crimes that could be committed in its dilated circumference, securing at the same time the treasures and goods found in these ruined houses and in the huts and rooms of the citizens who have taken refuge in gardens, the countryside, and the surrounding areas."[11] Yet at the same time he interpreted the postearthquake turmoil as a reflection of the breakdown of the city's spatial organization, he racialized the crime wave, placing the blame squarely on the black or the racially mixed plebe population.

Blacks were both marginal and essential in Lima. In legal terms, the sixteenth-century demarcation of Spanish America into two republics, European and Indian, had not stipulated a clear position for blacks and mixed groups. Although blacks were almost invariably identified as occupying the bottom rung of the social hierarchy, doubts about their exact rank and religious status continued throughout the colonial period. Slaves confronted the horrors of this institution, while free blacks faced different forms of discrimination and injustice. The work that the majority of them found as day laborers and hustlers brought them enough to eat and little

16 Blacks in Funeral Procession. *Source:* Simón Yanque (Esteban de Terralla y Landa)
    Lima por dentro y fuera, illustration by Ignacio Merino, 192 (Paris, 1854).

else. Yet they had a visible role in the city's public life, secular and religious, and some people of black descent had climbed socially and economically. Blacks were important members of the militias, *cofradías,* and some artisan guilds. Their massive presence prompted members of the colonial upper echelons to fret that Lima had become a "fundamentally black" city.[12] This ambiguous situation became clear in the uprisings and rebellions of the eighteenth century. Spanish forces regularly counted on black soldiers and spies, recalling the military battles of the conquest, yet rebel groups also recruited blacks.[13]

In light of colonial criminal discourse and the place of blacks in Lima, it is not surprising that commentators saw them as the culprits behind the series of crimes that followed the earthquake. Many fugitive slaves had survived on petty theft and highway robbery—the infamous *bandoleros* of the coast—whereas some free blacks would complement their menial jobs as itinerant vendors or day laborers with illegal acts. For the destitute, the opened doors of ruined houses or clothing and jewelry found on the shocked or the dead offered a tempting opportunity at a time when

160   customary social and disciplinary codes had been overturned and the normal venues for a meal lost. On the other hand, late colonial society had deeply racialized crime, casting all blacks as inherently prone to crime and other forms of dishonor. Many also blamed blacks for the spreading of diseases.[14]

The upper classes did not view Indians as inborn criminals. They did treat them warily, however, debating their adherence to the Catholic Church and questioning their loyalty to the Crown. These concerns proved correct in the years following the earthquake, as groups composed of Indians and people of mixed race escalated their fight against what they perceived to be injustice and marginalization. The earthquake had weakened the symbols and seeming strength of Spanish rule.

Indians in Lima: Laborers, Nobles, and Conspirators

Indians provided the labor and goods that allowed the city to rebuild. They hauled wood, sand, rocks, reeds, lime, and other materials; sold potatoes, hot peppers, coca leaves, a rich variety of fruits, and other products from the Andes and the coast and jungle; and made adobes and assisted in other construction tasks. Lima, however, could not always count on their cheap labor. Some Indians drafted to work after the earthquake returned to their nearby villages to tend their crops. Lima was also the home of many "noble Indians," who claimed descent from the Inca elite and thus special rights.

Indians moved far beyond their customary role as laborers, petty merchants, and nobles in June 1750, when authorities uncovered a conspiracy by a group of Limeño Indians based in El Cercado to kill and expel the Spanish. Priests learned of the plan and alerted the viceroy. The plans included burning roofs, flooding streets, taking over the Plaza Mayor, and executing Europeans. Although the Spanish rapidly and brutally repressed the conspirators, their concerns about broader connections proved well founded when a more sustained and violent revolt took place in nearby Huarochirí, the Andean area directly to the east of Lima. In this case, rebels killed more than a dozen authorities and mobilized supporters in an extensive area. The earthquake had both revealed and increased the vulnerability of Spanish rule. Viceroy Manso de Velasco and other authorities felt threatened from below, along two fault lines: geological as well as cultural and racial.

The role of rebel is a familiar one among eighteenth-century Andean people, as hundreds of riots, revolts, and rebellions shook the area. The Tupac Amaru rebellion from 1780 to 1783 constituted the largest uprising in colonial Spanish America, spreading throughout much of western South America, humiliating the viceregal forces, and forcing much of the population to choose sides.[15] Historians have used these social movements as a window to understand Peru under the Bourbons and as an opportunity to place Indians at the center of history. In this regard, the El Cercado and Huarochirí uprisings examined here shed light on, among other topics, opposition to the Spanish, divergent understandings of colonialism, and the obstacles to multiclass and multiracial social movements. There is a danger, however, in situating them in a long line of uprisings. This perspective tends to culminate in the Tupac Amaru and Tupac Katari rebellions or the Wars of Independence in the early nineteenth century. The rebels are too easily cast as "precursors" to independence when, in fact, they had quite different objectives, inspirations, and tactics. "Downstreaming" takes the participants out of their context and puts them into a Manichean struggle of "Andean people" versus the Spanish. The social base, language, and platform of the El Cercado and Huarochirí participants differed greatly from those of the uprisings of later decades.

Viceroy Manso de Velasco's reaction to the events indicates the ambiguities and contradictions of Bourbon policy toward Andean Indians. Fulfilling the Bourbon objective of increasing remittances to Spain and decreasing local autonomy required heightened exploitation (higher head tax, more labor drafts, and the forced sale of goods) and the weakening of the venerable kuraka tradition of partial self-rule. Authorities recognized that these policies were unpopular and thus increased the likelihood of riots, insurrections, and even rebellion, increasingly common throughout the century. Moreover, replacing ethnic or local kurakas with outsiders was costly and complicated. But the problem moved far beyond the political and economic cost of increasing state power and revenues. As Manso de Velasco's writings on the El Cercado and Huarochirí events indicate, authorities recognized that the division of Peru into neat caste groups was by this point a fiction. He lamented Lima's messy social organization and the "weak" European population. He also regretted how the city "de-Indianized" Indians, granting them different worldviews and material culture and thus weakening their differentiation from other groups. Although he hinted that the divisions among Peruvians were debilitating, he saw the integration of Indians as impossible or impractical and ultimately sought to restore the shaky foundations intended to separate the two republics. The Crown itself had vacillated, unsure whether the Enlightenment idea of the breakup of corporate groups and identities, a project that by definition had to target Indians, could function in Peru. The viceroy and other authorities in Peru believed it was impossible. These contradictions played out in the midst of demands from Spain to increase revenues and alarming defiance in the viceroy's own front yard, the Plaza Mayor and the city's hinterland.

El Cercado and Huarochirí also demonstrate the complexity of Indians' aspirations and ideologies in the mid–eighteenth century. Historians have long correlated the increasing demands by the Bourbons and growing insurgency in the Andes. These elements can be seen in Huarochirí, as kurakas who felt their position weakening played a large role, and rebels made their hatred for the colonial authority, the *corregidor*, painfully clear. Yet another key grievance motivated Indian discontent—their demands to gain full access to the religious orders. This underscored the centuries-long effort by Indians to annul their definition or demarcation as "New Christians" and thus inferiors to Europeans. Changing the definition would mean that they were "religious adults" rather than unruly children, putting into danger the ideological foundations of Spanish colonialism. The crucial text motivating Indians during this period was a petition by three Franciscan friars that demanded that the Spanish open the mendicant orders to indigenous people, a demand which questioned colonial rule, since these campaigns situated the Incas as monarchical predecessors to the Spanish and thus extended to them equal aristocratic rights. The Indian nobility of Lima (no doubt looked down upon by the Cusco indigenous nobility) echoed this and other complaints in their effort to gain recognition as equals to the Spanish. Their ideas and actions differed greatly from those of the indigenous peasantry who participated in dozens of Andean uprisings. Therefore, in this chapter I pay considerable attention to the Franciscan text *Representación verdadera* (True representation) as well as to the jockeying by Lima's Indians in the festivities of 1748 celebrating the coronation of Fernando VI.

What role did the earthquake itself play? As soon as he surveyed the devastated city on October 28, the viceroy worried that it would destabilize Lima's material and spiritual order to the point that Spanish rule was in danger. He never separated the physical destruction of the earthquake from the social mayhem it prompted (or threatened). Both fault lines, the seis-

mic and the social or racial, needed to be addressed. He therefore rushed
to rebuild, secure the state's monopoly on firearms, and prevent the formation of links between Lima and its hinterland and the threat posed by the
ongoing rebellion of Juan Santos Atahualpa.

Juan Santos Atahualpa "Apu Inca" (Inca lord), a mestizo probably from
Cusco, arrived in the western Amazon, or montaña, in 1742 and declared
his right as a descendent of the executed Emperor Atahualpa to resurrect
the Incan empire. He crafted a multiethnic movement that included Afro-
Peruvians (slaves and former slaves), highland Indians and mestizos, and
natives from the Amazon basin. For more than a decade his forces kept the
colonial state at bay, defeating three major military expeditions and inching
ever closer toward Lima and the coast. Atahualpa's forces halted Franciscan evangelization in this frontier zone, killing more than twenty friars and
forcing many back to the coast. In the aftermath of the earthquake, Manso
de Velasco and others worried that malcontents in Lima would link with
this uprising and extend the fighting into all of central Peru, coast, Andes,
and jungle.[16]

The viceroy recognized deep social and economic dangers involving
Indians, yet, lacking a solution and pressed by Madrid, he ultimately sought
to restore the status quo. Indians used the rebuilding period to push their
various agendas, just as other groups had, sustaining projects that could assume a deeply subversive nature. In addition, the catastrophe had brought
to the fore alleged premonitions by Santa Rosa about her city's destruction
and the return of the Incas in 1750. The viceroy and his inner circle were
not alone in seeing the years after the earthquake as perilous, as a time of
radical change.

Lima 1747

Viceroy Manso de Velasco found many reasons to worry about the Indian
population. Since 1735, more than a dozen riots, revolts, uprisings, and
rebellions by Indians had targeted viceregal authorities and, in fewer cases,
priests. Some were local riots such as that in Lucanas in 1736, when Indians
stoned the mayor for having struck a former Indian mayor. Others spread
beyond a town or district, linking disparate social groups and regions.
Viceroy Castelfuerte (1724–36) imposed a policy of tightening tax collection through new censuses, closer control of authorities, and the taxation

164 of mestizos, and it met with widespread opposition, prompting mestizo-Indian alliances.[17] Authorities fretted that the Juan Santos rebellion would spread into the Andes and down to Lima. In his memoir, Viceroy Superunda warned that Indians "have not forgotten their ancient Kings and see the Spanish as usurpers."[18] The lack of arms in Lima as well as the small percentage of Europeans troubled the viceroy. Recognizing that the chaotic state of Lima could foster discord and facilitate the work of rebels, he hurried the rebuilding efforts, stressing the connection between resettlement and sociopolitical stability.

Indian disgruntlement with the Spanish hinged on several issues. Throughout the eighteenth century, the colonial state raised tax and labor demands. Kurakas found it increasingly difficult both to appease the Indians they represented and to satisfy the state. Many were replaced by people without local roots. These "interim *Kurakas*" sought to profit rapidly and frequently provoked widespread Indian displeasure.[19] The riots and rebellions that struck fear into authorities throughout the eighteenth century expressed deep opposition to diverse types of exploitation and the intrusion of nonlocal authorities, a threat to local political autonomy. Indigenous people challenged increased taxes and labor demands as well as the misdeeds of authorities through nonviolent means — negotiation and the court system primarily — and collective action. In the uprisings studied here, rebels expressed and built on the widespread opposition to various forms of exploitation as well as to the encroachment and abuses of non-indigenous authorities.

Taxes, the labor draft, and invasive authorities were not the only grounds for complaints by Indians. In 1748, the Franciscan friar Calixto Tupak Inca published *Representación verdadera y exclamación rendida y lamentable que toda la nación Indiana hace a la Majestad del Señor Rey de las Españas y Emperador de las Indias . . .* (True Representation). This remarkable text publicized deep resentment over Indians' exclusion from the religious orders, a grievance that ultimately put into question Spanish rule and influenced the rebels of Lima and the hinterland. Based on the prophet Jeremiah's Lamentations, the harrowing account of the destruction of Jerusalem by the Babylonians, and deeply steeped in the apocalyptic thought of the late baroque, the *Representación verdadera* indignantly protested the barriers blocking Indians from the Church, particularly from the mendicant orders.[20] Its primary complaint was that Indians could be only *donados*, members of an order who paid a small dowry, professed vows, and worked as virtual servants, and not friars.[21] Fray Calixto, however, moved far beyond this demand and criticized the Spanish for not enforcing their laws, for preventing Indians from rising in both the Church and the State, and for allowing widespread exploitation and the demise of authority.[22]

The *Representación* and a similar text, the *Planctus Indorum* (1750), written in Latin presumably by Fray Isidoro de Cala y Ortega, also a Franciscan, have been interpreted as reflections of "an Inca national movement," "creole nationalism," apocalyptic baroque thought, late scholasticism, and enlightened reformism.[23] All of these interpretations are partially correct, as these different elements can be found in the two works. The *Representación* as well as the *Planctus* moved far beyond the core argument about the rights of Indians to be full-fledged members of the mendicant orders and the Church. They also ruminated on the Incas and the injustices of Spanish rule, particularly the dissonance between theory and practice. The *Representación* repeatedly blamed authorities in Peru for not implementing what the Crown intended and thus requested permission for Fray Calixto to travel to Madrid to meet the king and queen so that Indians, in his persona, could "see them, know and adore them, show them our scars, face to face."[24] Both texts criticized the Juan Santos movement, yet pointed out that the lack of Indian friars and the abandonment of Christian ideals had nudged some toward radical action.[25] Juan Carlos Estenssoro has shown how the demand by Indians to be allowed into the priesthood formed part of a broader effort to eschew the definition of Indians as New Christians and deem them instead Old Christians. This would dissolve one of the fundamental tenets of colonial social stratification, a key distinction between Europeans and Indians, and thus constituted a far-reaching demand.[26] The text reflected frustration with the vacillations of Bourbon policies in terms of allowing Indians into the mendicant orders as well as deeper concerns about the threat to the prerogatives of Indians posed by the Crown's reforms.[27]

Fray Calixto was born in Tarma, Peru, in 1710, the son of a Spaniard and a royal Indian woman, a descendent of Inca Tupac Yupanqui. He entered the Franciscan order as a *donado* in 1727 and spent time in Lima, Spain, Guatemala, and Charcas (Upper Peru, or modern-day Bolivia). He may have had contact with the Juan Santos rebels in 1744.[28] He sent the *Representación verdadera*—which was published in Lima without all the required permissions—to kurakas throughout Peru in 1748 in an attempt to raise money to go to Spain to present it to the king. In Quillabamba, Cuzco, he gained the support of Friar Isidoro de Cala y Ortega, who accompanied him on his extraordinary trip to Spain. He also had the encouragement of Fray Antonio Garro. Many authors believe that either Cala y Ortega or Garro rather than Fray Calixto was the author of the *Representación*; scholars also debate who the author of *Planctus* was.[29]

Fray Calixto failed in his efforts to obtain funds from Lima's Indian Cabildo to present his case in Madrid. Instead, he took a more economical and clandestine route. Fray Calixto and Cala y Ortega left Cuzco on September 25, 1749, and reached Buenos Aires on February 15, 1750. They hid in Buenos Aires until they were able to sneak into Brazil and take a ship from Rio de Janeiro on April 19 that arrived in Lisbon on July 20. From Portugal they sent a copy of the *Representación* to the pope via a banker who was traveling to Rome. They furtively went to Madrid, dodging an arrest order, but once there realized that gaining an audience with the king was unlikely. Instead, they waited for the king outside his country estate and miraculously managed to hand the manuscript to him as he opened the window of his coach during an evening promenade on August 23.[30] Days later, they were told that the king and his ministers had read it and that it had caused "a great stir."[31] In the following weeks, Cala y Ortega met with authorities in Madrid to explain the accusations of the *Representación*, and both friars accounted for their odyssey to their Franciscan superiors in Madrid. They were not immediately punished by their order or by the court, but the arrival in Madrid of the viceroy's report on uprisings in Lima and nearby Huarochirí, which implicated "two Franciscans friars," impeded any serious review of the complaints found in the *Representación*. On May 9, 1751, the Royal Council deemed the text "subversive" and prohibited its diffusion in Peru.[32] Their incredible good luck in handing the document to the king had ended with the untimely arrival of the report.

In Madrid, Calixto continued to write to the king. In early 1751, he cast himself as a noble loyal to his majesty as well as to the Inca kings. He decried how good Catholics in Peru had been forced out of the Church, into the mountains, and back to idolatry. He begged the king to "help quiet that Kingdom, if not, fatal consequences could occur."[33] In late 1751, Fray Calixto was sent to Valencia, where he was to become a *lego*, or full brother. He returned to Peru and continued his quixotic and possibly subversive actions. Fray Isidoro de Cala was denied permission to hand over the manuscripts to the pope and was retained but not imprisoned in Spain. He continued to lobby the Crown. Ultimately the two friars succeeded. In 1766, King Carlos III granted Indians the right to enter the mendicant orders, to study in any religious school, and to ascend in religious and governmental hierarchies.[34]

As the *Representación* and other documents indicate, the Incas were a crucial symbol in debates and political movements throughout this period. Noble Indians, at the same time that they tried to open the door to the Church and thus discard the New Christian/Old Christian distinction, sought to represent the Spanish and Incas as a continuous monarchy. Since the sixteenth century, the Indian elite had struggled to achieve recognition for their nobility. In the eighteenth century, these efforts at times carried a subversive message and could stoke the flames of rebellion. These were not, however, mere intellectual projections sponsored by nobles or rebel leaders. For the Indian masses, the constantly re-created memory of the Incas, "the Andean Utopia," had an overtly seditious nature and encouraged a variety of dissident projects.[35] Common people evoked and remembered the Incas. For example, an anonymous French Jesuit noted in the 1740s or 1750s that in Chincha, to the south of Lima, "these Indians affectionately conserve the memory of their Incas, and they get together from time to time to celebrate their memory. They sing verses in their honor and play lugubrious and moving songs on their flutes, which incite the compassion of everyone who hears them.[36] The invocation of the Incas, disgruntled Indian nobles, and mass Indian sedition merged in the events of the 1740s.

El Día de Lima

In January 1747, news reached Lima that King Philip V had died on July 9, 1746, and that his son had succeeded him as King Fernando VI.[37] Ceremonies were held in a temporary church in the Plaza Mayor in August, after those who had taken refuge there were relocated. In recognition of the sorry state of Lima as well as the need to mourn Philip V, the viceroy postponed celebrations for the new king until September 23, Fernando's birthday. The lengthy celebrations were halted in October in order to commemorate the earthquake and then resumed in early 1748.[38]

168   The celebration for the new king presented serious problems for the viceroy. On the one hand, how could a devastated city with thousands of homeless, many ill, and just about everyone in mourning hold elaborate, lengthy festivities? The Plaza Mayor could be cleared only temporarily, and debris cluttered all of the city's streets. Did Lima have the stability, space, and resources to celebrate the coronation of Fernando? On the other hand, some clerics questioned whether it was appropriate to celebrate at all in a time of such need, when God's wrath had just been unleashed. In Spanish America, the official rituals—masses, processions, and sanctioned "diversions"—were typically followed by more carnivalesque activities in which the lower classes expressed and enjoyed themselves. Concerned guards of the city's moral codes did not like these more boisterous, unrestrained celebrations.

The viceroy and his inner circle recognized the challenges in organizing proper festivities. Nonetheless, the viceroy considered the news about succession in Spain a "stimulation to evict those living in huts and shacks in the Plaza Mayor" and, in general, to remove people from gardens, plazas, and areas outside of the city walls and return them to their residences.[39] Favorable accounts of the viceroy's efforts in the Noticia Annalica and El Día de Lima stressed the viceroy's stunning success in preparing the city for the festivities, using it as a symbol of the city's resurgence.

El Día de Lima, a two-hundred page account of the celebration of the coronation of Fernando VI, describes the depths of Lima's descent following the horrendous earthquake and its reemergence thanks to its inhabitants' enthusiastic response to the viceroy's energetic measures. The text has frequent classical allusions, referring, for example, to Pliny the Younger on Mount Vesuvius and to Virgil on the sacking of Troy. Arguing that earthquakes are the worst of all catastrophes, the author compares resurgent Lima favorably to Troy, Athens, Carthage, and Sparta and thus labels Lima a "Phoenix."[40] The author noted that Lima "came to terms" with earthquakes and miraculously prepared for the celebration with "all magnificence." He continued, "Everything was hurried, yet everything was magnificent. And for those who had seen the city devastated, it was shocking to see it so well supplied. It seemed that nature had also been moved by joy and it had done its underground business, producing jobs instead of precious metals."[41] Not only had the population been swayed by Manso de Velasco's efforts, but the earth itself, the culprit behind the city's woes, had also amended its ways. Accounts emphasized how citizens worked tirelessly to clear the streets for the September procession. El Día de Lima celebrated a glorious triumph over rubble and idleness.[42]

On September 22, 1747, church bells rang from midday to mark the eve of the festivities to celebrate the new king. People dressed in their finest clothing, and the elite rode in their best coaches to see the arches and sculptures that venerated Fernando VI. The following day, representatives of corporate groups and institutions such as the Real Audiencia attended mass in the morning. The viceroy's coach was a "shining sign that such admirable pomp was the glorious triumph of happiness."[43] In the afternoon, militia battalions representing major corporations such as the nobility and the Cabildo lined up with their finest regalia and horses in the Plaza Mayor to embark on the royal cavalcade. Though the epidemics that plagued Lima after the earthquake had thinned the noble corps, they had not diminished their enthusiasm for pageantry.[44] Led by the royal banner, or pendón, the procession passed the triumphal arch with its elaborate artwork and then moved south to the second stage at La Merced church. It returned to the Plaza de Armas on the wonderfully named Guitarists and Shopkeepers streets and proceeded seven blocks east, passing the massive Concepción convent, to the Santa Ana plaza, where the third stage awaited. As large as the Plaza Mayor, Santa Ana allowed room for the elaborate rituals that proclaimed the new king. The procession left from the northwest side of the plaza, site of the Discalced San José monastery, and headed back toward the Plaza Mayor. In front of the Dominican Saint Thomas school stood the Mint, which had lined the pavement along its block with silver. From the Mint's balcony, officials threw coins with the effigy of Fernando VI, prompting mayhem as the plebe pushed and shoved to collect them. The fourth stage was in the next block, at the Inquisition plaza. Additional stands had to be built because the earthquake had destroyed the Inquisition's elaborate balcony. The procession then returned to the Plaza Mayor, the viceroy retiring from public view just before sunset. Fireworks, plays, and other festivities followed for eight days. The viceroy assumed a discrete role but offered judicial pardons and other dispensations.[45]

El Día de Lima explained that the ceremonies ended in October as people dedicated themselves to penitence to commemorate previous earthquakes, particularly that of October 20, 1687, and also the most recent one. The viceroy decided to suspend further festivities until February, when the Francis-

170 cans' evangelization campaign, the "universal missions," would be completed. Behind this decision lurked vigorous debates about the propriety of holding public festivities. The Cathedral Chapter argued that they would undermine the compunction the city's residents had shown and thus invite once again "divine indignation" already manifested in "repeated earthquakes." In a document from November 1747, the members of the chapter contended that in light of the harsh conditions caused by the earthquake and ensuing epidemics and aftershocks,

> nothing could be more prejudicial to the good customs necessary to placate divine wrath than the introduction of these profane celebrations, that normally produce in the plebeian, common people unbridled *relajación*, inciting robberies and other excesses . . . corroding in a few days all the progress that the preachers, through their pious zeal, and virtuous and repentant people, through their good examples, have made, to the point that, increasingly irritated, divine justice would unload its final blow or allow the calamities to resume.[46]

The members also addressed the viceroy's obsession with quick resettlement, noting that the festivities exacerbated the shortage of overseers, artisans, and workers.[47]

The city council retorted that the celebrations were not only an obligation, but also an important pledge to God by honoring the new king. They contended that norms could be followed so as not to provoke, once again, divine retribution. The viceroy recognized the difficult decision, the balance between "pledging to God the primary respect that he is due, without overlooking the King and what his Majesty deserves."[48] He put Pedro Bravo de Lagunas y Castillo in charge of creating guidelines. The most notable act was the decision to not hold bullfights, in order to save money and avoid boisterous behavior. Nonetheless, the festivities were to take place early in the coming year, before Lent.

The viceroy was not simply caught between the divergent views of the Cathedral Chapter and of the city council on festivities and the common good. He also was ambivalent about the festivities. As noted previously, he disliked Lima's ostentatious public life and, in good Bourbon absolutist fashion, sought to restrain it. He no doubt worried about expenses, yet also recognized that the preparation for the September promulgation had accelerated his efforts to return people to their houses and to clean up the streets. The chaotic, carnivalesque nature of baroque festivities could potentially cause more permanent subversion of social order. The masking of identities, the mixing of people, and exuberant multiday parties always disquieted the ruling classes.

The festivities in February 1748 included many plays, operas, and concerts. The second courtyard of the viceregal palace was converted into an amphitheater. The first play, Calderón de la Barca's *Ni Amor se Libra de Amor*, developed the Lima-as-Phoenix symbolism. Fireworks illuminated the Plaza Mayor, drawing large crowds. The pageant organized by Lima's Indian nobility—the final but highly significant event of the February festivities—was remarkably ornate and fascinating. It also justified some of the perturbation over these rituals.

The viceroy and representatives of key institutions and corporations took their seats in the Plaza Mayor, which was spruced up with trees and plants to represent spring. Don Antonio Chayguaca, one of the noble Indian leaders of the procession, had the honor of sitting next to the viceroy to serve as his "interpreter."[49] Dressed in fine European clothing, leaders of the Indian council and militia regiment described to the audience the significance of the ritual and fulfilled the requirement of requesting permission. Representatives of the Gran Chimu, the pre-Inca ruler of the north coast, led the parade. Following him were the Gran Taumpa, called the ambassador of the Incas, *Ñustas*, or royal ladies, and the *Coya*, or queen, all dressed in elaborate native dress. Attendants cared for the Inca "sovereigns," carrying them on gold thrones.

Huascar Inca, the Cusco-based pretender to Inca sovereignty when the Spanish arrived, began the presentation of the Incas. Atahualpa, the northern candidate captured and killed by Pizarro's forces, was noticeably absent.[50] The eleven previous Incas followed, all elaborately dressed and surrounded by attendants, dancers, and elaborate props. For example, the queen of Capa-Yupanqui, deemed the sixth Inca, wore "60,000 pesos worth of jewelry."[51] Numerous other kings, ambassadors, and kurakas accompanied Manco Capac, the first Inca. Among much finery, three associates carried a banner that stated, "Long Live the Catholic King Don Fernando VI, King of Spain, and Emperor of the Indies."[52] Bringing up the rear, a triumphal float pulled by eight horses and covered with gold and jewels displayed a painting that evoked the symbols of the Spanish crown—a lion on top of the globe.

El Día de Lima applauded the procession's refined pageantry, which

172   stressed Indians' loyalty. It again lauded Lima's accomplishment—"a city reduced to dust, closer to the tomb than to the display of its magnificence"—in organizing such regal and beneficial festivities. Comparing the celebrations in Lima to Rome's circuses and spectacles, the author asked rhetorically, "How might it glow in its zenith if it shines so in its nadir?"[53] The viceroy and other authorities shared this satisfied appraisal of the festivities for the new king. Yet tensions and the sign of impending problems emerged. In the *Representación*, Fray Calixto complained that Indians had performed last, "as was always the case." He complimented their performance as "the most plausible, lucid, happy, and grandiose" seen in the last two centuries and perhaps superior to those of ancient Rome. Nonetheless, two weeks after the festivities a Spanish mayor had sentenced a noble indigenous woman, a leading performer in the performance, to public humiliation for a small infraction. The friar complained that Europeans were treated differently from "Indians, mestizos, and mulattoes, blacks and other vile and plebeian people" and stressed the constant injustices of the system. The root cause was the lack of Indian authorities and the distance between the Crown and its corrupted representatives in Peru.[54] He also mentioned "meetings after the royal festivals" in which he expressed his ideas.[55] Fray Calixto did not invent or exaggerate this frustration and anger in order to bolster his campaign. Some of the participants in the parade in 1748 were already moving beyond the staged veneration of the Incas, acting upon their grievances and anger against the Spanish.

El Cercado

On June 21, 1750, a priest from San Lázaro across the Rimac River told Viceroy Manso de Velasco that he had learned in confession that some of the city's Indians had been meeting in the hills next to a meadow to the north, a popular recreation site called Amancaes, to prepare an uprising. The following day a Franciscan cleric added more details. A free black employee of his had heard rumors about a planned uprising and had met some of the leaders. The viceroy told the friar to convince his employee to attend another meeting on June 24 in order to provide a full report. Over many drinks, the man gleaned the major facts of the conspiracy.[56]

The rebels planned to take advantage of the celebrations for San Miguel el Arcangel (Saint Michael, September 20), when the usual celebratory chaos overtook the city and many participants carried arms, real or fake. They envisioned breaking into the armory at the viceroy's palace and taking "muskets, pistols and even swords" from the European population. At midnight, under the guise of fireworks and dressed in white shirts, they were to light the thatched roofs of the huts on the outskirts ("that subsisted due to the earthquake") and divert the Rimac River into the city.[57] One source mentions that the Indians planned to shout that the ocean had reached Lima, exploiting the deep fears of an even more destructive tsunami.[58] With the city's residents panicked and slowed by the mud, rebels would then take over the palace and five hundred men would storm the Callao presidio. Fifty men stationed at each of the four corners of the Plaza Mayor were to kill those fleeing their houses. Key authorities would be executed, particularly *chapetones* (a derogatory term for Spaniard), with the assassin gaining the title of his victim.[59] Slaves would be freed and Catholicism respected, "with a small number of clergy from each of the orders" remaining. Some wanted to crown Juan Santos, the Amazonian rebel, while others preferred rule by a noble council.[60] According to the viceroy, they sought to "reestablish their ancient Empire."[61]

The viceroy put Pedro José Bravo de Castilla, a member of the Real Audiencia and a critical advisor, in charge of the investigation. With the information gained from the informant, officials captured three leaders just before dawn on June 26 in a pottery shop in the Cocharcas neighborhood.[62] Many Indians, particularly those from nearby provinces, lived and worked in Cocharcas, in the Santa Ana district adjacent to the city's eastern gate.[63] Their testimony "a toda diligencia" (with full diligence) led to the capture of eight more participants, although others were able to flee.[64] On the morning of July 22, Miguel Surichac, Santiago Walpa Maita, Melchor de los Reyes, Antonio Cabo, Gregorio Loredo, and Julian Ayala were dragged by horses, hanged, and quartered in the Plaza Mayor. Their heads, skin peeled off and salted, were exhibited on bastions of the city's walls, and their quartered body parts were placed near their meeting places as gruesome reminders of the penalty for subversion.[65] Two suspects were sent to Ceuta, the Spanish enclave in north Africa, and two to the Callao presidio. A "quasi Spaniard" accused of serving as their scribe was given two hundred lashes in public.[66] A battalion of Indian nobles attended the grisly execution. The viceroy noted dubiously their acceptance of the punishment and promised them favors for their loyalty. In his words, "This

174   solemn demonstration was sufficient."[67] He also observed, however, that some Indians, driven by "fear or guilt," had fled the city to avoid possible retaliation and violence.[68]

The leaders of the abortive insurgency were Indians and mestizos, many of them artisans. Not from the poorest strata of Lima, they had the resources, experience, contacts, and worldview to plan an uprising. One source labeled Miguel Surichac the "General," Francisco García Jiménez Inca as second-in-command, and Pedro Santos as number three. Surichac, a mestizo, had worked for an important figure, Don Alonso Santa, and accompanied him on his assignment as corregidor. He had thus learned to read and write and perhaps had been in touch with Juan Santos.[69] Jiménez Inca, a captain of the potters' guild and a leading figure in Santa Ana as well as in his native Huarochirí, had hosted many of the conspirators' meetings. He had owned a house with some shops on the street of the Mint that was demolished by the earthquake.[70] Santos was a surgeon, a less vaunted profession at the time than today, from Saña on the northern coast. The viceroy believed he had been a recruiter and had burned the lists of followers to prevent further arrests. Santos initially escaped but was captured and executed in September.[71] One document classified Cabo as another "principal instrument." Ayala, described as being part Spaniard, apparently drew the map of the rebels' plan.[72] About the others little is known except that Loredo was deemed "part Spanish" and Hualpa Maita had an indigenous name.

In a letter of September 24, the viceroy noted that the rebels had been planning the uprising for more than two years. He acknowledged their grievances about the mistreatment of Indians by local authorities, yet stressed that "above all, they are exasperated by their exclusion from the priesthood, with all the positions going to Spaniards, sentiments supported by two Franciscan clergy." In a slightly different draft of this letter he mentioned "a manifesto published without permission by two clerics of little talent." He was referring, of course, to Fray Calixto and Fray Cala y Ortega.[73] He also mentioned the participation of three of the leaders in the pageantry in 1748. Indeed, Jimenez had played Inca Roca while Santos had portrayed the king of the pre-Inca northern Chimu kingdom, the Great Chimu Capac.[74] The rebels had met frequently since March, changing the place and time to avoid suspicion. They swore their faith to the cause in front of a crucifix and believed they could attract slaves to their movement.

The viceroy fretted that Cabo, a devout Indian who behind his religiosity hid a "mortal hatred and aversion towards the Spanish," had disseminated the idea that the rebels were fulfilling Santa Rosa de Lima's prognostication about the return of the Incas in the year 1750.[75] Several versions of this purported prophecy circulated in Lima after the earthquake. The historian Flores Galindo believed it took on new life when it became entangled with elite fears of an Indian takeover of the city. Santa Rosa's alleged vision had been converted into an apocalyptic belief that rising waters would dislodge the Spanish and lead to Indian rule, saved because their neighborhood lay farther to the east. Dating from the late seventeenth century, this apocryphal prophecy prompted multiple invocations of Santa Rosa and her association, curious in light of her Lima background, with the Incas and even subversive movements. For example, in 1704, the Inquisition prohibited linking her with the cult of the Incas in paintings. Both the *Representación* and the *Planctus* associated her with indigenous demands.[76]

Manso de Velasco acknowledged that disaster had been averted because "the Spanish live carefully, and we do not lend our arms to anyone except legitimate defenders of the Crown, because all these Indian and Black People bear us no good will."[77] The viceroy was about to pardon some of the participants when he learned that Jiménez also was involved in a broad uprising in nearby Huarochirí. He immediately abandoned all display of benevolence by the colonial state.

Huarochirí

The Andean province of Huarochirí looms over Lima to the east. The events of 1750 highlighted its importance to the capital. One account reported that the uprising prompted a shortage of "potatoes, lard, bacon, and other food" in Lima. The author pointed out that the humidity and relatively high temperatures of the coast—in contrast to Andean frigidity, particularly in the winter, when the uprising took place—made it impossible to store produce for more than a few days.[78] A description of Huarochirí written just after the uprising began by calling it "Lima's breadbasket."[79] In the eighteenth century, travelers to the central Andes and jungle followed a trail that began next to the Lurín River, passing through the town of Huarochirí itself. In more modern times, trains and cars took a route slightly to the north, along the Mantaro River.

The viceroy called Huarochirí the throat of Peru, meaning that it connected the head, Lima, to the body, the Andes and the Amazon basin.[80] He worried that rebels could cut Lima off from the interior. If they were to join the ongoing subversion of Juan Santos in the Amazon, they would have Lima surrounded and control much of central Peru. One account of the Huarochirí conflict asserted that if it spread to Tarma, Juan Santos's western front, "the kingdom was doomed."[81]

Jiménez Inca traveled to Lahuaytambo in June 1750 to marry María Gregoria de Puipuilibia, the daughter of a cacique. During the wedding and patron saint festival he recruited supporters for the uprising, taking advantage of his now-extensive kin ties. Once he learned that his fellow conspirators had been captured or were in hiding, Jiménez Inca accelerated his efforts. His new father-in-law, Don Juan Pedro de Puipuilibia, the kuraka of Lahuaytambo, and Don Andrés de Borja Puipuilibia, newly named kuraka of Huarochirí, agreed to join him. Like many midcentury kurakas, they chafed at continuing pressure to supply laborers for the labor draft, the *mita*, and inflexible demands to collect the head tax. The decline in population since an epidemic in the 1730s had made this increasingly difficult, and their pleas for a new census to document the decline and thus lower the tax burden had been turned down by the viceregal government.[82]

News of Jiménez Inca's activities prompted quick action by the viceroy, and this in turn forced the rebels to react. Manso de Velasco sent José Antonio de Salazar y Ugarte, the corregidor of Huarochirí, to arrest Jiménez Inca. On July 19, Salazar left Yauli, a small mining town, to search for him in Huarochirí. They captured María Gregoria, but even after the painful humiliation of a whipping she would not give precise information about the whereabouts of her husband and the other rebels. Francisco de Araujo y Río, the former corregidor of Huarochirí, and his son-in-law, Juan José Orrantia, the brother of Huarochirí's parish priest, joined the Spanish forces in Huarochirí, confident they would quickly capture the leaders and stifle the uprising. Andrés de Borja Puipuilibia, the kuraka, duped the Spanish, telling them he would bring them the rebel leader. On the night of the twenty-fifth rebels descended from the hills and assembled in the house of Lorenzo Saxamanta, one of the leaders. The leaders had written to the indigenous authorities throughout the province to gain their support.[83]

Agustín Chuquiri, the mayor of Huarochirí, slipped away to warn the Spanish, most of whom were staying in the town council building; others were in the priest's house half a block away. Chuquiri told them to take up their guns, as more than four hundred rebels, who counted on supporters in the surrounding provinces of Canta, Yauyos, Jauja, Tarma, and Bombon, were preparing to kill them. When the Spanish soldiers paid little attention, striking him and telling him to arrest the rebels himself, he fled. An Indian woman, María Inés, also warned them, but to no avail.[84] The rebels began to ring the church bells after ten in the evening, yelling for the Spanish to come out. They killed one of Salazar y Ugarte's soldiers, Thomas Chirito, when he ventured to the priest's house. The besieged Spaniards in the town council house, who had twenty-seven muskets, eighteen pistols, and gunpowder, could not agree on a plan. Some wanted to shoot their way through the rebel forces while others preferred to wait. When the rebels set fire to the roof, Salazar y Ugarte and others took refuge in the building's central patio, hauling the province's documentation and tribute money with them. Seven others stormed out, wounding several rebels. They made it to the outskirts of town but were surrounded and stoned to death.

Stones thrown by the rebels over the town council walls and into the patio had wounded most of the nine who remained. On Sunday morning, the twenty-sixth, a trusted mulatto assistant sent by Salazar y Ugarte to scout the situation, particularly the status of those barricaded in the priest's house, was killed. Desperate, Salazar instructed his men to divide the four thousand pesos from the town treasury and stuff it along with any documentation in their clothes and to flee together toward the priest's house. Their pessimism at this point was clear: they sought a confessor in order to "die as good people."[85] Rebels quickly captured three of them, executing one immediately. Three more died in the plaza, while Salazar, suffering from a gunshot wound in the jaw, made it to the priest's house but could not convince the soldiers to open the door. A stone thrown by a woman knocked him off the wall he was trying to climb, and a young man named Joseph Chepinto finished him off with a lance. The rebels cut the throats of two of the prisoners yet pardoned the dark-skinned Thomas de Robladillo, who posed as a member of the Indian elite. Drinking and eating with the rebels after being on the brink of execution, Robladillo promised he would recruit four thousand men for the rebels. They named him a sergeant and let him leave town. He did not return.

The rebels gave the petrified priest two hundred pesos from the money taken from Salazar for masses for the dead Spaniards. They also requested

178 a mass for their troops and paid local women to prepare the noon meal. Someone warned Araujo y Río and Orrantia, who were still in the priest's house, that all Spaniards were to be killed. Taking bread and cheese for what they hoped would be an escape to Lima, they fled out the back door and were not noticed for several blocks. A woman who had gone for water, however, spotted Orrantia and alerted the rebels, who quickly seized him. One of them, Miguel Caruajulca, told Orrantia not to worry—he would not hurt the brother of "his priest." He asked Orrantia for his sword and then killed him with it.

The group that had escorted Robladillo out of town chanced upon Araujo and brought him back to town. The rebel captain Cristobal Ventura told him that the Indians were bitter about his abusive behavior when he was the corregidor and ordered him to carry heavy rocks on his back, in imitation of Indians sent to the mines. Ventura claimed this would alleviate the bitterness toward him and preempt punishment. It proved, however, to be simply an initial humiliation, highly symbolic in this rocky mining area. Araujo screamed to no avail that if he were freed he would pay anyone who defended him generously and would donate two thousand pesos to build a church in the town of Tupicocha, where Ventura was from. But Ventura and others beat him to death with sticks. They took off his clothes, put a piece of cheese in his mouth and a piece of bread in his hand, and left him on the outskirts of town. The revulsion the rebels felt for the former corregidor was evident.[86]

The rebels moved quickly to extend their control of the region. Jiménez Inca ordered his Indian troops to block roads and to stand guard in the peaks over narrow passages in order to bombard the enemy with stones. He sent Francisco Santa Cruz with two hundred men to confront any troops from Lima and ordered Captain Joseph de Irazabal to burn bridges. Jiménez Inca and his father-in-law returned to Lahuaytambo, leaving four hundred men to guard Huarochirí. Their goal was to incite all the towns of the province to "rise up in arms."[87] The Lima newspaper *La Gazeta de Lima* claimed that they wrote appeals to other towns in the area urging them to join the uprising and "take revenge for those executed in Lima."[88]

The news of the rebels' initial victory prompted great anxiety in Lima. The proximity of Huarochirí precluded Lima's residents from dismissing the events as distant chaos. Accounts stressed the irrational violence of the rebels, an interpretation that reflected the fear in Lima and served to cast the insurgents as dangerous others. In his memoirs, the viceroy described how thirteen authorities and their servants "were killed with cruel and barbarous demonstrations of the rebels' fury."[89] An anonymous account declared that the rebels cut out and ate Araujo's tongue and dipped bread in the blood of the Spanish who had been beheaded. They then threw the bodies to the dogs.[90]

The exaggerated depictions of the rebels and the broad fear in Lima should not be confused with panicky inaction. The viceroy reacted firmly. On August 3 the Marqués de Monterrico y Conde del Puerto (whose real name, Don Melchor Malo de Molina, is equally evocative) led a battalion of over five hundred armed men on horseback toward Huarochirí. The rebels, however, were already beset by internal divisions and key losses. Local priests and others condemned and belittled the rebels, emphasizing their extreme views and minimal chance for success and thus the danger of supporting them. Francisco Melo, a Spaniard who was called in from the mines at Yauli to lead the counterinsurgency (and who left a wonderfully detailed account of his efforts), sent forged letters to local leaders who the insurgents might recruit that stressed the violence and divisions of the rebels and the strength of the viceregal forces. These planted doubts as well as fear and thus stymied recruitment. For example, the kuraka of Chaclla, Pedro Julcarilpo, found this letter in his patio, addressed to a loyalist in another town:

> Beloved compadre:
>
> I received your letter, in which you asked permission to kill my compadre Pedro Julcarilpo and bring me his head. Do not do it, because I know that he is a loyal vassal of His Majesty, and once he knows that I am on my way to Huarochirí with more than 400 soldiers armed with good muskets, he will quickly come personally to give me the obedience that he owes to the King my Lord. If he does not, you may execute him as you offered, cutting off his head, and I will reward you in the name of his Majesty.[91]

The already vacillating Julcarilpo fled. Melo sent letters like this one throughout the province, sowing discord and pessimism. He also used his extensive kinship connections as well as his knowledge of Quechua to gain supporters.

On August 2, the villagers of Langa seized Don Juan Pedro Puipuilibia and his brother, Don Andrés, and handed them over to authorities. On August 3, the day the viceroy's repressive force left Lima, a group recruited by Melo waited for Jiménez Inca as he left San Damián to meet with Francisco Santa Cruz in Cocachacra. Upon seeing the group, the rebel leader threw himself down a steep canyon in order to escape, but an Indian watching the mules in the gully hit him with a rock and helped capture him. Melo's forces as well as those of the Marqués de Monterrico captured all of the rebel leaders within fifteen days. By August 10, Melo himself had over five hundred prisoners "of both sexes and different ages."[92] Initial supporters returned to their communities, hopeful that retribution would not reach them.

Melo ordered much of the region to attend the executions in Huarochirí on August 17 and confirm their allegiance to the king. He forgot to warn his soldiers he had done so, and when more than two thousand Indians appeared on the hills above the town on August 13, some panicked and grabbed their guns. At that moment Melo happened to be interrogating Francisco Santa Cruz, who stood up, believing that perhaps the Indians were coming to liberate him. Melo threw the shackled Santa Cruz across the room "like a hazelnut."[93] Melo had struggled to convince the terrified Indians of the region to attend the ceremony. To his great satisfaction, Indian nobles from Lima arrived, and shouts of "Long Live the King of Spain, our Lord" rang out in the days preceding the ritual. A war council confirmed the death sentence for the seven leaders. Melo recommended that they delay announcing the general pardon for Indian participants in order to maximize the drama of the ritual.

On August 17, soldiers dragged seven leaders of the rebellion into the plaza in Huarochirí one by one. Because there was no hangman present, they were shot before being hanged and quartered. Santa Cruz, whose knowledge of history and erudition had impressed Melo, stunned the crowd when, after being shot eight times in the head, he cried out, "Madre mia, Santa Rosa, I put my soul in your hands to be presented to our Lord, Jesus Christ." Melo ordered that he be put out of his misery with a shot to the lungs.[94] Other prisoners were tied to the gallows, whipped, and, in an act designed to humiliate them, shorn. The commander then posted the general pardon in the corners of the plaza. The brutal, precise ritual hit another snag, however, when they discovered that no one knew how to quarter the seven bodies. Melo ordered that members of the mulatto battalion from Lima do the best they could at midnight. The body parts were exhibited throughout the region as a warning to "coming generations."[95] In the following days, the soldiers burned rebels' houses and salted their fields.[96]

The conspiracy of El Cercado and the Huarochirí uprising were intimately connected. Not only was Jiménez Inca a leader of both, but throughout the late 1740s, Indians from Huarochirí who resided in or worked in Lima proved to be agitators.[97] The viceroy acknowledged the correspondence that flowed between Lima and Huarochirí (and neighboring Canta) and the efforts of the leaders to link them. It pleased him, however, that the subversion had not moved beyond Lima and its Andean hinterland. What most worried him were possible connections with the Juan Santos uprising to the east.

"The Dominated Seeks to Evade"

These events led the viceroy to write about Indians and Spanish rule in Peru. His letters afford valuable insights into the tangled social ideas and practices of the era. They are not the mere frustrated venting of a harried viceroy but rather important testimony on the perplexities and contradictions of eighteenth-century thought. As we have seen throughout this book, Manso de Velasco, by now Conde de Superunda, exhibited a clear absolutist plan for rebuilding Lima and for containing the Church. Even though he had to struggle and compromise to put the plan into practice, he advanced a coherent vision and practical, widely accepted emergency measures. His thoughts and policies on Indians, in contrast, seem muddled and contradictory. In hindsight, it is clear they portended the difficulties the Bourbons would have in maintaining their grip on the Andes.

In a letter dated September 24, 1750, Manso reported to the king on the eruption, repression, and implications of the uprising. He began by bitterly noting that despite their "humility," Indians had a disposition toward "insolent thoughts." The gruesome reminders of the penalty for subversion—rebels' body parts displayed in central locations—had only made them more secretive. In fact, he implied that the repression and its constant reminders encouraged them to seek alliances with blacks and to adopt an "all or nothing" revolutionary strategy.[98] The viceroy also referred to Indians' predisposition to alcohol.[99] In his eyes, the insolent, secretive, and drunk Indians posed a constant serious threat.

Manso then briefly evaluated the interpretation, "vulgarly" extensive, that the uprisings had been caused by the mistreatment of Indians by corregidores and priests. Although cognizant of the misbehavior and "excesses" of secular and religious authorities—he alludes to them frequently elsewhere—the viceroy dismissed this argument in a single sentence. He countered that the rebel leaders themselves had no compassion nor did the rebels have any grounds for complaint. Instead, he probed the nature and status of Indians, blaming the breakdown of the social and cultural barriers between Indians and Europeans for prompting envy and thus putting impertinent thoughts into their brains. In his view, the division between Indians and Europeans, the sixteenth-century notion of two republics, was easier to maintain in provincial towns and communities, under the careful guidance of authorities, than in Lima, which, by contrast, presented many challenges. He noted that Indians migrated or were brought to the capital to take jobs in the "mechanical trades" that the Spanish rejected. Once there,

> the common clothing that they use without distinction, new forms of hygiene [aseo], and the noble cloth that they wear (about which it is inconvenient to make changes), spoils them and makes it unbearable for them not to be allowed into certain professions and dignitary positions; if these were to be given to them, it would mean handing over our domination to them or raising them to the status in which, with more encouragement and means, they will try to retake it.[100]

The viceroy thus captures how early modern cities weakened hierarchies more easily enforced in the countryside—Indians worked in higher status jobs, wore the same clothing as others, and even donned the elaborate fashions of the upper classes, leading them to demand fuller access to caste-limited jobs and positions. In addition, Indians in Lima did not pay the head tax, the ultimate marker of "Indianness."

   In light of this analysis, Manso's next paragraph is surprising. In a sprawling sentence, the viceroy concedes that "the true and permanent cause of Indians' restlessness" is that in all other conquered nations the dominated and dominant blend through marriage, and after a few generations "they are mixed up, becoming a single people" with uniform loyalty to the sovereign. The only distinction is that of origins. Yet in Peru "the diversity of customs, the accident of colors, or the vileness of the dominated" did not allow these connections or mixing. The two nations remain separated, and under the influence of "malcontents and malignant geniuses . . . the dominated seek to evade what they view as the oppression of their freedom, and to change a government, although just and orderly, for which they have an enduring hatred."[101] The viceroy seems momentarily to lament Peru's virtual segregation, which he otherwise attempts to fortify or restore in order to avoid further problems.

In the end, however, his musings justify colonial social divisions. The viceroy points to festivities like those of 1747 and 1748 for the new king as an example of Indians' disdain for the Spanish and nostalgia for the Incas. He describes their representation of "their old Kings" and the tears and sadness that the dress and dances evoked. Here he noted that three of the participants "had paid with their lives" for these emotions—they had participated in the Cercado and Huarochirí uprisings and had been executed. He called for noble Indians not to be separated from the "common festivities" and to celebrate with other Indians. The sixteenth-century distinction between noble and common Indians had followed Spanish notions of social hierarchy and had granted them a useful mediator; by the eighteenth century, it had become dangerous.[102] In 1750, the viceroy prohibited the participation of Incas in civic and religious festivities.[103]

Manso recommended that the laws and decrees regarding (and protecting) Indians be strictly enforced and that they be given forums to voice their discontent. He then suggested measures to diminish the Indian presence in Lima, "the most efficient and solid solution to avoid the risk of more restlessness."[104] For example, he sought to prohibit priests and corregidores from bringing young boys to work in the city's houses and churches, where they often learned trades such as sewing, furniture making, and shoemaking. This acculturation made them difficult to "reduce to their towns" and also made them easy prey to Indians and others with subversive ideas. Bringing young Indian boys and girls to the city endangered the by-then weakened structure imposed by the Spanish in the sixteenth century, whereby Indians were at least partially isolated and controlled by secular and religious authorities.[105] The viceroy was calling for the separation he had lamented in a previous paragraph. It was, however, a suggestion; he knew that any sort of large effort to "re-Indianize" Indians spatially or ideologically was impossible.

Manso further recommended that the European population remain vigi-

184 lant (he labeled the events of Huarochirí "stupid carelessness") and that they maintain well-organized troops and armories throughout the kingdom. He mentioned his efforts to rebuild the city after the earthquake, efforts which had made it safer and thus increased the will of people to enlist in the militias. Yet these social and urbanistic efforts had a limit. The Spanish had to be prepared to fight rebels. His penultimate sentence noted the worrisome lack of arms, many of which were already in use in the struggle against Juan Santos.[106]

In the 1740s, the Juan Santos rebels repelled several Spanish offensives. In fact, in 1752, Juan Santos's forces entered the Andean town of Andamarca, the closest they ventured to the coast. The viceroy's concerns in the years after the Cercado conspiracy and the Huarochirí uprising that Indians were increasingly disgruntled and prone to violent action were not unfounded.[107] His insistence that there were ties between the conspirators and Franciscan renegades also proved correct. In 1753, Fray Calixto returned to Peru from Spain. After a period in Charcas, Upper Peru, he was back in Lima by 1756 and quickly came under suspicion. The corregidor of the Indian neighborhood, Don José Hurtado, reported suspicious meetings in "one Indian's house, the shops of leading Indians and master craftsmen, with spies at the door, and, most frequently, in the cell of a Franciscan in the San Francisco el Grande monastery, Fray Calixto." The viceroy reported that Fray Calixto also visited many Indians, staying for days and gathering an "entourage" to promote "the old complaints that Indians were not given jobs and were not allowed in the orders."[108] In addition, Fray Calixto protested that the punishment of the rebels in 1750 had been excessive and sought the means to return to Spain to lodge a complaint once again.[109] The viceroy put Don Pedro Bravo del Rivero in charge of the case.

With the permission of the Franciscans, the authorities arrested Fray Calixto and confiscated his papers. They claimed that the material confirmed his subversive nature and disobedience. The Consejo de Indias approved of his detention and decreed, in November 1577, that he be removed from Peru. After a long journey—the ship broke down in Chile—the fifty-year-old friar reached Cádiz in September 1760. Carefully guarded by other priests, he was taken to the isolated Franciscan convent of San Francisco del Monte in the Adamuz desert (Sierra Morena, Andalucía). In 1765, he pleaded with his superiors for clemency in regard to his harsh treatment, citing his bad health. He never returned to Peru.[110]

In the months and years after the earthquake, Viceroy Manso was able to impose his emergency measures on Lima and Callao, preventing shortages as well as riots and looting. He also succeeded in hastening the city's rebuilding. His plans to rein in the power of the upper classes and the Church proved more difficult to implement. Both groups supported him on some measures but fought his more powerful reforms aimed at their autonomy and wealth. In the end, a compromise was reached. Indians proved even more difficult. In the eighteenth century, the Spanish sought constant increases in tax revenues, centered in the Andes on the Indian head tax, and imposed a growing number of outsiders in local offices, thereby endangering and redefining the kuraka office. At the same time, colonial officials worried about the exploitation of Indians and the impact this could have on the fiscal system and social stability. Yet the contradictions moved far beyond the tension between colonial extractions and continued colonial rule. As the musings of Manso de Velasco examined above indicate, the colonizers knew that the separation (and exploitation) of Indians was at the heart of the problem, but also at the heart of colonial rule. Full-scale integration was impossible, yet it seemed too late to shore up the division between the by-now theoretical or mythical "two republics."

Manso understood that in ordering priests and others not to bring young Indian children to Lima he was not going to solve the problem. In fact, Indians were already presenting their own proposals, envisioning their own alternative worlds, taking action. As we have seen, the term *Indian* referred to many different groups, each of which had its own grievances, plans, and utopias. Unifying them would prove difficult, if not impossible. But from the perspective of the viceroy, the social instability of Peru in its entirety, particularly the fragile domination over the Indian majority, meant that the absolutist capital that he and others envisioned would prove unachievable. While buildings could be reconstructed, dress codes imposed, and corporate groups restrained, lingering social tensions, injustices, and contradictions could not, as became increasingly and painfully clear in the following decades, easily be patched over.

Aftershocks and Echoes

There is no doubt that Peru, more than a country of fiction, of legend, or of comedy, as some would have it, is a country filled with history. The past awaits and speaks to us, from every corner: from pre-Hispanic ruins, from the colonial temples and the republican battlegrounds, from the fables about towering mountains or Cyclopean walls as well as from romantic narrow streets or the crossroads of forgotten paths.
—RAÚL PORRAS BARRENECHEA,
Perspectiva y panorama, 40–41

Epilogue

In 1758, the Conde de Superunda requested that he be relieved of his position as viceroy of Peru. Almost seventy years old, he yearned to retire in Spain. Carlos III granted his request two years later, and on October 27, 1761, a day shy of the earthquake's fifteenth anniversary, he sailed from Callao for the return to Spain. Yet a calm retirement did not await the count. In Lima, the official review of his tenure as viceroy, the *juicio de residencia*, cited many accusations. Critics charged the viceroy and his aides with favoritism and with collecting millions of pesos of silver, gold, and other treasures that the tsunami had washed away. His defenders coyly and correctly answered that heavy metal doesn't float—the sea had swallowed it, and lucky treasure-seekers and ransackers had taken the rest. Manso was ultimately exonerated of these and other charges, but the long trial proved humiliating and costly.[1]

More troubles awaited him on his return voyage. His

boat docked in Havana, Cuba, just as the English were planning their as-
sault on the island, "the Pearl of the Caribbean," one of the many fronts in
the worldwide Seven Years' War (1756–63). The captain-general of Cuba,
Juan de Prado Portocarrero, formed a war junta and, following protocol,
put Manso de Velasco, the senior officer on the island, in charge, at least
nominally. The Cuban forces held out for two months, but the English took
the island in August 1762. A military court in Cádiz, Spain, tried Manso for
this defeat. In 1765 the court handed down the shockingly stern sentence
of a ten-year suspension of military duties and honors, a stiff fine, and
banishment from his home. Now seventy-seven years old, Manso moved to
Granada rather than his native La Rioja and struggled to make ends meet.
In an unexpected ironic twist, the previous archbishop of Peru and Manso
de Velasco's implacable enemy, Pedro Antonio de Barroeta, allowed him
to stay in his archbishop's palace in Granada. Barroeta had been assigned
there in 1758. The archbishop cared for the Conde de Superunda until he
died on January 5, 1767.[2]

Subsequent viceroys in Peru pushed through many of the reforms that
Manso de Velasco and Louis Godin had originally envisioned. Riots in
Madrid in 1766 had prompted stricter social control measures and a more
manageable urban organization on both sides of the Atlantic Ocean. In the
distant colony, the authorities divided Lima into four quarters, named new
officials, improved lighting, water, and sanitation, and rationalized the
division and demarcation of space. Manso de Velasco's successor, the Catalan Manuel de Amat, changed the face of Lima by constructing new public buildings such as the Acho bullring. He enforced the expulsion of the
Jesuits in 1767, the most extreme act in the struggle between the Crown and
the religious orders.[3] In Lima, groups reacted to these and other changes as
they had responded to the postearthquake reconstruction: by giving wary
support when convenient, dogged opposition when not, and cautious ambivalence in general. The central fault lines stressed here—Bourbon absolutism versus baroque piety and varying notions of order and disorder and
of what Lima should and shouldn't be—continued to mark urban struggles
in the latter half of the eighteenth century and beyond.

Important features of the relationship between Spain and Peru, vividly
seen in the Manso de Velasco–Marqués de Ensenada correspondence,
persisted, shaping the Bourbon Reforms. Spain was hesitant to spend
its wealth in the Americas, dubious about the possibility of "civilizing"

the dark-skinned lower classes and wary of those born in the Americas. The Crown wanted to weaken but not banish the Catholic Church, with the exception of the troublesome Jesuits, whom they expelled. Depleted financially by the wars with England and France, Spain demanded more and more revenue from its American colonies. In the words of John Lynch, "They spent the eighteenth century pushing up [Peru's tax] share from 2 to 40 percent, by taxing colonists, tightening control, and fighting off foreigners. In the process they gained a revenue and lost an empire."[4]

The discursive battle also intensified. The anonymous "Description of Lima," written in the 1770s, dismissed Lima as a sinful backwater where the repugnant dark-skinned lower classes and elite women mixed and men were feminized by the city's active social life. The Spanish botanist Hipólito Ruíz, who reached Lima in 1777, did not hide his scorn for the city's social customs, ridiculing women's dress and the city's habits. After describing the innate weakness of Indians, blacks, and mulattos, he surmised, "The sum total of much of this, making up a physical monstrosity, naturally produces a moral monstrosity: this multiplied perversity of tendencies and passions is picked up by the unfortunate Spaniard, who is born, reared, and nurtured by them, unless—as rarely happens—some good fortune separates him from it."[5]

Esteban Terralla Landa, a Spaniard who arrived in Peru as part of Viceroy Theodoro de Croix's entourage in 1782, wrote the most acidic account of Lima, a long satirical verse entitled "Lima, Inside and Out." The title underlines the guiding argument that beneath the seeming splendor of the city and its inhabitants lay a corrupt, degenerate core. In the eyes of Simón Ayunque, the narrator, impoverished, superficial women disguised themselves under their fancy clothing while the facades of the houses hid "rusticity and dereliction."[6] Besides denigrating the city's filthy streets, disturbingly porous racial hierarchies, and general vanity, he repeatedly casts the women of Lima as courtesans who must sell themselves to the highest bidder. He describes women who, after an extravagant evening stroll, have to make do with half a piece of bread for dinner. Aging *tapadas*, after years spent in ornate clothing and coaches, have nothing to their name. He deemed this "divine justice/for their natural arrogance/and because in their youth/they appreciated nothing/making fun of everything/and now time makes fun of them."[7] He scorns their false piety—their claims of a monastic life—noting their beautiful bodies yet warning of their "lion souls" and defining them as "angels with nails."[8] Race again plays a role in this vain luxury—blacks are granted too much freedom, and their proximity taints the lives of the upper classes.

The denunciations of Lima continued during the War of Independence. For example, the Spanish commander Jerónimo Valdés repeatedly complained that Lima "corrupts the morals of the soldiers" and weakened the spirit of commanding officers.[9] Spain's policies and discourse, however, are only one side of this story. More important were the deep opposition in the Americas to these policies and the reaction to this disdain.

On the one hand, the Peruvian upper classes applauded efforts by the colonial state to tame the unruly lower classes. The fear of the plebe pushed the Lima merchant elite into an uneasy alliance with Spanish forces.[10] In the late eighteenth century, Lima officials targeted gambling and drinking, seen as vices that presumably led blacks in particular to disobedience and dishonesty. These efforts formed part of a program of increased disciplining of *casta* and black unruliness. The specter of disobedient plebes subverting the City of Kings from within and growing bands of maroons and bandits from outside continued to terrify the elite and others well beyond the grim aftermath of the earthquake-tsunami. The anxiety reinforced class lines.[11]

On the other hand, while the fear of the lower classes boosted support for the different viceroys' urban reforms, the upper classes were, not surprisingly, loath to give up their prerogatives—their distinguished houses, flamboyant public behavior, and favored economic position. They approved the effort of the king's representatives to rein in the lower classes but opposed efforts to weaken their own power or to raise their taxes. Their dogged opposition to Godin's architectural reforms was not an anomaly; in subsequent decades, they proved themselves capable of resisting change.[12]

Church leaders continued to fight secularization, stressing the clergy's ever more crucial role in times of trouble. For example, religious authorities emphasized the need for the Church and faith in the midst of the tumultuous Tupac Amaru uprising in the 1780s. The conflicting ideas about the role of the Church seen in the earthquake's aftermath clashed over and over. Bourbon reformers believed that weakening the presence of the Church would aid both Madrid and Peru. Representatives of the Church argued that it would only accelerate Peru's economic and moral decline. Discussions about the Church's internal order and economic power continued to mark

190   these attacks and counterattacks.[13] Neither the Lima upper classes nor the Church accepted Bourbon absolutism and regalism without a fight.

Moral reformers continued to target Lima's women and their improper attire, thereby demonstrating the failure of previous campaigns. Much of the city had ostensibly supported these campaigns, yet no sea change in public behavior took place. Limeños might respond to preachers' calls for moral reform, joining them in processions and crowding the confession booth for a few days, but they did not radically alter their risqué dress and public flirtation. Nonetheless, the people of Lima feared divine punishment, seeing God's hand in earthquakes and other calamities, and continued to turn to their saints and their lush public religiosity to defend themselves. Viceroys and archbishops failed to steer them away from their baroque practices.[14]

The social fissures that the earthquake and tsunami uncovered widened in the late eighteenth century and early nineteenth. The concerns about the unruly nature of the city's lower classes, the disobedience of blacks, and the potential subversion of Indians fortified stereotypical discourse about these groups' incorrigibility and dangerousness. Reformers decried gambling, drinking, and other plebeian vices, while authorities fretted about the growing number of maroons and bandits who targeted travelers to and from Lima. The exasperation with lower-class disobedience and the specter of black violence escalated. The fear of Andean uprisings evident in the events of El Cercado and Huarochirí proved clairvoyant. Riots, revolts, and rebellions increased in size and number with each passing decade, building up to the massive Tupac Amaru and Tupac Katari uprisings of the 1780s. As the lower classes expressed their opposition to the Bourbon Reforms and, more widely, Spanish colonialism, these events fostered the interpretation of Indians as deceitful and possibly heretical savages, deepening the Lima–Andes divide.[15]

In sum, the tensions evident in the aftermath of the earthquake-tsunami simmered for decades. Groups, institutions, and individuals opposed Spanish efforts to empower the state, weaken the Church and other corporate bodies, increase tax revenues, and control the lower classes. Nonetheless, they did so for different reasons and could not unite in any enduring way. This fractured opposition marked Peru in the wars of Independence. Resistance to colonial rule was widespread, but groups and regions had disparate motivations and goals. For example, Cusco and other Andean areas distrusted Lima, deeming centralism as Peru's key problem. Lima, on the other hand, viewed the Andean insurgents with skepticism and even fear. Patrician merchants and provincial intermediaries disagreed about tax policies, while liberals and conservatives battled over the role of the Church. Elites and plebes had wildly different notions about public behavior and social control. These and other divisions, evident following the earthquake, continued to mark postcolonial Peru.

Is this book about Lima in 1746 relevant to the City of Kings in the twenty-first century? The population has soared from fifty thousand to over seven million, with a massive presence of Andean migrants, and Pizarro's old checkerboard, or *damero*, now constitutes only about 5 percent of the city. Many residents of the more distant neighborhoods, where the very poor and the very rich live, never venture into the downtown area. *Tapadas* can be found only on tacky posters, and a depressingly small number of colonial houses, balconies, and facades has survived the centuries. Parts of downtown Lima can take the traveler back to the eighteenth century—the San Francisco church, the Torre Tagle and other mansions, and some colonial houses now crowded with hundreds of people. Recent decades have seen some interesting projects to preserve what remains of colonial Lima. Yet most of the city dates from after World War II, including the teeming *barriadas*, shantytowns, and slums. Upper-class neighborhoods enjoy more trees, better streets, and lots of security guards (*huachimanes*, a Quechua-sounding term taken from the English *watchman*), but they also lack physical reminders of the colonial era.

   Yet the museums and monuments of downtown Lima, *el centro*, are not the only relics of the earthquake-tsunami era. The multitudes that join in the Señor de los Milagros procession in October as well as the fervent devotion to saints, new and old, indicate that the push to replace baroque religiosity with more intimate forms of devotion never fully succeeded. Piety and sensuality still combine in fascinating ways.

   The other fault line—the disagreement over order and disorder—also continues to characterize Lima. Today, the public demands stronger measures against crime, bad driving, tax evasion, and other problems. Nonetheless, Limeños cringe at and flaunt governmental efforts to increase social control. This demonstrates an understandable distrust of the state, a historical legacy that has only deepened in recent decades. Self-interest

192   might be another explanation—people want other people's vices to be corrected, not their own. It also indicates, I believe, a disagreement about exactly which measures should be taken and by whom, the virtual definition of what occurred after October 28, 1746. Limeños can agree in vague terms on the problem—today it would be crime—but disagree about the solution. Ultimately, they differ on their understanding of what Lima is and what it can be; who is a Limeño and who isn't. Although Lima is no longer the Bourbon City of Kings, the social divisions, the discourse about the city and its inhabitants, and the political fragmentation that marked 1746 continue to echo.

One Earthquakes, Tsunamis, Absolutism

1 It was estimated to have been between 8.0 and 8.6 on the Richter scale. For technical descriptions of the earthquake, see Giesecke and Silgado, *Terremotos*; Silgado, *Historia*; Dorbath, "Assessment," esp. 574–75, Beringhausen, "Tsunamis."

2 On tsunamis, see González, "Tsunamis!"; Dudley and Lee, *Tsunami!*; and a valuable Web page: http://www.usc.edu/dept/tsunamis/peru/index.html. For data, see Lockridge, "Tsunamis in Peru-Chile."

3 In his "Carta o diario," Llano Zapata refers to destruction in the coastal valleys of Chancay, Huarua, Barranca, Supe, and Pativilca as well as Cerro de la Sal and the Lucanas volcano. Llano Zapata, "Carta," Odriozola, *Los terremotos*, 95. In his "observaciones," he cites a letter from a Jesuit missionary who described tremors that occurred in Quito (today Ecuador), over eight hundred miles from Lima, on October 28. Llano Zapata, "Observación diario," 136; see also 141. For Huancavelica, see Archivo General de Indias (hereafter AGI), Lima, Leg. 643; for Huarochirí, Melo, "Diario," 59–60. For a summary, see Silgado, *Historia*, 31; for a map, see Lockridge, "Tsunamis," 19.

194

4　Conde de Superunda, *Relación*, 259.

5　Llano Zapata, "Carta," 71–72.

6　Bernales Ballesteros, *Lima*, 325.

7　Ovando, "Carta," 50–51. See also Guillermo Lohmann Villena's introduction to the work of Miguel Feijoo de Sosa, *Relación*, 28–29.

8　Ovando, "Carta," 51.

9　Llano Zapata, "Carta," 81–95; Llano Zapata, "Observación," 132.

10　I thank Ryan Crewe of Yale University for detective work on these publications.

11　Lozano, "Relación," 36.

12　Ibid., 38.

13　Preuss and Kuroiwa, "Urban Planning," 277. Callao residents apparently did not flee inland once the earthquake occurred. In this period, people did not necessarily understand the relationship between earthquakes and tsunamis, particularly in a place such as Lima, where earthquakes were common and tsunamis much less so.

14　Montero del Aguila, "Desolación," 3; Arrus, *El Callao*, 194–96; Ovando, "Carta," 52.

15　Conde de St. Malo, *A Voyage*, 84.

16　Lozano, "Relación," 42; Llano Zapata, "Carta," 98.

17　Lozano, "Relación," 41; Ovando, "Carta," 53.

18　Conde de Superunda, *Relación*, 260. Lozano, "Relación," 41, also has information on remains.

19　The fact that individuals had taken pieces of the San Fermín raised the ire of Ovando. Ovando, "Carta," 62. On the sale of the remains of the San Fermín, see Archivo General de la Nación (Peru), (hereafter AGN), Factoría Mayor, Libro de Cuentas, C-15, Leg. 267, c. 1270, 1747. On the warehouses, or *bodegas*, see the anon., *Individual*, 156.

20　Montero del Aguila, *Desolación*, 174.

21　The quote is from the spiritual biography of Fr. Pedro Mont, found in Papió, *La Historia*, 256.

22　Anon., *Individual y verdadera relación*; Odriozola, *Terremotos*, 161–62; Montero del Aguila, *Desolación*, 174.

23　Sánchez Rodríguez, "La ruina," 172.

24　Llano Zapata, "Carta," 80.

25　Lastres, "Terremotos," 151; see also Sánchez Rodríguez, "La ruina," 180. In the 1750s, the Franciscans sought to protect their virtual monopoly on funeral cloth. See AGI, Lima, Leg. 542, tertiary order of San Francisco.

26　Manso, "Informes," (see AGI, Lima, Leg. 541 as well).

27　Esquivel y Navia, *Noticias*, 2:351. Lozano refers to him as Alfonso de los Rios, Lozano, "Relación," 42.

28　Llano Zapata, "Carta," 74; Ovando, "Carta," 51.

29　Llano Zapata, "Relación del auto particular," 386; Medina, *Historia del Tribunal*, 2:289–91.

30 In his enlightening review, Darnton recognizes that it is perhaps not the best term. Darnton, "It Happened," quote on 60.

31 See the introduction by Scott, *Enlightened Absolutism*.

32 Classic works on the Bourbon Reforms include Lynch, *Spanish Colonial*, and Fisher, *Government and Society*. Recent titles include Fisher, *Bourbon Peru*; Fisher, Kuethe, and McFarlane, *Reform*; Guardino, *The Time*; Guimerá, ed., *El reformismo*; Pearce, "Early Bourbon Government." Much work has been done in the past decade or so on the social content of the reforms. See Premo, *Children*; Twinam, *Public Lives*; Stern, *The Secret*. I have reviewed some of this literature, particularly that in Spanish, in Walker, "Introducción. Dossier: Los Andes."

33 Mills, Taylor, Lauderdale Graham, *Colonial Latin America*, 406. The key texts on the baroque in Peru are Mujica, ed. *El Barroco Peruano*, vols. 1, 2.

34 Fundamental for this theme is Voekel, *Alone Before God*; see also Peralta, "Las razones."

35 One key study is Maravall, *Culture of the Baroque*. On Lima, see Bromley, "Fiestas caballerescas," who cites thirty-five annual festival days, 216; Osorio, "The King"; Ramos Sosa, *Arte Festivo*.

36 See especially Pearce, "Early Bourbon Government." Moreno Cebrián, *El virreinato del Marqués de Castelfuerte*.

37 Key studies include Cañizares, "Postcolonialism"; Poole, *Vision*; Pratt, *Imperial Eyes*; Liebersohn, *The Travelers' World*. Their debt to Edward Said and his *Orientalism* is obvious.

38 In fact, the 1746 catastrophe has been the subject of much recent research. See Aldana Rivera, "¿Ocurrencias?" and Oliver-Smith, "El terremoto," both in a two-volume work edited by Virginia García Acosta; Quiroz Chueca, "Movimiento"; Pérez-Mallaína Bueno, *Retrato*; Sánchez Rodríguez, "La ruina." The literature on cities and catastrophes is massive. I found particularly useful Massard-Guilbaud, "Introduction: The Urban Catastrophe," and Oliver-Smith, "Anthropological Research."

39 Voltaire, *Candide*; and "Poem on Destruction of Lisbon." See the introduction and articles in Johns, *Dreadful Visitations*.

40 Regular clergy are those priests and nuns such as the Franciscans, Dominicans, and Jesuits who live by a special set of rules in a religious community. The Jesuits are not a mendicant order, i.e., those whose income was supposed to come primarily from alms. Seculars are the diocesan clergy, directly responsible to the bishop.

Two   Premonitions of the Destruction of Lima

1 Llano Zapata, "Carta," 72–73.

2 Llano Zapata, "Respuesta dada." He noted that it was "natural" that he knew a great deal about them, as he was "born and raised in Lima, where these insults are most common." On earthquake theories of this period, Taylor, "Eighteenth-Century Earthquake Theories"; Oeser, "Historical." The French

196   scientist Amadée Frezier, whose writings on early eighteenth-century Peru will be much cited in this book, was inclined toward the latter explanation. Another view of the causes of earthquakes, in reference to one in Trujillo in 1759, can be found in Feijoo de Sosa, *Relación Descriptiva*, 35–36.

3   Porras Barrenechea, *Perspectiva*, 14.

4   Quoted in Oeser, "Historical," 30. See also Clark, "Science, Reason, and an Angry God."

5   Cevallos, *Respuesta a la carta.*

6   For a list of aspirants, see Glave, *De Rosa*, 148. Sánchez-Concha B., *Santos*, also has valuable information.

7   Glave, *De Rosa*, 148–49. On Ursula and visionaries in Lima, see Van Deusen, *The Souls of Purgatory*, 40–49. On Ayllón, see Estenssoro, *Del paganismo*, 468–92.

8   Estenssoro, *Del paganismo*, 480–81.

9   Whenever I bring up my research with a Peruvian, I almost invariably receive a comment or question referring to the role of Santa Rosa or el Señor de los Milagros.

10   Córdova Salinas, *Vida, virtudes*, cited in Mujica Pinilla, *Rosa*, 329. See also Córdova Salinas, O.F.M., *Crónica Franciscana*, 539–49, esp. 542–43. Soon afterward, Father Solano predicted a massive earthquake in the city of Trujillo, north of Lima, a prophecy that came true fifteen years later. Córdova Salinas, O.F.M., *Crónica Franciscana*, 542. The three punishments are war, famine, and plague. Apocalypse, 6, 2.

11   Cited in Morgan, *Spanish-American Saints*, 84.

12   Mujica, *Rosa Limensis*, 329; Morgan, *Spanish-American Saints*; Córdova Salinas, O.F.M., *Crónica Franciscana*, 542. On Santa Rosa and the 1687 earthquake, see Odriozola, *Terremotos*, 22.

13   Llano Zapata, "Observación diaria crítica," 128–29. On Sr. de los Milagros, see Banchero, *La verdadera historia*; Rostworowski de Diez Canseco, *Pachacamac y el Señor*; Locke, "Catholic Icons"; anon., *Lima: Paseos*, 86–87. The latter is an excellent guide to historical Lima.

14   Locke, "Catholic Icons," 188–89.

15   Biblioteca Nacional (Madrid), Ms. 9375, Copia de papeles varios, siglo XVII, ff. 139–40. See also Pérez-Mallaína Bueno, *Retrato*, 407–09, and Moreno Cebrián, "El regalismo," 246.

16   "Relación que arruinó a Lima el 20 de Octubre de 1687," Odriozola, *Terremotos*, 23–32. One priest invoked Father Castillo and the shaking stopped, 26.

17   Suárez, "Ciencia, ficción."

18   Glave, *De Rosa*, 343, for "baroque fatalism"; 343–66 for events.

19   Pacheco Vélez calls them a "symbol of baroque plentitude." Pacheco Vélez, *Memoria y utopia*, 241. Günther Doering and Lohmann Villena, *Lima*, 125–26. Viceroy Marqués de Castelfuerte (1724–36) added a wall to the north side along the Rimac River. I thank Adrian Pearce for pointing this out.

20   For Lima's woes in the 1740s, see the summary in Lohmann Villena, "Victorino

Montero del Aguila." On the epidemic, Pearce, "The Peruvian Population"; on
pirates and other maritime threats to Callao and Lima, see Lohmann Villena,
Las defensas militares, and Flores Guzmán, "El enemigo frente a las costas," in
Rosas Lauro, *El miedo en el Perú*. For a strong overview of the Andes in the eigh-
teenth century, see Andrien, *Andean Worlds*, chaps 7, 8, and for rebellions, see
O'Phelan Godoy, *Un siglo de rebeliones*.

21 Mujica, "El Arte y los Sermones," in Mujica, *El Barroco Peruano*, esp. 219–38.

22 On Fernández de Córdoba, see Vargas Ugarte, *Impresos*, 6:116–203, which includes a document on the daily routine of the Spiritual Houses. On fear in
Europe, see the pathbreaking Jean Delumeau, *El miedo en occidente*. For Peru,
see the recent book edited by Claudia Rosas Lauro, *El miedo en el Perú*.

23 Baltazar Moncada, *Descripción de la casa*.

24 Ibid., 3–4.

25 For an astute analysis, see Mujica, *El Barroco*, 250–55.

26 Cited by Lavrin and Loreto L., eds., *Monjas y beatas*, introduction, 12. Mujica, *El
Barroco*, 8–12. I learned a great deal from Schutte, *Aspiring Saints*; Weber, *Teresa
of Avila*; Sánchez Ortega, "Women as Source."

27 Rubial García, "Los Santos Milagreros," 55.

28 *Beatas* were religious women who had taken simple vows rather than the complete solemn vows of nuns. *Alumbradas* were women who claimed to have direct contact with God; they were considered false mystics and a sect in early
modern Spain.

29 Schutte, *Aspiring Saints*, chap. 3. On visionaries in Lima, see Van Deusen, *The
Souls of Purgatory*, 40–49.

30 Chatellier, *The Religion of the Poor*, 58–59.

31 Izaguirre, *Historia de las misiones franciscanas*, 2:39. The literature on the development of the Franciscans is vast. Particularly enlightening is Chatellier, *The
Religion of the Poor*.

32 Heras, *Los franciscanos y las misiones populares*.

33 Manso de Velasco, *Informes*, "Informe del Cabildo Eclesiastico," 2. See also
Papió, *La Historia d'Escornalbou*, particularly the biography of P. Fr. Pedro Mont
for descriptions of their work.

34 Heras, *Los franciscanos y las misiones populares*; Egaña, *Historia de la Iglesia*, esp.
1065–68; Esquivel y Navia, *Noticias cronológicas*, 2:264–69.

35 Archivo Histórico Nacional (Madrid; hereafter AHN), Inquisición, Leg. 1651,
in papeles sueltos.

36 AGI, Lima, Leg. 819, Cartas y Expedientes tramitados en el Consejo.

37 On their conflict, see Pérez-Mallaína Bueno, *Retrato de una ciudad*, 227–42;
Moreno Cebrián, "Introducción," Conde de Superunda, *Relación*, 52–56. On
Barroeta as a reformer, see Estenssoro, "Modernismo, estética." An important
source on Barroeta is Potau, *Lágrimas de Lima*.

38 José Durand, Prólogo, *Gaceta de Lima*, vol. 2. (1762–65), apéndice 1, "La despe-
dida del Arzobispo Barroeta," 21.

198   39   Estenssoro, "Modernismo, estética." See also Vargas Ugarte, *Historia de la Igle-sia*, vol. 4, esp. 144–47.

40   AHN, Inquisición, Leg. 1651, expediente 2, 16 de noviembre, 1756. Also found in AHN, Inquisición, Leg. 2206, exp. 4.

41   AHN, Inquisición, Leg. 1651.

42   Ibid, 6v.

43   Ibid, 7v.

44   Along with Amos and St. Paul, the prophet Jeremiah, chapter 5, is also mentioned twice. Ibid., 2v, 18v.

45   Ibid, Barroeta, February 20, 1757.

46   Ibid.

47   AGI, Lima, Leg. 807, November 7, 1756.

48   AHN, Inquisición, 2206, doc. from January 24, 1757.

49   Millar Carvacho, *La Inquisición de Lima*, 2:118.

50   Ibid, 118–19.

51   This theme is well covered by Pérez-Mallaína Bueno, *Retrato*, 182–87. Egaña, *Historia de la Iglesia*, 822.

52   On this theme, I have followed Bilinkoff, "Confessors, Penitents." See also Coakley, "Friars as Confidants."

53   AHN, Inquisición, Leg. 1651.

54   Ibid. f. 3.

55   Mujica, *Rosa Limensis*, 329. See also Iwasaki, "Mujeres al borde."

56   Mujica, "El arte y los sermones," *El Barroco Peruano*, 1, 227–28. Ramón Mujica relates it to the diffusion of sermons by San Vicente Ferrer (d. 1419).

57   AHN, Inquisición, Leg. 1651.

58   Her testimony is found ibid., January 7, 1757. (ff. 80–83).

59   Ibid.

60   Ibid. On the discernment of spirits, see Schutte, *Aspiring Saints*, chap. 3.

61   AHN, Inquisición, Leg. 1651.

62   See Schutte, *Aspiring Saints*, 47: "Visions from God are always glorious, pure, chaste, comforting, and lasting, whereas those from the devil are very often disgusting and frightening and always of short duration."

63   AHN, Inquisición, Leg. 1651.

64   The Lisbon earthquake took place at approximately 9:30 A.M., 3:30 A.M. in Lima, an unusual time for a nun to be praying but certainly not impossible.

65   Ibid.

66   Ibid.

67   Ibid. Alcántara mistakenly refers to Joseph rather than to Juan Garro.

68   Ibid.

69   Although the Plaza de Acho was inaugurated in 1766, bullfights were held in the pampa there well before then, particularly as fundraisers after the earthquake. Bravo de Lagunas y Castilla, *Discurso histórico-jurídico*.

70   AHN, Inquisición, Leg. 1651. King Ferndinand VI's wife, the Portuguese

Barbara de Braganza, was unpopular in Spain. John Lynch deems her "a notoriously avaricious woman and largely unloved in Spain." Lynch, *Bourbon Spain*, 158.

71 Llano Zapata, "Carta," 104.

72 Espinosa refers to "a religious woman from the Descalzas de San Joseph convent," while Parra names her. AHN, Inquisición, Leg. 1651, 44v and 50. Papió, *La Historia d'Escornalbou*, 255, also refers to the 1737 Panama fire.

73 Llano Zapata, "Carta," 104.

74 Rizo Patrón, *Linaje, Dote, y Poder*, 82.

75 On Pablo de Olavide and his family, see Defourneaux, *Pablo de Olavide*; Olavide, Estuardo Nuñez, ed. *Pablo de Olavide, obras selectas*.

76 Llano Zapata, "Carta," 81.

77 AHN, Inquisición, Leg. 1651. On Santa Rosa, see Mujica, *Rosa Limensis*; Flores Araoz, et al., *Santa Rosa de Lima*; Graziano, *Wounds of Love*.

78 AHN, Inquisición, Leg. 1651.

79 Ibid.

80 Ibid.

81 Ibid.

82 Ibid. 45v–46.

83 Kagan, *Lucrecia's Dream*, 86; note the contrast with Adas, *Prophets of Rebellion*.

84 For a summary, see Millar Carvacho, *La Inquisición de Lima (1697–1820)*, 121–22.

85 AGI, Lima, Leg. 651, Duplicado (via reservada), Virrey Amat.

Three   The City of Kings: Before and After

1 The literature on the founding of Lima includes Cobo, *Historia de la Fundación de Lima*; Günther Doering and Lohmann Villena, *Lima*; Durán Montero, *Lima en el Siglo XVII*; Rostworowski de Diez Canseco, *Señoríos indígenas*; Bromley and Barbagelata, *Evolución urbana*; and Gutiérrez Arbulú, ed., *Lima en el siglo XVI*, particularly the environmental history by Gilda Cogorno Ventura, "Tiempo de Lomas." On Spanish urban planning, see Kagan, *Urban Images*, especially chap. 2; Durston, "Un régimen urbanistico."

2 Cited in Higgins, *Lima*, 31.

3 Cited by Jean-Pierre Clement, "El nacimiento," 83.

4 Günther Doering and Lohmann Villena, *Lima*, 122–25, which includes maps. See also Mariátegui Oliva, *El Rimac*; on the indigenous population, see Charney, *Indian Society*; on leprosy, see Warren, "Piety and Danger," Cascajo Romero, *El pleito de la curación*.

5 Kagan, *Urban Images*, 169–76; Durán Montero, *Lima en el siglo xvii*, esp. 19–21.

6 Arrus, *El Callao*; Lequenda, "Descripción del Puerto del Callao."

7 Key works include Lowry, "Forging an Indian Nation," Charney, *Indian Society*, and Vergara Ormeño, "La población indígena." Although focused on Cusco,

very valuable is Garrett, *A Shadow of Empire*. Estenssoro, *Del paganismo*, is informative and groundbreaking. In contrast to the great majority of Indians in Peru, those who resided in Lima did not maintain communal land and thus did not pay tribute.

8 Haitin, "Late Colonial Lima," 281–82; Lowry, "Forging an Indian Nation"; Estenssoro, *Del paganismo*, part 3.

9 For their origin in Africa, see Aguirre, *Breve Historia*, 25–26; Bowser, *The African Slave*.

10 Flores Galindo, *Aristocracia y plebe*, 95–138; for a list of monastery slaves, see Van Deusen, *Between the Sacred*, 173. On Indians owning slaves, see Cobo, cited in Higgins, *Lima*, 48–49.

11 Aguirre, *Breve Historia*, 127–37; and Jouve Martín, *Esclavos*, 41–43.

12 This summary takes liberally from Aguirre, *Breve historia*. On the anxieties that the city had become predominantly black, Jouve Martín, *Esclavos*, 22–24.

13 One study tabulates 452 Spaniards immigrating to Lima in the first half of the eighteenth century. Turiso Sebastián, *Comerciantes españoles*, 57. The statistic is from Haitin, "Late Colonial Lima," 279.

14 The questions of race and *limpieza de sangre*, or purity of blood, in the early modern Spanish world are much debated. The classic study is Mörner, *Race Mixture*; recent contributions include Herzog, *Defining Nations*; Martínez, "The Black Blood." I would like to thank Matt O'Hara for his help on this question.

15 On debates about mestizas in early colonial Peru, see Burns, *Colonial Habits*. The figure from 1613 is from Durán Montero, *Lima*, 56; that from 1792, from Haitin, "Late Colonial Lima," 279. On the concept of two republics, see Borah, *Justice by Insurance*.

16 These calculations were probably low, as two thousand individuals, mostly slaves and militia members, dodged the census. Fisher, *Government and Society*, 251; Haitin, "Late Colonial Lima," 279–281. On the term *casta*, see Estenssoro, "Los colores de la plebe."

17 Conde de Superunda, *Relación*, 229.

18 Pérez Cantó, *Lima*, 44–48 discusses these census numbers. For an overview, see Cahill, "Colour by Numbers."

19 Estenssoro, "Los colores de la plebe"; Aguirre, *Breve Historia*, 40–48.

20 Mörner, *Race*, 56–60; Cahill, "Colour by Numbers," 338–39.

21 Estenssoro, "Los colores de la plebe," and Wuffarden, "Los lienzos," both in *Los cuadros del mestizaje de Amat*. The literature on the *cuadros de castas* has increased. See among others Katzew, *Casta Paintings*, and the catalogue, Romero de Tejada ed., *Frutas y castas ilustradas*.

22 For a recent monograph that demonstrates the importance of age and childhood in social differentiation, see Premo, *Children of the Father King*.

23 Panfichi, "Urbanización temprana," Ramón, "Urbe y orden."

24 Debates about the weight of the Creole-Peninsular divide continue. Key works

include Flores Galindo, *Aristocracia y plebe*; Lohmann, *Los ministros*, passim; Turiso Sebastián, *Comerciantes españoles*.

25   Brading, *The First America*; Lavallé, *Las promesas ambiguas*; Wuffarden, "La ciudad"; Cummins, "A Tale of Two Cities"; Kagan, *Urban Images*, esp. 169–86 (Lima and Cuzco). On saints, see Jouve Martín, "En olor"; Sánchez-Concha B., *Santos*.

26   Lowry, "Forging an Indian Nation," 30–31; Cosamalón, *Indios detrás*. A valuable source is Cook, *Numeración general*.

27   Summarized in Jouve Martín, *Esclavos*, 31–33.

28   St. Malo, *A Voyage to Peru*, 78.

29   Biblioteca Nacional de Madrid, ms. number 11026, Descripción de Lima," 65.

30   Montero del Aguila, "Noticia Annalica," 179–80. For the agricultural production around Lima, see Haitin, "Late Colonial Lima," 139–41; Flores Galindo, *Aristocracia y plebe*, 30–53; Vegas de Cáceres "Una imagen distorsionada."

31   "In Lima I learned nothing about Peru." Alexander Von Humboldt, letter to don Ignacio Checa, January 18, 1803, Nuñez and Petersen, *Alexander von Humboldt*, 214–15.

32   For a description of the incorporation of pre-Hispanic building materials and techniques, see Juan de Ulloa, *Viaje*, 44–46. Secondary sources include Harth-Terré and Márquez Abanto, *Las Bellas Artes*; Bernales Ballesteros, *Lima, La Ciudad*; Dorta, *La arquitectura barroca*; San Cristóbal, *La casa virreinal*.

33   Harth-Terré and Márquez Abanto, *Las Bellas Artes*; Ramirez and Walker, "Cuentas y cultura." For an evocative summary of colonial architecture, see Hardoy, "Two Thousand Years," 34.

34   Wuffarden, "La plentitud, esp. 40–42; Pacheco Vélez, *Memoria y utopía*, 224–70; Bernales Ballesteros, *Lima, La Ciudad*, 227–90.

35   Porras Barrenechea, *Perspectiva*, 29. See Eugenio Lanuza y Sotelo, a Franciscan who visited Lima in the 1730s, for more compliments about interior design, *Viaje ilustrado*, 106. For another perspective on domestic life and sociability, see Mannarelli, *Pecados públicos*.

36   Flores Galindo, *Aristocracia y plebe*, 78–80.

37   An anonymous French priest noted that "in the large houses there is commonly a room built to be earthquake-proof." Nieto Velez, "Una descripción del Perú," 286. For an inventory of the *oratorios*' contents, see Archivo Arzobispal de Lima (AAL), Capillas y oratorios, 1612–1915.

38   Sánchez Rodríguez, "La ruina," 69.

39   On *quincha*, see Llano Zapata, "Respuesta dada"; Rodríguez-Camilloni, "Tradición e innovación."

40   See Hipólito Ruiz, who was in Peru in the late 1770s, in Schultes and de Jaramillo-Arango, *The Journals*, 54; see also Kagan, *Urban Images*, 169–71.

41   Juan and Ulloa, *A Voyage*, 176–77; the Spanish version is found in Ulloa, *Viaje a la América meridional*, vol. b, 44. I have changed the translation of *bajaraque*

202

(from the indigenous language of Taino) to *wattle and daub*. Curiously, both this term as well as quincha (Quechua) are from indigenous languages. The English version has both Antonio de Ulloa and Jorge Juan as the authors; the Spanish only Ulloa. Juan Pimentel refers to Ulloa as the "principal author" of the account. Pimentel, *viajeros científicos*, 51.

42 Ricardo Ramírez conducted the research in the notary records, providing not just quantitative material but his own interpretations and ideas.

43 Critics contended that "in no other place in Christendom are there so many and such large bells, especially in the churches of the regular orders." AGI, Lima, Leg. 522 and Leg. 393. All of the accounts refer to the chilling mix of screams, groans, and pleas for help with the sound of tumbling buildings and aftershocks.

44 Llano Zapata, "Carta," 75.

45 Ibid, 73.

46 Conde de Superunda, *Relación*, 247.

47 Valdivieso y Torrejón, *Allegación Jurídica*.

48 Sánchez Rodríguez, "La ruina," 100–102; Llano Zapata, "Observación diaria," esp. 138–39; Ramírez and Walker, "Cuentas y cultura material," passim. The best summary, Bernales Ballesteros, *Lima, La Ciudad*, 293–303.

49 AGI, Lima, Leg. 509.

50 Sánchez Rodríguez, "La ruina," 102–06.

51 Llano Zapata, "Observación diaria," 132–38; Llano Zapata, "Carta," 101.

52 Anon., *Individual y verdadera*, 152. See also Lozano, "Relación," 39.

53 De Larreta, "Letras anuas," 135. Lozano states that only two priests in Callao survived. Lozano, "Relación," 41. On the Franciscans, Lozano, "Relación," 41; Llano Zapata, "Carta," 99. Many Dominican priests who were in Callao for a special mass were also victims.

54 AGI, Lima, Leg. 509.

55 Bravo de Lagunas, *Voto Consultivo*, 156.

56 Sánchez Rodríguez, "La ruina," 150–51; Pérez-Mallaína Bueno, *Retrato*, 60–62.

57 Conde de Superunda, *Relación*, 262. Lozano, "Relación," 40.

58 Llano Zapata, "Carta," 74–75. Montero del Aguila also noted that many "did not make it to the sacred" (no lograron lo sagrado) and were buried in plazas and streets. Montero del Aguila, *Desolación de la ciudad*, 174.

59 Lozano, "Relación del Terremoto," 40; Montero del Aguila, *Desolación de la ciudad*, 174. On horses and mules, see AGI, Santa Fe, Leg. 572, Correspondencia de Sebastián de Eslava, virrey del Nuevo Reino de Granada, "Consideraciones de las pérdidas del Callao y Lima año de 1746." I suspect that Montero del Aguila, a key ideologue of Manso de Velasco, wrote this frank report, much cited here.

60 Llano Zapata, "Observación," 141–42; Llano Zapata, "Carta," 97; see O'Phelan Godoy, "Una rebelión abortada," 10–14.

61 Llano Zapata, "Carta," 95–96; the figure is on 97; 71–76.

62 Llano Zapata, "Carta," 81, 94.

63 St. Malo, *A Voyage*, 88–89.

64 Llano Zapata, "Carta," 72, and "Observación," passim; Sánchez Rodríguez, "La ruina," 133–36; Conde de Superunda, *Relación*, 262. For medical information, see the account of a meeting of doctors concerned about fevers. John Carter Brown Library, Noticias del Perú, vol. 2, #8, no title, begins "Haviendo se experimentado en esta ciudad," Lima, 27 de junio 1749.

65 John Carter Brown Library, Noticias del Perú, vol. 2, #8, no title, begins "Haviendo se experimentado en esta ciudad," Lima, 27 de junio 1749. On medicine, see Bustíos Romaní, *Cuatrocientos años*; Warren, "Piety and Danger."

66 On the city's hospitals, see Cahill, "Financing Health Care"; Perez Cantó, *Lima*, 24–28; Aguirre Medrano, *Historia de los hospitales*; Moreno Cebrián, "Introducción," 37–39; Conde de Superunda, *Relación*, 215–17.

67 AGN, notarios, Francisco Estacio Meléndez, 1748, protocolo 379, fs. 1551–1558 and 1751, prot. 387, f. 736–742,

68 Cascajo Romero, *El pleito de la curación*, 16–19; and Bravo de Lagunas y Castilla, *Discurso histórico-jurídico*, esp. 165–66.

69 Ovando, "Carta," 53.

70 Conde de Superunda, *Relación*, 262–63.

71 Llano Zapata, "Carta," 76.

72 Gálvez, *Calles de Lima*, 114.

73 AGN, Cabildo, Justicia Ordinaria, Criminales, Leg. 14, exp. 8.

74 AGN, Cabildo, Causas Civiles, Leg. 18, c. 302, 1758.

75 AGN, Casa de Moneda, C. M. 069. Luis Agustín Gonzáles Soberal.

76 Nieto Vélez, "Testimonio sobre el venerable," 385.

77 Anon., *True and Particular* (1748), 3.

78 AGI, Lima, Leg. 416.

79 Ovando, "Carta," 56.

80 Ovando, "Carta," 52, 56–58.

Four Stabilizing the Unstable

1 Hohenberg and Lees, *The Making of Urban Europe*, 137–71, quote from 151. The literature is vast. I found particularly useful the essays in Millon, ed., *The Triumph of the Baroque*, and McClain, Merriman, Kaoru, eds., *Edo and Paris*. Mumford, *The City in History* is always insightful; on Latin American, see anon., *La Ciudad Hispanoamericana*; Hünefeldt, "El crecimiento de las ciudades."

2 Cited in Mignot, "Urban Transformations," *Baroque*, 318. The attacks of September 11, 2001, in the United States prompted much rethinking about disaster, rebuilding, and memory. Two notable books emerged from this: Vale and Campanella, eds., *The Resilient City*; Ockman, ed., *Out of Ground Zero*.

3 Moreno Cebrián, "Introducción," Conde de Superunda, *Relación*, 17–19; Saénz-Diez, *Los riojanos*, 151–87; Salvat Monguillot, "En torno," passim.

204

4   Pearce, "Early Bourbon Government," 18.

5   Moore, *The Cabildo in Perú*, 51–53; Harth-Terré, "Bicentenario de un infausto suceso," 12–15. Guardino, *The Time of Liberty*, 28–29, notes this for Mexico.

6   Conde de Superunda, *Relación*, 257–58.

7   For more names, see Moreno Cebrián, "Introducción," Conde de Superunda, *Relación*, 20. See also Lohmann Villena, *Las relaciones*, 129–32. Despite their similar names, Bravo de Lagunas and Bravo del Rivero were not related. They had married sisters, however, and Hervoso was the godfather of one of Bravo del Rivero's children. Pérez-Mallaína Bueno, *Retrato*, 238. On the Audiencia members, see Burkholder and Chandler, *Biographical Dictionary*.

8   Lohmann Villena, *Las relaciones*, 131.

9   AGI, Lima, Leg. 523; Pérez-Mallaína Bueno, *Retrato*, 232–52; Warren, "Piety and Danger," 36–40.

10   AGI, Lima, Leg. 787. See also Quiroz Chueca, "Movimiento de tierra," for accusations about other wrongdoing in Callao.

11   AGI, Lima, Legs. 642 and 643. This is discussed in Pérez-Mallaína Bueno, *Retrato*, 119–24; Pearce, "Early Bourbon Government," passim.

12   Cited in Rodríguez Villa, *Don Zenón de Somodevilla*, 56.

13   On Ensenada, see Gómez Urdáñez, *El proyecto reformista*; Stein and Stein, *Silver, Trade, and War*, 234–39; Rodríguez Villa, *Don Zenón de Somodevilla*; Pearce, "Early Bourbon Government."

14   AGI, Santa Fe, Leg. 572, Correspondencia del Virrey Sebastián Eslava.

15   Ibid.

16   Ibid. On this more humble and personal notion of devotion, see Voekel, *Alone Before God*.

17   AGI, Santa Fe, Leg. 572, Correspondencia del Virrey Sebastián Eslava.

18   AGI, Lima, Leg. 643, letter dated July 15, 1747.

19   Valdivieso, *Allegación Jurídica*, 28b and 30b; Lozano, "Relación," 36.

20   AGI, Lima, Leg. 416, March 1747. The New Tax was a despised duty on agricultural and industrial goods that lasted from 1742 until 1752 and was destined for defense.

21   AGI, Lima, Leg. 596, citing a 1751 report.

22   AGI, Lima, Leg. 540.

23   For some examples, see Pérez-Mallaína Bueno, *Retrato*, 361.

24   AGN, Notarios, Francisco Roldán, 1747, protocolo 930, f. 613–39, 710–27. 141; 77; 78.

25   AGI, Lima, Leg. 415. The viceroy used the term *arrabales*, a term of Arab origin that referred to areas outside city limits.

26   AGI, Lima, Leg. 511 (p. 14). Officials of the Inquisition, for example, took refuge in the fields of the San Felipe School. Medina, *Historia del Tribunal*, 290.

27   Llano Zapata, "Carta," 83.

28   AGI, Lima, Leg. 444. For the stolen wood, AGN, Cabildo, Leg. 1, exp. 11.

These sources note that the thieves sold their loot in Acho and the Alameda, both in Rimac. There are dozens of references to stolen wood.

29 Archivo del Cabildo Metropolitano, Lima, Cédulas Reales y otros papeles, November 18, 1747; AGI, Lima, Leg. 983. Ulloa had commented favorably on the smell of the plaza just years before. See Ulloa, *Viaje a la América meridional*, 78; on the stench of the Mexico City plaza, see Brading, "The City in Bourbon Spanish America," 71–72.

30 AGI, Lima, Leg. 983.

31 Conde de Superunda, *Relación*, 263.

32 On the hesitancy to rebuild, see the viceroy's letter to Carvajal, July 31, 1747. Cited in Vargas Ugarte, *Impresos Peruanos*, vol. 4 (Manuscritos Peruanos en las bibliotecas de América), 221.

33 On bread and social control in France, see Kaplan, "Provisioning Paris." The literature on this topic in Europe is extensive.

34 Conde de Superunda, *Relación*, 260; Llano Zapata, "Carta," 75–76.

35 Flores Galindo, *Aristocracia y plebe*, 21–29; Ramos, *Trigo chileno*; Bravo de Lagunas, *Voto Consultivo*; Pérez-Mallaína Bueno, "La utilización interesada"; Haitin, "Late Colonial Lima."

36 Bravo de Lagunas, *Voto Consultivo*.

37 Conde de Superunda, *Relación*, 69; anon., "Individual y verdadera," 158–59.

38 AGN, Cabildo, Leg. 1, exp. 10, January 1747. One baker, Don Zipriano de Tejada, argued that the rules shouldn't apply to him because he gave away much of his bread and his best product had special ingredients (wine, sesame seeds, etc.) and sold out despite its high price. AGI, Lima, Leg, 446.

39 AGI, Lima, Leg. 986, from February 26, 1756. This was just one of many controversies about wheat and bread. Lawsuits dragged on for years over who was to cover the cost of wheat lost in Callao's warehouses. See Pacheco, "Por parte" for one perspective.

40 AGI, Lima, Leg. 444, July 26, 1746.

41 For a table on these debts, see Moreno Cebrián, "Introducción," Conde de Superunda, *Relación*, 88; for military expenditures, see Pérez-Mallaína Bueno, *Retrato*, 116–17, who charts the increased expenditures.

42 AGI, Tribunal de Cuentas Oficios Reales y sus dependencias, Leg. 1127, 1 de agosto 1746.

43 AGI, Lima, Leg. 643, November 1, 1746.

44 AGI, Lima, Leg. 643.

45 Moreno Cebrián, "Introducción," Conde de Superunda, *Relación*, 73, 91–94; Vargas Ugarte, *Historia General del Perú, Virreinato*, 270–71.

46 Pearce, "Huancavelica 1700–1759," 696.

47 Mumford, *The City in History*; Tilly, *Coercion, Capital and European States*. On the improvement, see Pérez-Mallaína Bueno, *Retrato*, 116–18.

48 AGI, Lima, Leg. 642 and 643.

49 Pérez-Mallaína Bueno, *Retrato*, 127–29; the documentation is once again from AGI, Lima, Leg. 643.

206

50 Pérez-Mallaína Bueno, *Retrato*, 121–24.

51 Kaplan, "Provisioning Paris," quotes on 175 and 208–09.

52 Llano Zapata, "Carta," 91.

53 AGI, Lima, Leg. 983.

54 AGI, Lima, Leg. 511. Information about seemingly futile price controls in 1747 is also found here.

55 AGI, Lima, Leg. 511.

56 Montero del Aguila, *Noticia Annalica*, 179–80, for both the slave and Indian remark. See also Barriga, *Los terremotos*, 303–05, for Arequipa examples.

57 Archivo del Cabildo Metropolitano, Lima, Acuerdos Capitulares, Libro XVI, p. 31; see also Pérez-Mallaína Bueno, *Retrato*, 115–16.

Five Obstacles to Urban Reform

1 They considered the Lurigancho valley at the foot of the San Bartolomé hill, to the east. AGI, Lima, Leg. 511.

2 Günther Doering and Lohmann Villena, *Lima*, 130.

3 AGI, Lima, Leg. 511, 27b; the Cathedral expenditures of 357,157 pesos comes from Pérez-Mallaína Bueno, *Retrato*, 123.

4 AGI, Lima, Leg. 511, 32–37. On the earthquake and *censos*, see Aldana Rivera, "¿Ocurrencias del Tiempo?" 167–94.

5 Officials in Lisbon made a similar decision after the 1755 earthquake there.

6 Lafuente and Mazuecos, *Los caballeros*; Poole, *Vision, Race, and Modernity*, chap. 2; Whitaker, *Mapmaker's Wife*.

7 This stay in Peru hurt his reputation in France, as de La Condamine and Bouguer, by now his enemies, questioned his lack of publications and his collaboration with the Spanish Crown. After attempting to regain his place in Paris scientific circles, he died in Cádiz in 1760, the director of the Armada's Coast Guard Academy. Lafuente and Mazuecos, *Los caballeros*, esp. 142–46, and, for a portrait, 61; Philip Keenan, "Astronomy in the Viceroyalty," 297–305; Harth-Terré, "Bicentenario." See also Histoire de l'Académe Royale des Sciences, "Eloge de M. Godin."

8 Tobriner, "Earthquakes and Planning," and "La Casa Baraccata." Maxwell, "Lisbon: The Earthquake"; Fraile, "Putting Order."

9 Hardoy, *Two Thousand Years*, 34.

10 Hohenberg and Lees, *The Making*, part 2; Mignot, "Urban transformations."

11 AGI, Lima, Leg. 511, 17–18.

12 Cited in Vargas Ugarte, *Historia General del Perú*, 4:263.

13 AGI, Lima, Leg. 511, 17–18. Authorities frequently discussed ways to force Indians to work in the city, although in this case no policy was established. For an example, see Bravo de Lagunas, *Voto Consultivo*.

14 On the tangled finances of this family, see Rizo-Patrón, *Linaje, Dote, y Poder*, 145–46.

15 Pérez-Mallaína Bueno demonstrates that Don Manuel de Silva y la Banda, a

promiment lawyer and one of the litigants, wrote the longer text from May.   207
Pérez-Mallaína Bueno, "La utilización interesada," 80.

16   AGI, Lima, Leg. 511, 65.

17   He referred to Partida 3, Ley diez, Titulo 32. Alfonso X, *Las Siete Partidas,* 2:184.

18   AGI, Lima, Leg. 511, 67.

19   Ibid. 67–90.

20   Ibid.

21   AGI, Lima, Leg. 419.

22   AGI, Lima, Leg. 511.

23   AGI, Lima, Leg. 984.

24   Pérez-Mallaína Bueno highlights the rhetorical merits of this document. Pérez-Mallaína Bueno, "La utilización interesada."

25   Durán Montero, *Lima en el Siglo XVII,* 40–41.

26   They also lost their store and many investments. Pablo de Olavide wrote a short novel about the disaster entitled *Teresa o el terremoto de Lima.* In Olavide, *Obras selectas,* 193–216.

27   They did not address counterarguments such as the wealth of owners in these areas or the viceregal state's preference for this core area.

28   AGI, Lima, Leg. 511, 92.

29   Kagan, *Urban Images,* 21. See also Goldthwaite, *The Building of Renaissance Florence,* 69–83; and for Lima, Wuffarden, "La Ciudad y sus Emblemas," 59–75.

30   AGI, Lima, Leg. 511, 205–20.

31   Conde de Superunda, *Relación,* 264–65.

32   AGI, Lima, Leg. 511, 2, letter from June 20, 1748.

33   Conde de Superunda, *Relación,* 265–66.

34   Susy Sánchez provides a list that dates from 1749, the mint, to 1791, the Sagrario Church. Sánchez Rodríguez, "La ruina de Lima," 332–34.

35   De la Barra, *Historic Monograph;* Arrus, *El Callao,* passim; Rodríguez Casado and Pérez Embid, *Construcciones militares,* 108–26.

36   Sánchez, *Sermon que en la missa de accion de Gracias por la Reedificacion.* See anon., *Pompa Funeral,* for laudatory rhetoric toward King Fernando and his efforts to rebuild the cathedral.

37   In fact, the earthquake made the houses seem even lower, as much of the rubble remained on the streets, raising them slightly and making the houses appear sunken. Harth-Terré and Márquez Abanto, "Las bellas artes," 187. On architectural changes, see Ramón, "Urbe y Orden," 318; Basadre, *La multitud,* 101–05; Günther Doering and Lohmann Villena, *Lima,* 133–39. For a description, particularly the plainer facades, see von Tschudi, *Testimonio del Perú,* 80–92. In the late 1770s, Hipólito Ruíz wrote, "Now the houses are very low, with the exception of a few whose owners, regardless of the threat of earthquakes, have built them up again." Evans Schultes and von Thenen de Jaramillo-Arango, trans., *The Journals of Hipólito Ruíz,* 55.

38   Hector Velarde, *Arquitectura peruana,* 106–07.

208 39 Anon., *Pompa Funeral*, 58.

40 AGI, Lima, Legs. 419, 420.

41 Biek, "Louis XIV and the Cities," 71.

Six Licentious Friars, Wandering Nuns

1 Van Deusen, *Between the Sacred*, 126, 176–77; Pérez-Mallaína Bueno, *Retrato*, 315; see also AGI, Lima, Leg. 984. Bernard Lavallé calculates a similar percentage, 18 percent of the European women of the city in the same year: 820 out of 4,359 Spaniards. Cited in Margarita Suárez, "El Poder," 165.

2 On this process, see Ramón Joffré, *La muralla*, 92–100.

3 Bernales Ballesteros, *Lima*, 219–24, 298–99.

4 Gálvez, *Una Lima*, 30–47.

5 Vicuña Mackenna, "Lima en 1810," Porras Barrenechea, *Pequeña Antología*, 255.

6 Israel, *Radical Enlightenment*, esp. chaps. 21, 28, who emphasizes the work of Feijóo; Thomas, *Religion and the Decline*.

7 Roberto Fernández outlines a "triple operation." Fernández, *La España*, 232–328. David Brading, "Boubon Spain," 116; Antonio Acosta, "La reforma"; Herr, *The Eighteenth-Century Revolution*.

8 Pearce, "Early Bourbon Government," for a list and summary, 185–88; Acosta, "La reforma."

9 Taylor, *Magistrates*. For second half of century, Brading, *The First America*, chaps. 21, 22.

10 Martin, *Daughters*, 204–05; anon., *Lima: Paseos*, chap. 6.

11 Vargas Ugarte, *Historia de la iglesia*, 4:2–3.

12 Martin, *Daughters*, 179. Van Deusen, *Between the Sacred*, 173–74.

13 AGI, Lima, Leg. 521, 1725.

14 Van Deusen, *Between the Sacred*, 173.

15 AGI, Lima, Leg. 555, Expediente sobre alborotos. . . . For a more detailed summary, see Martin, *Daughters*, 273–79.

16 Moreno Cebrián, "El Regalismo," 230–32.

17 Ibid., 242; see also his introductions to the memoirs of Viceroy Castelfuerte and Viceroy Manso de Velasco. Moreno Cebrián, *El virreinato del Marqués*; Moreno Cebrián, introduction to Conde de Superunda, *Relación*.

18 *Relación*, AGI, Lima, Leg. 413; also Moreno Cebrian, "El Regalismo."

19 *Relación*, AGI, Lima, Leg. 413. The Real Academia Española defines *concupiscence* as "deseo de bienes terrenos y, en especial, apetito desordenado de placeres deshonestos." *Oxford English Dictionary*: Eager or inordinate desire; immoderate sexual desire, lust; Theology: desire for worldly things.

20 *Relación*, AGI, Lima, Leg. 413, 11. "Los Religiosos conventuales andan como bagando por ciudad solos, y de corta hedad, asi a pie como a mula en sillas indesentes y contrarias a su estado por lo costoso de ellas, y muchos con estriberas de Plata entrando publicamente en la casa de meretrices, y pasandose

a la puerta de ellas . . . y muchos llevando su concubina delante en la misma   209
Mula a los paseos publicos."

21   Moreno Cebrián, "El Regalismo." 238. On the epidemic, see Pearce, "The Peruvian Population," 69–104.

22   AGI, Lima, Leg. 413, document dated Dec. 20, 1730, from Virrey Castelfuerte to VM. "La causa principalisima de que subsistan con tan porfiado teson las calamidades, atrasos, y aversos sucesos de tan experimentados terremotos, con que el cielo castiga continuamente a este afligido reyno."

23   Frezier, A Voyage, 231.

24   Juan and Ulloa, Discourse and Political Reflections, a translation of their Noticias Secretas.

25   Poole, Vision, esp. chaps. 2, 3. Maza, The Myth, 53–61; Roche, France in the Enlightenment, esp. chaps. 17–19.

26   In 1956, Father Luis Merino made a parallel argument. In order to discount the accusations by Juan and Ulloa, he emphasized that the debate about the orders dated from the late seventeenth century and that Juan and Ulloa did not have that great an influence on discussions in Madrid. Merino, "Estudio crítico."

27   Pearce, "Early Bourbon Government," 190–96; Taylor, Magistrates, 15–16; 84; Sánchez Bella, Iglesia y estado, 121–22.

28   Brading, Church and State, 63.

29   AGI, Lima, Leg. 643, December 10, 1746; also Lima, Leg. 984; see also Pérez-Mallaína Bueno, Retrato, 137.

30   An almost identical version of this letter is in AGI, Lima, Leg. 415, Dec. 10, 1746 ("tremendo golpe"). For Manso's objections to the regulars and the conventos grandes, see his memoirs, Conde de Superunda, Relación, 203–10. Also valuable is the introduction by Alfredo Moreno, esp. 44–49, a detailed summary of these issues.

31   AGI, Leg. 984, 65. "Si no havia relaxado su observancia a lo menos la havia dispensado de modo que ha sido asunto de la detracción de los extrangeros y Españoles que pasan a aquellos Reynos y extrañan las licenciosas libertades con que ellos viven."

32   AGI, Leg. 643, letter from December 18, 1748. See also AGI, Lima, Leg. 1596, for extensive documentation on regulars and rural parishes.

33   Ibid. He reiterates this point in his memoirs: ". . . la repugnancia con que se restituyen los que han vivido algún tiempo en libertad." Conde de Superunda, Relación, 199.

34   Ibid. In this letter, he refers to scandals in Quito involving the Franciscans, a clear reference to Jorge Juan and Antonio de Ulloa's Noticias secretas de América.

35   Biblioteca del Palacio Real, Madrid (BPR), II/601 1036994, Colección Histórica de los documentos de los despachos de Indias," f. 8. The Jesuits were largely excluded from the reforms of the period. Not only was Rávago a member of the king's inner circle (and other members were sympathetic to this order as well) but the overriding concern about whether the orders made sufficient money to sustain themselves, a strength of the Jesuits, insulated them from the focus of criticism. This would, of course, change.

36 On Carvajal and Ensenada, see Gómez Urdáñez, *El proyecto reformista de Ensenada*; Rodríguez Villa, *Don Zenón de Somodevilla*; Fernández, *La España moderna*; Pearce, "Early Bourbon Government"; Brading, "Church and State"; John Lynch, *Bourbon Spain*, chap. 5.

37 For a list of the members, see Sánchez Bella, *Iglesia y estado*, 124.

38 For a detailed guide to administrative reforms, see Margarita Gómez Gómez, *Forma y expedición*. For a reinterpretation of the Bourbon period, see Pearce, "Early Bourbon Government."

39 BPR, Colección Histórica, f. 1–3, and 9. Some of the letters are found both in the AGI and the Junta's summary, but not all of them.

40 BPR, Colección histórica, f. 12.

41 Perez-Mallaína Bueno, *Retrato*, 321.

42 Bernales Ballesteros, *Lima*, 295–303.

43 Sánchez Bella, *Iglesia y estado*, 132

44 AGI, Lima, Leg. 643, Letter from December 18, 1748.

45 BPR, Colección Histórica, 19v.

46 For a good summary, see Brading, *Church and State*, 62–64.

47 Brading notes the surprising lack of study on secularization in Peru. Adrian Pearce demonstrates the general impact that secularization had—the reduction in the number of *doctrinas* held by the orders—and provides leads for further study. Brading, *Church and State*, 67–68; Pearce, "Early Bourbon Government." See also Taylor, *Magistrates*, 83–87.

48 Burns, *Colonial Habits*, 64.

49 Arnold J. Bauer, "The Church," 707–33. On the *censos* in colonial Lima and the preponderance of the convents, see Hamnett, "Church Wealth"; Suárez, "El poder"; Pérez-Mallaína Bueno, *Retrato*; on censos and the Inquisition in Peru, see Millar C., *Inquisición y sociedad*; Quiroz, *Deudas olvidadas*.

50 See chapter 2.

51 AGN, Escribano Estacio Meléndez, 1747, prot. 374, fol. 13v–16.

52 AGI, Lima, Leg. 509, November 17, 1746. These accounts not only describe the dire situation of the houses and their owners, but also outline the complexity of the censos. Most cases discuss multiple censos on each property owed to different institutions.

53 AGI, Lima, Leg. 415. "Ninguna buena razón dictaba, que los dueños de ellas quisiesen sacrificar sus caudales, y dedicarlos a repararlas, para que reviviese un censo extincto, quando a menos costo podían comprar otros solares libres."

54 AGI, Lima, Leg. 352.

55 For example, a document from December 1746 referred to "private pacts" in which the interest rates were dropped. AGI, Lima, Leg. 509, December 1746. See also Quiroz, *Deudas olvidadas*, 47–54, on this controversy.

56 AGI, Lima, Leg. 415.

57 AGI, Lima, Leg. 509, p 54b. See 75v on the possibility of the Santo Toribio

(Bethlemites) Hospital closing. "Parece que solo se tuvo presente la equidad 211
para los dueños de las fincas, como si los censualistas fuesen indignos de ella,
por ser hospitales, que distribuyen sus rentas en la curación de los enfermos,
en que tanto interesa la caridad y beneficio publico."

58   AGI, Lima, Leg. 509, document from Silva, p. 389.
59   AGI, Lima, Leg. 509, 391–98v.
60   Alvarez de Ron, Representación Jurídica, 6.
61   Points made by Bauer, "The Church," and Pérez-Mallaína Bueno, Retrato.
62   This is summarized in Pérez-Mallaína Bueno, Retrato, 90–91.
63   Alvarez de Ron, Representación.
64   Valdivieso y Torrejón, Allegación Jurídica.
65   AGI, Lima, Leg. 352. Also Leg. 509.
66   AGI, Lima, Leg. 509, 483–539.
67   Pérez-Mallaína Bueno, Retrato, 303–05.
68   AGI, Lima, Leg. 352.
69   The slow payment was not a sign of anticlericalism: the viceroy was a devout
     man.
70   For the dizzying bureaucratic journey, see AGI, Lima, Leg. 509, and Pérez-
     Mallaína Bueno, Retrato, chaps. 10, 11. I found material on the censo battle not
     only in the thousand-page Legajo 509 but in at least half a dozen other legajos
     as well.
71   AGI, Lima, Leg. 352; also Leg. 509.
72   AGN, Notarios, Manuel de Echeverz, 1747, prot. 219, 1003–11.
73   On the Church in the latter decades of the eighteenth century, see García
     Jordán, Iglesia y poder, introduction and chap. 1; Peralta, "Las razones"; Vargas
     Ugarte, Historia de la Iglesia and Concilios Limenses.

Seven   Controlling Women's Bodies

1   Papió, La Historia d'Esconalbou, 255–56. I want to thank Nuria Sala I Vila for
    providing me with this obscure work.
2   Ibid, 258–59.
3   Ramírez, Soli deo Honor.
4   Hohenberg and Lees, The Making, 157.
5   Porras, Perspectiva y panorama, 66. For Mumford's quote, see Mumford, The City
    in History, 351.
6   Anon., El Día de Lima; see Ruiz Cano, Júbilos de Lima, and Fernández de Castro,
    Elisio peruano for descriptions of eighteenth-century ritual in Lima.
7   Betagh, "Captain Betagh's Observations," 9–10.
8   Paz, Sor Juana, 70.
9   Work on travel literature include Cañizares, "Postcolonialism avante la let-
    tre?"; Poole, Vision, Race, and Modernity; Pratt, Imperial Eyes.
10 Fuentes, Lima: Apuntes históricos, 101.

212   11   Ibid, 102.

12   Leon Pinelo, *Velos en los rostros*. The Peruvian historian José de la Riva Agüero labeled it a mix of the Arab *embozo* and the Tarifa (Andalusia) shawl, Riva Aguero, "La conquista y el virreinato," 396.

13   León Pinelo, *Velos en los rostros*, 248–52.

14   Ibid, 341–43.

15   Glave, *De Rosa*, 349; Basadre, *La multitud*, 77–81; also Mugaburu, *Chronicle of Colonial Lima*, 318, who refers to condemnation of homosexual activities in seventeenth-century Lima.

16   García Calderón, *Para una Antología*, 13–14.

17   Ibid, 11.

18   Poole, *Vision, Race and Modernity*, 90–92.

19   Hunt, *Governance of the Consuming Passions*, esp. 28–34.

20   Ibid. 84–85.

21   For analyses of clothing, see Cruz de Amenábar, *El Traje*, and O'Phelan Godoy, "El vestido." For an overview of changes in Europe as well as in the study of clothing, see Roche, *The Culture of Clothing*.

22   Frezier, *A Voyage*, 219.

23   Ibid. See Pablo Macera, *Viajeros franceses*, 38–39, for a summary of Frezier's superficial visit and observations.

24   Avalos de Matos, trans., "Lima de 1700 vista por De la Bardinais Le Gentil," 119–22, 295–304, quotes from 298. See Poole, *Vision, Race, and Modernity*, for French notions of the Andes.

25   Descola, *Daily*, 81. Macera derides Bachelier as a simple plagiary of Frezier, Macera, *La imagen francesa*, 37; Estuardo Nuñez defends him from these charges. Nuñez, *Viajes*, 82–83.

26   Captain Betagh, "Captain Betagh's Observations," 1813, 7–8.

27   Ibid., 10.

28   Ibid.

29   Ibid.

30   Ibid., 10–12. On English masculinity in this period, see Roberts, "Pleasure Engendered."

31   Juan and Ulloa, *A Voyage*, 193.

32   Ibid., 196.

33   Ibid.

34   Ibid., 201.

35   Ibid., 199.

36   Ibid., 200.

37   St. Malo, *A Voyage*, 75.

38   Ibid., 76–77, quote on 77.

39   Nuñez, *Cuatro Viajeros Alemanes*, 31.

40   See Peralta Ruíz and Walker, "Viajeros naturalistas, científicos."

41   AGI, Lima, Leg. 987; AGI, Lima, Leg. 984.

42   The literature on Juan and Ulloa is vast. I have benefited from Andrien, "The Noticias Secretas"; Brading, *The First America*, chap. 19; Lafuente and Mazuecos, *Los caballeros*; Merino, "Estudio crítico"; Pimentel, *Viajeros científicos*; Saumell, "Introducción," in Ulloa, *Viaje a la América meridional*. Conversations with Víctor Peralta have also been a great help.

43   Mary L. Pratt emphasizes the need to incorporate "contestatory expressions from the site of imperial intervention," yet correctly notes that these debates about colonial society cannot be neatly divided into Spanish versus Creole (or dominant versus subaltern). See her introduction, esp. 2–4. Pratt, *Imperial Eyes*.

44   Both cited in Basadre, *La multitud*, 78.

45   O'Phelan Godoy, "El vestido," 108–09; Earle, "'Two Pairs of Pink Satin Shoes'"; Earle, "Luxury, Clothing and Race."

46   These are reprinted in Konetzke, *Colección de Documentos*, vol. 3, tomo 1, "Pragmática contra el abuso de trajes y otros gastos superfluos," Madrid, February 10, 1716, doc. #92, pp. 124–34, which refers to the 1691 document; "Real Decreto Aprobando un bando del Virrey del Perú para moderar el exceso en los trajes que vestían los negros, mulattos, indios y mestizos," San Ildefonso, September 7, 1725, doc. # 114, p. 187.

47   Earle, "Luxury, Clothing and Race," 222.

48   Earle, "'Two Pairs of Pink Satin Shoes,'" and "Luxury, Clothing and Race." Hunt, *Governance*.

49   Berg and Eger, Introduction, *In Pursuit of Luxury*; Rico, "Criptoburguesía y cambio económico."

50   Maza, *The Myth*, chap. 2, quote from 55.

51   Sempere y Guariños, *Historia del Luxo*; Cañizares-Esguerra, "Eighteenth-Century Spanish Political Economy."

52   See Rico, "Criptoburguesía y cambio económico."

53   Quoted ibid., 36.

54   Andrés de Munive, September 11, 1734, in Vargas Ugarte, *Impresos*, 6:201–03 (1949); also found in Medina, *La Imprenta en Lima*, 3:175–76.

55   Andrés de Munive, September 11, 1734, in Vargas Ugarte, *Impresos*, 6:201–03 (1949).

56   Konetzke, *Colección de Documentos*, vol. 3, tomo 1, "Real Decreto Aprobando un bando del Virrey del Perú para moderar el exceso en los trajes que vestían los negros, mulattos, indios y mestizos," San Ildefonso, September 7, 1725, doc. # 114, p. 187.

57   Moreno Cebrián, *El virreinato del Marqués de Castelfuerte*, 69.

58   Ibid., 546. His memoirs were written by Pedro de Peralta Barnuevo.

59   Vargas Ugarte, *Historia de la Iglesia*, 4:271–72. The document is in the Vargas Ugarte Collection in the Ruiz de Montoya University, "Auto del Obispo de Arequipa, D. Juan Cavera de Toledo, reprimiendo el abuso de los trajes femininos sobre todo en Moquegua," 1735.

214

60 "Trajes inhonestos de las mujeres, de D Pedro Bravo del Rivero, Obispo de Arequipa," found in the Vargas Ugarte Collection in the Ruiz de Montoya University 1744.

61 Medina, La Imprenta en Lima, 435–36.

62 Llano Zapata cited the sentence on covering body parts, although transcribing the arm cover reaching "the fist" rather than the elbow. Llano Zapata, "Carta," 92.

63 I did not find this decree, but it is cited in Papió, La Historia, 258.

64 Cited in Vargas Ugarte, Historía de la Iglesia, 4:144.

65 Cruz de Amenábar, "El Traje," 95–99.

66 AGI, Santa Fe, Leg. 572.

67 Ibid. On Montero del Aguila, see Lohmann Villena, "Victorino Montero del Aguila."

68 Lanuza y Sotelo, Viaje Ilustrado, 109.

69 Manso de Velasco, "Informes que hacen al Rey," Lima, 175?.

70 Ibid, the document is from the Cabildo Eclesiástico Metropolitano.

71 Ramírez, Soli Deo Honor, Title page and p. 1.

72 Ibid., introduction.

73 Ibid.

74 Ibid., from Provincia de Doce Apóstoles.

75 Ibid.

76 Quoted in Heras, O.F.M., Los Franciscanos y las misiones populares, 25. I have a copy of this account thanks to the dogged efforts of Claudia Rosas in the Archivo Storico of the Propaganda Fide Congregation, Rome. Fray Joseph de San Antonio, "Viva Jesús." Fondo S. C., America Meridionales, 3:207–08.

77 In Konetzke, Documentos, vol. 3, tomo I. "Consulta del Consejo de las Indias sobre una representación del misionero capuchino Fr. Mariano de Junqueras para reformar las costumbres relajadas del Perú," Madrid, August 25, 1789, 660–63. He also condemned the city's convents and monasteries.

78 Ibid.

79 Mercurio Peruano, February 10, 1791, "Carta escrita a la sociedad sobre los gastos excesivos de una Tapada."

80 Quoted in Pratt, Imperial Eyes, 167.

81 Lastarria, El manuscrito del Diablo, 236.

Eight   The Lima and Huarochirí Rebellions

1 Flores Galindo, Aristocracia y plebe.

2 The study by Jesús Cosamalón should have prompted more debate and discussion. Cosamalón, Indios detrás de la muralla.

3 In Mexico City, "overt expressions of racial prejudice seldom occurred among plebeians." Cope, The Limits, 76; Flores Galindo, Aristocracia y plebe, refers to a "permanent ethnic tension" in Lima and provides some examples, 168–

80; quote from 169. Criminal trials of the period are full of racial and sexual insults. For a lively example, see AGN, Cabildo, Justicia Ordinaria, Leg. 3, cuad. 3, 1749. On Indian-black relations, see Restall, *Beyond Black and Red*.

4 AGN, Notarios, Manuel de Echeverz, 1747, prot. 219, 1003; AGN, Notarios, Francisco Estacio Meléndez, 1749, Prot. 381, 1187. These are just two of many examples.

5 Montero del Aguila, *Desolación*, 7.

6 Llano Zapata, "Carta," 84–85, 77.

7 Anon., *Individual y verdadera relación*, Odriozola, *Terremotos*, 161–62; Montero del Aguila, *Desolación*, 174.

8 AGI, Lima, Leg. 511, letter from June 20, 1748.

9 Ovando, "Carta," 54–55. The marquis also mentions the rumor of the kidnapping of a religious woman, perhaps a nun. Lower-class insurgency, urban chaos, and possible sexual abuse of a nun—all of the city leaders' nightmares were present.

10 Llano Zapata, "Carta," 72–73.

11 Archivo Histórico Municipalidad Metropolitana de Lima, Libro de Cabildo, tomo 35, 1730 a 1756, folio 156, January 1, 1747.

12 The term is from Jouve Martín, who is referring to the late seventeenth century. Jouve Martín, *Esclavos de la ciudad letrada*, 22–23.

13 In the 1780s, the Tupac Amaru rebellion decreed the abolition of slavery despite the fact that the southern Andes, the rebels' base, had a minuscule black population.

14 Flores Galindo, *Aristocracia y plebe*; Aguirre, *Agentes de su propia libertad*; Velázquez Castro, *Las máscaras*; Warren, "Piety and Danger." Vivanco, "Bandolerismo colonial."

15 The literature on Tupac Amaru is vast. Leading studies include O'Phelan Godoy, *Un siglo de rebeliones*; Lewin, *La rebelión de Tupac Amaru*; and Stern, ed., *Resistance, Rebellion, and Consciousness*.

16 In 1752, after their greatest military success, their actions stopped. On Juan Santos, see Stern, "The Age of Andean Insurrection," in Stern, ed., *Resistance, Rebellion, and Consciousness*; Varese, *Salt of the Mountain*; Flores Galindo, "La chispa y el incendio," *Buscando*, 93–107.

17 O'Phelan Godoy, *Un siglo de rebeliones*, 79–94, 111; for a table of uprisings, 297–307. See also Stern, "The Age of Andean Insurrection," in Stern, ed., *Resistance, Rebellion, and Consciousness*, esp., 49. Pearce, "The Peruvian Population."

18 Conde de Superunda, *Relación*, 247.

19 These tensions are summarized in Andrien, *Andean Worlds*, chap. 7; Larson, *Colonialism and Agrarian Transformation*; Sala I Vila, *Y se armó*; Spalding, *Huarochirí*, esp. chap. 9.

20 Fray Calixto Tupac Inka, *Representación verdadera*. EL SEÑOR DON FERNANDO VI, PIDIENDO LOS ATIENDA Y REMEDIE, SACANDOLOS DEL AFRENTOSO VIPERIO Y OPROBIO EN QUE ESTAN MAS DE DOSCIENTOS AÑOS.

EXCLAMACION DE LOS INDIOS AMERICANOS, USANDO PARA ELLA DE LA MISMA QUE HIZO EL PROFETA JEREMIAS A DIOS EN EL CAPITULO 5 Y ULTIMO DE SUS LAMENTACIONES. For apocalyptic thought, see the introduction by José María Navarro, *Una denuncia profética*, and Mujica, "El arte y los sermones" in Mujica, *Barroco* (2002), 218–306, esp. 222–38.

21 O'Phelan Godoy has shown that noble Indians, who because of their status passed the *pureza de sangre* test, had limited access to the priesthood in the eighteenth century. O'Phelan Godoy, "'Ascender al estado eclesiástico.'" On this topic, see also Olaechea, "Sacerdotes indios" and "Los indios en las órdenes."

22 Fray Calixto Tupac Inca, *Representación*, in Loayza, *Fray Calixto*; O'Phelan Godoy, "'Ascender al estado eclesiástico'"; Bernales Ballesteros, "Fray Calixto"; Vargas Ugarte, *Historia General del Perú, Virreinato*, 227–56.

23 Peralta, "Tiranía o buen gobierno," 68–69, for a summary of different perspectives.

24 Fray Calixto Tupak Inca, *Representación*, in Loayza, *Fray Calixto*, 19.

25 See Navarro, *Una denuncia profética*. . . . *Planctus*, 170, where it goes as far as to claim, "No es rebelión de indios, sino fuga de las crueldades de la tiranía; y son los españoles quienes realmente aparecen rebeldes al Rey Católico." See also 428–29. Fray Calixto Tupak Inca, *Representación*, in Loayza, *Fray Calixto*, 16–17, for Juan Santos.

26 This is a key argument of Estenssoro, *Del paganismo a la santidad*. See also his essay "Construyendo la memoria" in anon., *Los incas, reyes del Perú*.

27 On the vacillations, see O'Phelan Godoy, *La gran rebelión*, 47–63; Garrett, *Shadow of Empire*, chap. 4.

28 Bernales Ballesteros, "Fray Calixto," 6.

29 Vargas Ugarte and Bernales Ballesteros believe it was by Garro; Estenssoro contends that it was by Cala.

30 Bernales Ballesteros, "Fray Calixto," summarizes this adventure.

31 Cited by Bernales Ballesteros, "Fray Calixto," 8.

32 Ibid., 8–10; Peralta, "Tiranía o buen gobierno," 81.

33 Loayza, *Fray Calixto*, 67.

34 For the decree, which mentions Isidoro de Cala, see Vargas Ugarte, *Impresos Peruanos*, 6:126. For the buildup to this decree and earlier changes such as a royal *cédula* in 1697, see O'Phelan Godoy, *La gran rebelión*, 47–68; Muro Orejón, "La igualdad."

35 Flores Galindo, *Buscando un inca*. See also Estenssoro, "Construyendo la memoria."

36 Nieto Vélez, "Una descripción," 288. He believes that the text is from 1751. I suspect it might be earlier, as damage from the earthquake is not mentioned in the review of Lima.

37 In his memoirs, Superunda mentions that the news reached Lima on February 21, Conde de Superunda, *Relación*, 265; Victorino Montero de Aguila puts

the date in January, Montero del Aguila, *Noticia Annalica*, 185. El *Día de Lima* (1748) includes the official announcement, which reached Lima via Panama and Quito, El *Día de Lima*, 107–08.

38 Montero del Aguila, *Noticia Annalica*, 184–85. For one account, see anon., *Pompa Funeral*.

39 Conde de Superunda, *Relación*, 265.

40 Anon., El *Día de Lima*, 54–56.

41 Ibid, 122–23.

42 Montero del Aguila, *Noticia Annalica*, 185–86; El *Día de Lima*, 116.

43 El *Día de Lima*, 174.

44 Ibid, 165.

45 El *Día de Lima*. On colonial rituals, see Osorio, "The King in Lima"; Ramos Sosa, *Arte Festivo*; and, with a different focus, Lohmann Villena, El *arte dramático*.

46 Archivo del Cabildo Metropolitano, Lima, *Serie A, Acuerdos Capitulares*, Libro XVI, p. 31, November 1747, Cabildo to Viceroy. El *Día de Lima* refers to this argument on 202–03; see 209 for the "universal missions."

47 Archivo del Cabildo Metropolitano, Lima, *Serie A, Acuerdos Capitulares*, Libro XVI, p. 31, November 1747, Cabildo to Viceroy.

48 El *Día de Lima*, 209.

49 El *Día de Lima*, 263.

50 Juan Carlos Estenssoro has shown that the 1748 *mascada* formed part of an effort by the indigenous royalty to enter the category of Old Christian. In paintings and rituals, they cast Atahualpa as a traitor and thus presented his enemy, Huascar, who did not have descendents, as the link between the Incas and the Spanish crown. If this interpretation of a continuous monarchy were accepted, theoretically, the discrimination against Indians could not be sustained. Estenssoro, *Del paganismo a la santidad*, esp. 493–516.

51 El *Día de Lima*, 256.

52 El *Día de Lima*, 259.

53 Ibid, 264, 265.

54 Fray Calixto Tupac Inca, *Representación*, in Loayza, *Fray Calixto*, 19–20.

55 Cited in Pérez-Mallaína Bueno, *Retrato*, 366–67.

56 Carrió de la Vandera emphasizes the conspirators' drunkenness. Carrió de la Vandera, *Reforma*, 48–49.

57 The quote and the mention of white shirts come from AGI, Lima, Leg. 988, *Noticias desde Payta*.

58 Carrió de la Vandera, *Reforma*, 48.

59 "Copia de una carta escrita en Lima sobre el levantamiento de los indios en el año de 1750," Biblioteca Colombiana, Seville. An almost identical copy of this letter can be found in the British Library, MS., additional, 13,976. I cite the Seville version as it has a bit more material.

60 Ibid.

61 Loayza, *Juan Santos*, 161. The document is from AGI, Lima, Leg. 988

62 In his memoirs as well as in a letter from September 24, 1750, Superunda writes that he first heard of the conspiracy on June 21. Conde de Superunda, *Relación*, 247; also in Loayza, *Juan Santos*, 164. The anonymous account in the Biblioteca Colombina puts the date at June 26, 1750.

63 On Cocharcas, see O'Phelan Godoy, "Una rebelión abortada," 15–17.

64 Diligencia—from Loayza, *Juan Santos*, 163; the account in the Biblioteca Colombina, "Copia de una carta," used the term "dar tormento" to refer to the rough treatment or torture of the prisoners.

65 "Copia de una carta," Biblioteca Colombina; Loayza mentions that Ayala perhaps escaped. Loayza, *Juan Santos*, 167. See also the "Relación y verdadero romance que declara la inconsiderada y atrevida sublevación . . . ," an anonymous poetic account of the uprising. Reprinted in Sotelo, *Las insurrecciones*, 21–30.

66 "Copia de una carta," Biblioteca Colombina.

67 AGI, Lima, Leg. 642, letter to Ensenada, March 12, 1752.

68 Loayza, *Juan Santos*, 166–67; noted by Spalding, *Huarochirí*, 274.

69 O'Phelan Godoy, "Una rebelión abortada," 28; "Copia de una carta," Biblioteca Colombina.

70 See Spalding, *Huarochirí*, 275–93; O'Phelan Godoy, *Un siglo*, 114. On his house, see AGI, Lima, Leg. 983, "Testimonio de los autos seguidos . . . ," a suit by census holders seeking discounts.

71 Loayza, *Juan Santos*, 172; Vargas Ugarte, *Historia General del Perú, Virreinato*, 251.

72 On Cabo and Ayala, Loayza, *Juan Santos*, 165–66, 171–72.

73 AGI, Lima, Leg. 417, letter from September 24, 1750. This version is slightly less diplomatic than that found in AGI, Lima, Leg. 988, and published by Francisco Loayza, *Juan Santos*; the quote is found on 163. Repeated in letter of January 15, 1747. Loayza, *Fray Calixto*, 85; and AGI, Lima, Leg. 417, in which the viceroy refers to them as people of "little talent."

74 *El Día de Lima*, 255, 247. I did not find reference to a third rebel leader in this account.

75 Loayza, *Juan Santos* 165.

76 Flores Galindo, *Buscando un Inca*, 90; the history of the prophecies and her invocations is told in Mujica, *Rosa Limensis*, 340–47; Mujica, "Arte e identidad," in *Mujica Barroco* (1), 51–53, for Inquisition prohibition. See also O'Phelan Godoy, *La gran rebelión*, 37–45.

77 The quote comes from "Copia de una carta," Biblioteca Colombina. Information on the uprising from Loayza, *Juan Santos*, 161–78. These events are also summarized in Spalding, *Huarochirí*, 274–75. Loayza, *Juan Santos*, 172, mentions the map and Ayala and the participant who tried to join Juan Santos.

78 Don Sebastián Franco de Melo. "Diario Histórico del Lebantamiento de la Provincia de Huarochirí, y su Pacificación." Museo Mitre, Buenos Aires, 1767, 36. Ice was another important product.

79 Descripción, in Melo, "Diario Histórico."

80 In Loayza, *Juan Santos*, 169.

81 "Copia de una carta," Biblioteca Colombina.

82 Huarochirí is fortunate to have its historian—Karen Spalding. My review of the uprising parallels and builds from hers, as does my summary of the state of *kurakas*. For the demographic crisis of the early eighteenth century, see Pearce, "The Peruvian Population."

83 "Copia de una carta," Biblioteca Colombina; also O'Phelan Godoy, *Un siglo*, 113.

84 Melo, "Diario Histórico," 9b-10.

85 Melo, "Diario Histórico," 11b. See also *Gazeta de Lima*, 13 (1750), for a slightly different account. I thank Karen Spalding for providing me with a copy of this rare imprint.

86 Melo, "Diario Histórico," 12b-13b. For accusations against Araujo for abusive behavior as corregidor, see AGI, Escribanía de Camara, Leg. 526B.

87 Melo describes these efforts with admiration, Melo, "Diario Histórico," 14. See also Spalding, *Huarochirí*, 277.

88 "Excitándolos a la venganza de los castigados en Lima." *La Gazeta de Lima*, no. 13.

89 Conde de Superunda, *Relación*, 248. He acknowledged in the following paragraph, however, the Indians' use of letters, their organization, and quick assumption of control of roads and bridges.

90 These questionably gory details are in the Biblioteca Colombina account. A 1792 account by Miguel Cebrián y Martínez claimed that the rebels "followed their Gentile custom of drinking the blood of the cadavers." Deustua Pimentel, "Reminiscencias incaicas," 147. On tendentious accounts of rebel (Indian) violence and apostasy, see Walker, *Smoldering Ashes*, chap. 2.

91 Cited in Spalding, *Huarochirí*, 282, which highlights how the Spanish took advantage of internal divisions. See ibid., 272, for a summary of Melo. I've changed the translation slightly ("musket" for "shotgun").

92 Melo, "Diario Histórico," 40b. The Biblioteca Colombina account notes with satisfaction that the "heavy hand of punishment. . . . Taking lives and livestock" worked. "Copia de una carta," Biblioteca Colombina. For a poem by El Ciego de la Merced celebrating the marquis's heroics, see Fray Francisco del Castillo Andraca y Tamayo, *Obras*, 142-56.

93 Melo, "Diario Histórico," 43b.

94 Ibid., 49b.

95 Ibid., 45.

96 Ibid., 50-55; see also Spalding, *Huarochirí*, 288-91, for the execution.

97 Scarlett O'Phelan Godoy has found important ties between the Cercado conspirators and the Huarochirí uprising, particularly the suspicious behavior of Huarochirí potmakers (*olleros*) in Lima in the late 1740s. O'Phelan Godoy "Una rebelión abortada," 17-18.

220

98 Versions of this letter are found in AGI, Lima, Leg. 988, and Lima, Leg. 417; also in Loayza, *Juan Santos*; the quote is on 174.

99 Loayza, *Juan Santos*, 164, see also Loayza, *Fray Calixto*, 86, which refers to Indian drunkenness. Letter from January 15, 1757.

100 Loayza, *Juan Santos*, 175.

101 Ibid., 176.

102 Ibid. See also Ramón, "Urbe y orden," 305–06.

103 Mujica, "Arte e identidad," 30.

104 Loayza, *Juan Santos*, 177.

105 See also Carrió de la Vandera on "cholitos and cholitas" brought to Lima. Carrió de la Vandera, *Reforma*, 52–53.

106 Loayza, *Juan Santos*, 178; the quote "necio descuidado" is on 167. For more on the military situation, see AGI, Leg. 643, March 13, 1752; Campbell, *The Military*, chaps. 1, 2.

107 Varese, *Salt of the Mountain*; Flores Galindo, *Buscando un inca*, chap. 3, "La chispa y el incendio." Yet by 1756 the rebels stopped their incursions, and Juan Santos himself seemed to vanish.

108 Loayza, *Fray Calixto*, 87–91; or Bernales Ballesteros, "Fray Calixto," 11.

109 Loayza, *Fray Calixto*, 88.

110 Bernales Ballesteros, "Fray Calixto," 14.

Epilogue

1 AGI, Lima, Leg. 787.

2 Vargas Ugarte, *Historia del Perú, Virreinato*, 279–82. Barroeta would continue as Granada's archbishop until his death in 1775. For the accusations against the viceroy and his defense, see Manso de Velasco, "Confession del Theniente General Conde de Superunda." More documentation on Manso de Velasco can be found in the Fondo Samaniego in the Archivo Provincial de Alava, Sección: Fondos Especiales, Familia Velasco Superunda. I would like to thank Dr. Pilar Latasa for her help with these.

3 Lynch, *Bourbon Spain*, summarizes the Madrid riots and their impact, 261–68, the subject of much writing in Spain then and now. For the reforms' theoretical underpinnings, see Fraile, "Putting Order"; for their impact in Mexico, Viqueira Albán, *Propriety*, 210. On Amat and Lima, see Ramón, "Urbe y orden"; Vargas Ugarte, *Historia del Perú, Virreinato*, esp. 304–08; Walker, "Civilize or Control?" The key blueprint is Jorge Escobedo, *División de quarteles*. On Escobedo and his reforms, see Fisher, *Government and Society*, 69–71, 241–42, and Moreno Cebrián, "Cuarteles, barrios, y calles."

4 Lynch, *Bourbon Spain*, 21.

5 Schultes and de Jaramillo-Arango, *The Journals*, 56.

6 The quote comes from Alan Soons's introduction to the text. Esteban Terralla Landa, *Lima por dentro y fuera*, 1978 [1797], Soons, vii.

7   Terralla Landa, *Lima por dentro y fuera*, quote from 18, section on bread, 13.

8   Ibid., quotes from 15.

9   Jerónimo Valdés, "Refutación al manifiesto," in Conde de Torata, *Documentos para la historia*, 2:72. Cited in Marks, "Deconstructing Legitimacy."

10   Flores Galindo, *Aristocracia y plebe*, passim.

11   I discuss these campaigns briefly in Walker, "Civilize or Control?" See also Flores Galindo, *Aristocracia y plebe*, 153–55; Cosamalón, *Indios detrás de la muralla*. On the social impact and contradictions of the Bourbon Reforms, particularly insightful are Twinam, *Public Lives, Public Secrets*; Knight, *Mexico: The Colonial Era*, 240–69. On racial discourse and tensions in the eighteenth century, specifically regarding Afro-Peruvians, see Aguirre, *Breve historia de la esclavitud*; Flores Galindo, *Aristocracia y plebe*; Vélazquez Castro, *Las máscaras*.

12   The role of Lima's upper classes in the War of Independence has prompted intermittent debate. One classic and critical work is Bonilla and Spalding, *La independencia*; Flores Galindo, *Aristocracia y plebe*, is, once again, a key text. Marks, "Deconstructing the Legitimacy," which examines the city's merchants, should prompt a new round of debate and discussion.

13   Divisions with the Church also became more and more evident. The War of Independence (1808–25) brought these rifts to the surface, as some priests backed the patriot cause while others were steadfast supporters of the Spanish.

14   Documents in Vargas Ugarte, *Concilios Limenses* from 1769 and the Concilio of 1772 indicate the continued concern about immoral dress, priests' misbehavior (particularly concubines and gambling), the numbers of nuns, and the general moral disorder of the city. One priest ends his denunciation of the excess population of the convents by noting how this is tied to "two structural vices of colonial society, the propensity to waste and splendor and the disinclination to work and personal effort." Vargas Ugarte, *Concilios Limenses*, 3:168. On anguished reactions to earthquakes well after 1746, see the accounts in Odriozola, *Los terremotos*.

15   O'Phelan Godoy, *Un siglo*; Serulnikov, *Subverting Colonial Authority*.

Bibliography

Archives Consulted

Archivo General de la Nación (Lima)
Archivo San Francisco (Lima)
Archivo Arzobispal de Lima (Lima)
Archivo del Cabildo Metropolitano (Lima)
Biblioteca Nacional del Perú (Lima)
Universidad Ruiz de Montoya (Colección Vargas Ugarte)
    (Lima)
Archivo de Indias (Seville)
Biblioteca Colombina (Seville)
Archivo Histórico Nacional (Madrid)
Biblioteca Nacional (Madrid)
Archivo del Museo Naval (Madrid)
Biblioteca del Palacio Real (Madrid)
British Library (London)
Archivo Histórico de Propaganda Fide (Rome)
Library of Congress (Washington, D.C.)
John Carter Brown Library (Providence)
Harthe-Terré Collection, Tulane University Library
    (New Orleans)
Vatican Collection, St. Louis University (St. Louis)

224   Published Primary Sources
and Document Collections

Alfonso X, Rey de Castilla y León. *Las Siete Partidas del Soberano Rey don Alonso el Nono, nuevamente glosadas por el Licenciado Gregorio Lopez del Consejo Real de Indias de Su Majestad.* Vol. 2 (3). Madrid [Salamanca]: Boletín Oficial del Estado [Andrea de Portonaris], 1974 [1555].

Alvarez de Ron y Suñiga, Doct. Don Antonio Joseph. *Repressentacion Juridica, Allegato Reverente, que se haze por parte de las Religiones de esta noble Capital.* Al Excmo Senhor Don Joseph Manso de Velasco. Lima: Francisco Sobrino en Calle de Barranca, 1747.

Amat y Junient, Manuel de. *Memoria de Gobierno.* Edited by Vicente Rodríguez Casado and Florentino Pérez Embid. Seville: EEH-A, 1947.

Anon. *Individual y verdadera relación de la extrema ruyna que padeció la Ciudad de los Reyes, Lima, Capital del Reyno del Perú, con el horrible Temblor de tierra . . .* Lima: Imprenta que estaba en la Calle de las Mercaderes, 1746. Also in Odriozola, *Terremotos,* 148–71.

———. *Individual y verdadera relación.* México, Impreso en Lima reimpreso en México: Por la viuda de J.B. de Hogal, 1747.

———. *Puntual descripcion, funebre lamento, y sumptuoso tumulo, de la regia doliente pompa, con que en la santa iglesia metropolitana de la ciudad de los reyes, Lima, . . . reales exequias de la serenissima señora, la señora donha Mariana Josepha de Austria.* Lima, 1756.

———. *True and Particular Relation of the Dreadful Earthquake which happen'd at Lima the Capital of Peru . . .* Translated by Anonymous. 2d ed. London: Printed for T. Osborne in Gray's Inn, 1748.

———. *El Día de Lima. Proclamación real. Que de el Nombre Augusto de el Supremo Señor.* Lima, 1748.

———. *A True and Particular Relation of the Dreadful Earthquake which happen'd at Lima, the Capital of Peru, and the neighbouring Port of Callao, on the 28th of October, 1746. With an Account likewise of every Thing material that passed there afterwards to the End of November following. Published at Lima by Command of the Viceroy, and Translated from the Original Spanish, By a Gentleman who resided many Years in those Countries.* Edited by B. Franklin and D. Hall. Philadelphia: London Printed: Philadelphia Reprinted, and sold by B. Franklin and D. Hall at the New Printing-Office, near the Market, 1749, 1749.

———. *Por parte de los dueños de navios en la causa que siguen con los abastecedores de Pan de esta Ciudad, para que se declare que los Trigos que se perdieron en las Bodegas del Callao, con la Inundacion del Mar la noche del dia 28 de Octubre de 746 perecieron a los Abastecedores que los havian comprado, y no a los vendedores, sin embargo de que no se huviessen medido ni entregado por los Bodegueros, en los casos que separadamente se pondrán en este Papel, para que sin confusion se pueda dar una regla general comprehensive de todos.* Lima, 1749.

———. *Relacion y verdadero romance que declara la inconsiderada, y atrevida sublevacion, que intentaban hacer los Indios mal acordados y algunso Mestizos de la Ciudad de Lima. Se da razon de las promptissimas y bien ordenadas providencias que se dieron para embarazo de tan odiosa execucion, y del justo castigo que se dio a los culpados.* Lima, 1750.

———. *The Theory and History of Earthquakes containing . . .* London: J. Newberry and others, 1750.

———. *A True and Particular Relation of the Dreadful.* Boston: Printed and sold by D. Fowle in Ann-Street and Z. Fowle in Meddlestreet, 1755?

———. *Pompa Funeral en las exequias del Catholico rey de España y de las Indias Don Fernando VI, nuestro Señor que mandó a hacer en esta Iglesia metropolitana de Lima a 20 de Junio de 1760.* Lima: Imprenta de la Calle Real de Palacio, 1760.

Barbinais, Le Gentil de la. *Nouveau voyage autour du monde.* Amsterdam, 1727.

Barrenechea, Juan de. *Relox Astronomico de temblores de la tierra, secreto maravilloso de la naturaleza, descubierto y hallado por D. Juan de Barrenechea, substituto de la Cathedra de Prima de Mathematicas de esta Real Universidad de San Marcos de la Ciudad de Lima.* Lima: Imprenta Antuerpiana, que está en la Calle Real de Palacio, 1725.

Barroeta y Angel, Pedro Antonio. *Carta Pastoral que el Illmo. S. D. D. Pedro Antonio de Barroeta y Angel, Arzobispo de los Reyes, dirige al Venerable Clero, y Amado pueblo de su diocesis, con ocasion de las noticias, que se han participado de España del gran Terremoto, que el dia primero de Noviembre de 1755, se experimentó con grandes estragos en la Europa, y otras partes, para que con la prompta Penitencia aplaquen la Divina Justicia, que allá castiga, y acá nos amenaza.* Lima: Plazuela de San Christobal, 1756.

Betagh, Captain. "Captain Betagh's Observations on the Country of Peru, and Its Inhabitants, During His Captivity." In *A General Collection of the Best and Most Interesting Voyages and Travels in All Parts of the World; Many of Which Are Now Translated into English,* edited by John Pinkerton, Vol. 14, 1–29. London: Printed for Longman, Hurst, Rees, Orme, and Brown, Paternoster-Row; and Cadell and Davies, in the Strand, 1813.

Bouguer, M. "An Abridged Relation of a Voyage to Peru. . . ." In *A General Collection of the Best and Most Interesting Voyages and Travels in All Parts of the World; Many of Which Are Now Translated into English,* edited by John Pinkerton, Vol. 14, 270–312. London: Printed for Longman, Hurst, Rees, Orme, and Brown, Paternoster-Row; and Cadell and Davies, in the Strand, 1813.

Bravo de Lagunas y Castilla, Pedro. *Colección Legal de Cartas, Dictamenes, y otros Papeles en Derecho Dedicados al Sr. Dr. D. Francisco de Herboso y Figueroa.* Lima: Oficina de los Huérfanos, 1761.

Bravo de Lagunas y Castilla, Pedro José. *Voto Consultivo que Ofrece al Excelentissimo Señor Don Joseph Antonio Manso de Velasco.* Lima, 1755.

Bravo de Lagunas y Castilla, Pedro Joseph. *Discurso historico-juridico del origen, fundacion, reedificación, Derechos, y Exenciones del Hospital de SAN LAZARO de Lima.* Lima: Oficina de los Huérfanos, 1761.

Bravo del Rivero, Don Pedro. "Trajes inhonestos de las mujeres, de D Pedro Bravo del Rivero, Obispo de Arequipa." Lima, 1744.

Calatayud, Pedro, SJ. *Juizio de los Sacerdotes, Doctrina Practica y anatonima de sus conciencias, dispuestas en seis platicas que suele hazer al gremio Eclesiastico en sus missiones, y una Instruccion que da a un ilustradisimo señor Obispo, el M.R.P. Pedro de Calatayud. . . . dedicados al ilmo. Don Thomas Joseph de Montes, Arzobispo obispo de Cartagena y Murcia.*

226   reimpresión ed. Lima: Plazuela de San Christoval. Por Juan Joseph Gonzalez de
          Cosio, 1753.

Cangas, Gregorio de. *Descripción en diálogo de la ciudad de Lima entre un peruano práctico y
un bisoño chapetón.* Edited by Camilo G. Vicente and José L. Lenci, presentación e
introducción. Lima: BCR, 1997.

Carrió de la Vandera, Alonso. *Reforma del Perú.* Edited by Pablo Macera. Lima: Universidad Mayor de San Marcos, 1966 (1782).

Cavera de Toledo, D. Juan. "Auto del Obispo de Arequipa, D. Juan Cavera de Toledo,
reprimiendo el abuso de los trajes femininos sobre todo en Moquegua." Lima,
1735.

Cevallos, Doct. D. Josef. *Respuesta a la carta del Ilmo y Rmo. Señor D. Fray Miguel de San
Josef, Obispo de Guadix, y Baza, . . . sobre varios escritos a cerca del Terremoto. . . . por el Doct.
D. Josef Cevallos, Presbytero, Doctor Theologo, del Gremio, y Claustro de la Universidad de
Sevilla. . . . del Orden de San Agustín de esta Ciudad.* Seville: Imprenta de la Universidad
y Libreria de D. Joseph Navarro, Armijo, en Calle de Genova, 1757?

Cobo, Padre Bernabé. "Historia de la Fundación de Lima." In *Colección de Historiadores
del Perú,* vol. I, edited by M. González de la Rosa. Lima: Imprenta Liberal, 1882.

Cook, Noble David. *Numeración general de todas las Personas de ambos sexos, edades y calidades que se ha echo en la ciudad de Lima. año de 1700.* Lima: COFIDE, 1985.

Córdova Salinas, Diego de. *Crónica Franciscana de las Provincias del Perú.* Washington,
D.C.: Academy of Franciscan History, 1957 (1651).

Davin, Padre Diego. *Cartas edificantes, y curiosas escritas de las Misiones Estrangeras, y de
Levante Por algunos Missioneros de la Compañia de Jesus, traducidas por el Padre Diego Davin
de la misma Compañia.* 16 vols. Vol. 15. Madrid: Viuda de Manuel Fernandez y del
Supremo Consejo de la Inquisición, 1756.

De la Cruz, O.F.M., Fray Lauerano. *Descripción de los Reynos del Perú con particular noticia
de lo hecho por los Franciscanos.* Lima: PUC, Banco Central de la Reserva, 1999.

del Villar, Juan. *Relacion espantosa del Monstruo mas abominable que se ha descubierto en
mucho tiempo en este Reyno del Perú, y nuevo mundo de la America.* Lima: n.p., n.d.

Dunbar Temple, Ella. *La Gaceta de Lima del siglo XVIII. Facsímiles de seis ejemplares raros de
este periódico, Registro Histórico.* Lima: Universidad Nacional Mayor de San Marcos,
1965.

Eder, Francisco Javier. *Descripción de la Provincia de los Mojos en el Reino del Perú.* Translated by P. Fray Nicolás Armentia. La Paz: Imp. de "El siglo industrial," 1888.

Escobedo, Jorge. *División de quarteles y barrios e instrucción para el establecimiento de alcaldes
de barrio en la capital de Lima.* Lima, 1785.

Esquivel y Navia, Diego de. *Noticias cronológicas de la gran ciudad del Cuzco.* 2 vols. Lima:
Fundación Augusto N. Wiese, 1980.

Feijoo de Sosa, Miguel. *Relación descriptiva de la ciudad y provincia de Trujillo del Perú.*
Lima: Banco Industrial del Perú, 1984.

Fernández de Castro, Don Gerónimo. *Elisio peruano. Solemnidades heróicas, y festivas
demonstraciones de jubilos, que se han logrado en la muy noble, y muy Leal Ciudad de los
Reyes Lima, Cabeza de la America austral, y Corte del Perú, en la Aclamacion del excelso*

nombre del muy Alta, muy Poderoso, siempre Augusto, Catholico Monarcha de las Españas, y Emperador de las Americas Don Luis Primero . . . Lima: Francisco Sobrino, Impressor del Santo Oficio, en el Portal de los Escribanos, 1725.

Frezier, Mons. *A Voyage to the South-Sea and along the Coasts of Chili and Peru, in the Years 1712, 1713, and 1714. Particularly.* . . . London: Jonah Bowyer, 1717.

Hales, Stephen. *Some Considerations on the causes of earthquakes which were read before the Royal Society, April 5, 1750.* 2d ed., corrected ed. London: R. Manyby and H.S. Cox, 1750.

——. *Histoire des tremblemens de terre arrive's a Lima, capitale du Perout, Et Autres Lieux; Avec la Description du Perou, Et des recherches sur les Causes Phisiques des Tremblemens de Terre, par M. Hales de laSocieé Royale de Londres, & autres Phisiciens. Avec Cartes & Figures. Traduite de L'Anglois, Premiere Partie.* La Haye, 1752.

"Histoire de L'Académie Royale des Science, 1760, Avec les Mémoires de Mathématique & de Physique," Paris: L'Imprimerie Royal, 1761.

John Carter Brown Library. "A Facsimile of the First Issue of the GAZETA DE LIMA with a description of a file for the years 1744–1763." Boston: Merrymount Press, 1908.

Juan, Jorge, and Antonio de Ulloa. *A Voyage to South America,* Borzoi Books. New York: Alfred A. Knopf, 1964.

——. *Discourse and Political Reflections on the Kingdoms of Peru.* Edited by John Te-Paske. Norman: University of Oklahoma Press, 1978 [1826]. [Translation of Noticias Secretas.]

Konetzke, Richard. *Colección de Documentos para la Historia de la Formación Social de Hispanoamérica, 1493–1810.* 4 vols. Madrid: CSIC, 1962.

Lanuza y Sotelo, Eugenio. *Viaje ilustrado a los reinos del Perú.* Edited by Antonio Garrido Aranda and Patricia Hidalgo Nuchera, eds. Lima: PUC, 1998.

Leon Pinelo, Antonio. *Velos en los rostros de las mujeres: sus consecuencias y daños.* Vol. 4: *Curiosa Americana.* Santiago: Centro de Investigaciones de Historia Americana, Universidad de Chile, 1966 [1641].

Lequanda, José Ignacio. "Descripción del Puerto del Callao." In *Documentos Literarios,* edited by Manuel de Odriozola, Vol. 4, 369–83. Lima: Imprenta del Estado, 1874.

Liquori, Alfonso María (Saint Alfonso de Ligorio). *Discursos místicos.* Barcelona: Imprenta de Manuel Saurí, ed., 1842.

Llano Zapata, José Eusebio. *Carta o diario que escribió D. J. Eusebio de Llano y Zapata a su mas venerado amigo y docto corresponsal el Dr. D. Ignacio Chirivoga y Daza, canónigo de la sta. iglesia de Quito.* Lima: Con Licencia del Real y Superior Gobierno Reimpresa en Lima, Calle de la Barranca por Francisco Sobrino, 1747?

——. *Respuesta dada al rey nuestro señor D. Fernando el sexto sobre una pregunta, que S. M. hizo a un matematico, y experimentado en las tierras de Lima, sobre el terremoto, acaecido en el dia primero de noviembre de 1755.* Seville: López de Haro, 1756.

——. *Carta Persuasiva al Señor Don Ignacio de Escandon, Colegial Theologo, que fue en el Insigne y Mayor Colegio de San Luis de Quito, Thesorero de las Reales Caxas de Cuenca, Regidor, y Alcalde Ordinario de esta Ciudad, y Comandante General de las Tropas Auxiliares de*

228   la de Guayaquil, & Sobre Assunto de Escribir la Historia-Literaria de la America Meridional. Cadiz: Don Francisco Rioja, frente de Candelari, 1768.

———. *Memorias histórico, físicas, crítico, apologéticas de la América Meridional.* Edited by Ricardo Ramírez Castañeda, Antonio Garrido, Luis Millones Figueroa, Víctor Peralta, Charles Walker. Lima: IFEA, PUC, Universidad Nacional Mayor de San Marcos, 2005.

———. "Observacion diaria critico-historico-meteorologico, contiene todo lo acaecido en Lima desde primero de Marzo de 174- hasta 28 de Octubre del mismo. . . ." In Odriozola, *Terremotos,* 110–47.

Loayza, Francisco A. *Juan Santos, el Invencible: manuscritos del año de 1742 al año de 1755.* Lima: Imp. Domingo Miranda, 1942.

———. *Fray Calixto Tupak Inka. Documentos originales y, en su mayoría, totalmente desconocidos, auténticos de este apóstol indio, valiente defensor de su raza, desde el año de 1746 a 1760.* Edited by Francisco Loayza. Lima: Imprenta Domingo Miranda, 1948.

Lozano, Pedro, "Relación del terremoto." In Odriozola, *Terremotos,* 36–47.

Manso de Velasco, José. *Informes que hacen al Rey N.S. (Que Dios Guarde) y a su Consejo Real de Indias, El Virrey de Lima, Las Reales Audiencias, y a los dos reverendissimos Prelados Generales, Los Cabildos Eclesiasticos (en sedes vacantes) De Las Ciudades de Lima, la Plata, Bueno-Ayres y el Señor Obispo del Tucumán, y otras ciudades, y Villas mas populosas, del fruto que los Misioneros Apostolicos de la Religión Seraphica, y Colegio de Santa Rosa de Ocopa, han hecho con sus Misiones en las Provincias de Catholicas, y Gentiles del Reyno del Perú, y de los Misioneros Apstolicos, que han muerto flechados por la Fe.* Lima, 175?

———. *Confession del Theniente General Conde de Superunda, virrey que fué del Perú, y Vocal de la Junta, que por preventiva orden de S.M. se formó en la plaza de la Habana, para tratar, y deliberar quanto conviniesse a su defensa; empezada hoy tres de octubre de 1763 en su posada, en virtud del Acuerdo de la Junta de Generales del primero de corriente.* Madrid, 1763?

Member of Parliament in Town. *Reflections Physical and Moral, Upon the Various and numerous uncommon Phenomena in the Air, Water, or Earth, which have happened from the Earthquake at Lima, to the present Time. In a Series of Familiar Letters from a Member of Parliament in Town to his Friend in the Country.* London: A. Millar in the Strand, 1756.

Mercurio Peruano, 1791–95. Edición facsimilar. 12 volumes. Lima: Biblioteca Nacional del Perú, 1964.

Moncada, Doctor Balthasar de. *Descripción de la casa fabricada en Lima, corte del Perú, para que las Señoras ilustres de ella, y las demas mugeres devotas, y las que desean servir a Dios Nuestro Señor, pueden tener en total retiro, y con toda abstraccion, y direccion necesaria Los exercicios de San Ignacio de Loyola.* Seville: Joseph Padrino, Impressor y Mercader de Libros, en Calle Genova, 1757.

Montero del Aguila, Victorino. *Desolación de la ciudad de Lima, y Dilubio del Puerto del Callao. Cerrose esta relación en seis de noviembre de quarenta y seis, y sigue la calamidad, que dará matheria a mas larga explicación de los venideros sucessos.* Lima: Imprenta nueva, que estaba en la Calle de los Mercaderes, 1746. Also in Odriozola, *Terremotos,* 172–77.

———. *Noticia Annalica y Estado, que tiene el puerto del Callao, y la Ciudad de Lima, a el año cumplido de su desolación, y ruyna, que lo hace en este mes de Octubre de 1747.* Lima, 1747. Also in Odriozola, Terremotos, 177–193.

———. *Estado Político del Reyno del Perú, Ministros Relaxados: Thesoros con Pobreza: Fertilidad sin Cultivo: Sabiduria desestimada: Milicia sin Honor. . . .* Madrid, 1747.

Mugaburu, Joseph and Francisco. *Chronicle of Colonial Lima: The Diary of Joseph and Francisco Mugaburu, 1640–1697.* Translated by Robert R. Miller. Norman: University of Oklahoma Press, 1975.

Odriozola, Manuel de. *Terremotos. Colección de las relaciones de los más notables que ha sufrido esta capital y que la han arruinado. . . .* Lima, 1863.

———. *Documentos Literarios del Perú.* 11 vols. Lima: Imprenta del Estado, 1874.

Olavide, Pablo de. *Obras selectas.* Edited by Estuardo Nuñez, Biblioteca Clásicos del Perú, #3. Lima: Ediciones del Centenario Banco de Crédito del Perú, 1987.

Ovando, Marques de. "Carta que escribió el Marqués de Obando [sic]," in Odriozola, Terremotos, 47–69.

Pacheco, Doña Antonia. *Por parte de Doña Antonia Pacheco, se ponen en consideracion de V.S. los fundamentos de Derecho que hazen a su favor, para que en Justicia se le absuelva de la demanda puesta por los Dueños de los Trigos perdidos en la innundación de Callao.* Lima.

Papió, Joan. *La Historia d'Escornalbou. Facsímil del libro de.* Volls: Dep. de Cultura de la Generalitat de Catalunya, 1987 (1765).

Peralta Barnuevo, Pedro de. *Descripción de las Fiestas Reales.* Lima, 1723.

———. *Lima Fundada o Conquista del Perú.* Lima: Aurelio Alfaro, 1732 [1863].

Potau, D.D. Joseph. *Lágrimas de Lima en las exequias del Ilmo. Sr. D. D. Pedro Antonio de Barroeta y Angel, del Consejo de su Mag. Dignisimo Arzobispo, que fue de esta Santa Iglesia Metropolitana, y de la Granada, en donde falleció.* Lima: Imprenta de los Niños Huerfanos, 1776.

Ramírez Orta, Dr. D. Juan Agustín. *Soli Deo Honor, et Gloria Norte de Pureza, y claros desengaños, para persuadir a las mugeres, vayan honestas en sus trages, y escotes, Sacado de varios tratados de diferentes autores, que tratan largamente de esta materia. Por el Dr. D. Juan Agustín Ramírez, Canonigo Magistral de Calatayud, y Examinador Synodal del Arzobispado de Valencia. Reimpreso en Lima a diligencia de los RR. PP. Missioneros Apostolicos de San Francisco.* Lima: Imprenta nueva de la Calle de los Mercaderes, 1744.

Ruiz Cano y Galiano, Doctor Don Francisco Antonio. *Jubilos de Lima en Dedicación de su Santa Iglesia Cathedral, Instaurada (En Gran Parte) de la Ruina, que padeció con el Terremoto de el año de 1746. A Esfuerzos de el Activo zelo de el Exmo. Señor D. Joseph Manso de Velasco Conde de Super-Unda. . . .* Lima: Calle del Palacio, 1755.

———. *Lima gozosa descripcion de las festibas demonstraciones, con que esta ciudad, capital de la America meridional, celebro la Real proclamacion de el Nombre Augusto el Catholico Monarcha Señor Carlos III, nuestro señor (que Dios guarde).* Lima, 1760.

Sánchez, M. R. P., Juan. *Sermon que en la missa de accion de Gracias por la Reedificacion, o nueva construccion total del Hospital de San Lazaro de la Ciudad de Lima; Predico, en la Iglesia Parroquial del mismo Titulo, perteneciente a dicho Hospital, el M. R. P. Juan Sanchez de la Compañía de Jesus, el dia 23 de Abril de 1748. Lo dedica al Excmo. Sor. D. Joseph Antonio Manso de Velasco, Conde de Superunda . . .* Lima: Imprenta Nueva, que está en la Casa de los Niños Expositos, 1758.

230   Schultes, Richard Evans, and María José Nemry von Thenen de Jaramillo-Arango, translators. *The Journals of Hipólito Ruiz. Spanish Botanist in Peru and Chile 1777–1788.* Portland: Timber Press, 1998.

Sempere y Guariños, Juan. *Historia del Luxo, y de las leyes suntuarias de España.* 2 vols. Madrid, 1788.

St. Malo, Conde of St. *A Voyage to Peru; Performed by the Conde of St. Malo, in the Years 1745, 1746, 1747, 1748, 1749. Written by the Chaplain.* London: R. Griffiths, 1753.

Superunda, Conde de. *Relación de gobierno, Perú (1745–1761).* Edited and introduced by Alfredo Moreno Cebrián. Madrid: CSIC, 1983.

Taborga y Durana, D. Juan. "Vicario general de Arequipa, D. Juan Taborga y Durana sobre los trajes inhonestos de las mujeres 1747, dean de Arequipa." 1747.

Terralla Landa, Esteban. *Lima por dentro y fuera.* Edited by Alan Soons. Exeter: University of Exeter, 1978 [1797].

Torata, Conde de [Fernando Valdés y Hector] comp. *Documentos para la historia de la guerra separatista del Perú.* 4 vols. Madrid: Imprenta de la Viuda de M. Minuesa de los Rios, 1894–1898. Vol. 2: Valdés, Jerónimo. *Refutación que hace el Mariscal de Campo D. Jerónimo de Valdés del Manifiesto que el Teniente General D. Joaquín de la Pezuela imprimió en 1821 a su regreso del Perú.*

Tristan del Pozo, Don Juan Antonio. *Relacion Funebre, Poema Tragico, que del funesto terremoto acaecido en la corte del Perú y deplorable inundacion del presidio y Puerto del Callao, año de 1746.* Lima, 1746.

Ulloa, Juan de. *Viaje a la América meridional.* Edited by Andrés Saumell. Vol. b, *Crónicas de America.* Madrid: Historia 16, 1990.

Valdivieso y Torrejón, Dr. Don Miguel. *Allegación Jurídica por parte de los Vezinos Dueños de las casas de esta Capital, sobre la rebaja de los censos, por la ruina, que padecieron con el terremoto de 28 de Octubre de 1746.* Lima: Antonio Gutierrez en la imprenta que está en la Plazuela Marques de Otero, 1748, 1748.

Vargas Ugarte S.J., Rubén. *Manuscritos Peruanos en las Biblioteca de América.* 11 vols. Vol. 4, *Biblioteca Peruana.* Lima: Cia. de Impresiones y Publicidad, 1945.

———. *Relaciones de viajes.* Vol. 5, *Biblioteca Peruana.* 11 vols. Lima: Compañía de Impresiones y Publicidad, 1947.

———. *Impresos Peruanos Publicados en el Extranjero.* 11 vols. Vol. 6, *Biblioteca Peruana.* Lima: Cia. de Impresiones y Publicidad, 1949.

———. *Impresos Peruanos (1700–1762).* 11 vols. Vol. 9, *Biblioteca Peruana.* Lima: Cia. de Impresiones y Publicidad, 1956.

Voltaire. *Candide.* Edited by Daniel Gordon, translator, and introduction, *The Bedford Series in History and Culture.* Boston: Bedford/St. Martin's, 1999 [1759].

Von Tschudi, Johann Jakob. *Testimonio del Perú.* Lima: Consejo Económico Consultativo-Suiza-Peru, 1966.

Secondary Sources

Acosta Rodriguez, Antonio. "La reforma eclesiástica y misional (siglo XVIII)." In *Procesos americanos hacia la redefinición colonial*, edited by Enrique Tandeter, Jorge Hidalgo Lehuede, 349–74. Madrid: UNESCO, TROTTA, 2000.

Adas, Michael. *Prophets of Rebellion: Millenarian Protest Movements against the European Colonial Order*. Chapel Hill: University of North Carolina Press, 1979.

Aguirre, Carlos. *Agentes de su propia libertad*. Lima: PUC, 1993.

———. *Breve historia de la esclavitud en el Perú: Una herida que no deja de sangrar*. Lima: Fondo Editorial del Congreso del Perú, 2005.

Aguirre Medrano, Fidel. *Historia de los hospitales coloniales de hispanoamérica*. Vol. II, Peru. Miami: Editorial Interamerica, Inc., 1996.

Alayza Paz Soldan, Francisco. *"Temblores y terremotos" (Estudio Geo-Sismico y Constructivo)*. Offprint of Boletín de Minas. Lima: Talleres Gráficos P.T.C.M., 1935.

Aldana Rivera, Susana. "¿Ocurrencias del tiempo? Fenómenos naturales y sociedad en el Perú colonial," In *Historia y desastres en América Latina*, edited by Virginia García Acosta, 1:167–94. Lima: La Red-CIESAS, 1997.

Andrews, William D. "The Literature of the 1727 New England Earthquake." *Early American Literature* 7 (1973): 281–94.

Andrien, Kenneth J. "The *Noticias secretas de América* and the Construction of a Governing Ideology for the Spanish American Empire." *Colonial Latin American Review* 7, no. 2 (1998): 175–92.

———. *Andean Worlds: Indigenous History, Culture, and Consciousness under Spanish Rule, 1532–1825*. Albuquerque: University of New Mexico Press, 2001.

Angulo, Domingo. *La Metropolitana de la Ciudad de los Reyes, 1535–1825*. Lima: Lib. e Imprenta Gil, S.A., 1935.

Anon. *La Limeña*. Vol. 4, Festival de Lima. Lima: Concejo Provincial de Lima, 1959.

———. *La Ciudad Hispanoamericana: El Sueño de un Orden*. Madrid: CEHOPU (Centro de Estudios Históricos de Obras Públicas y Urbanismo, Ministerio de Obras Públicas y Urbanismo), 1992.

———. *Lima: Paseos por la ciudad y su historia*. 2d ed. Lima: Adobe Editores, 1999.

———. *Los incas, reyes del Perú. Colección Arte y Tesoros del Perú*. Lima: Banco de Crédito, 2005.

———. *Plaza Mayor*. Lima: Municipalidad de Lima, 1997.

———. *El urbanismo en el Nuevo Mundo: El ejemplo peruano*. Edited by Centro Cultural de España (Lima). Madrid: Ministerio de Educación, Cultura y Deporte, 2001.

Arrus, Dario. *El Callao en la epoca del coloniaje antes y despues de la catástrofe de 1746. Posición real y efectiva de la ciudad, en relación con el antiguo presidio, Fundación de Bellavista. Terremotos y piratas, datos histórico-cronológicos de los virreyes y gobernadores del Perú y de los sucesos más notables desde 1530–1829*. Callao: Imp. de "El Callao," 1914.

Avalos de Matos, Rosalía. "Lima de 1700 vista por De la Bardinais le Gentil, viajero francés del siglo XVIII." *Boletín de Lima* 22, no. 119–122 (2003): 295–304.

Banchero Castellano, Raúl. *La verdadera historia del Señor de los Milagros*. Lima: Inti-Sol, 1976.

232 Barriga, Víctor. *Los terremotos en Arequipa, 1582–1868; documentos de los archivos de Arequipa y de Sevilla.* Vol. 7, *Biblioteca Arequipa.* Arequipa: La Colmena, 1951.

Basadre, Jorge. *La multitud, la ciudad y el campo en la historia del Perú.* 3d ed. Lima: Ediciones Treintaitrés & Mosca Azul, 1980.

Bauer, Arnold J. "The Church in the Economy of Spanish America: *Censos* and *Depósitos* in the Eighteenth and Nineteenth Centuries." *Hispanic American Historical Review* 63, no. 4 (1983): 707–33.

Berg, Maxine, and Elizabeth Eger, eds. *Luxury in the Eighteenth Century: Debates, Desires and Delectable Goods.* New York: Palgrave Macmillan, 2003.

———. "In Pursuit of Luxury: Global History and British Consumer Goods in the Eighteenth Century." *Past and Present* 182 (2004): 85–142.

Beringhausen, Wm. H. "Tsunamis Reported from the West Coast of South America 1562–1960." *Bulletin of the Seismological Society of America* 52, no. 4 (1962): 915–21.

Bernales Ballesteros, Jorge. "Fray Calixto de San José Tupac Inca." *Historia y Cultura* 3 (1969): 5–18.

———. *Lima, La Ciudad y sus Monumentos.* Seville: EEH-A, 1972.

———. "Informes de los daños sufridos en la ciudad de Arequipa con el terremoto de 1784." *Anuario de Estudios Americanos* 24 (1972): 295–314.

Biek, William. "Louis XIV and the Cities." In *Edo & Paris: Urban Life and the State in the Early Modern Period,* edited by James L. McClain, John M. Merriman, and Ugawa Kaoru, 68–85. Ithaca: Cornell University Press, 1994.

Bilinkoff, Jodi. "Confessors, Penitents, and the Construction of Identities in Early Modern Avila." In *Culture and Identity: Early Modern Europe (1500–1800). Essays in Honor of Natalie Zemon Davis,* edited by Barbara B. Diefendorf and Carla Hesse, 83–100. Ann Arbor: University of Michigan Press, 1993.

Blanco, Lourdes. "Las monjas de Santa Clara: El erotismo de la fe y la subversión de la autoridad sacerdotal." In *En el nombre del señor: Shamanes, demonios y curanderos del norte del Perú,* edited by Luis Millones and Moises Lemlij, 184–98. Lima: BPP/ SIDEA, 1994.

Bode, Barbara. *No Bells to Toll.* New York: Charles Scribner's Sons, 1989.

Bonilla, Heraclio, and Karen Spalding. *La independencia en el Perú.* 2d ed. Lima: IEP, 1981.

Borah, Woodrow. *Justice by Insurance: The General Indian Court of Colonial Mexico and the Legal Aides of the Half-Real.* Berkeley: University of California Press, 1983.

Bowser, Frederick. *The African Slave in Colonial Peru, 1524–1650.* Stanford: Stanford University Press, 1974.

Brading, D. A. "The City in Bourbon Spanish America: Elite and Masses." *Comparative Urban Research* 8, no. 1 (1980): 71–85.

———. "Bourbon Spain and Its American Empire." In *Colonial Spanish America,* edited by Leslie Bethell, 112–62. Cambridge: Cambridge University Press, 1987.

———. *The First America: The Spanish Monarchy, Creole Patriots, and the Liberal State 1492–1867.* Cambridge: Cambridge University Press, 1991.

———. *Church and State in Bourbon Mexico: The Diocese of Michoacán 1749–1810.* Cambridge: Cambridge University Press, 1994.

Braun, Theodore E. D., and John Radner, eds. "The Lisbon Earthquake of 1755: Representations and Reactions." *Studies on Voltaire and the Eighteenth Century*, Vol. 2 (2005).

Bromley, Juan. *Virreyes, cabildantes y oidores*. Lima: Club del Libro Peruano, 1944.

———. "Fiestas Caballerescas, Populares y Religiosas en la Lima Virreinal." *Revista Histórica* 27 (1964): 200–220.

Bromley, Juan, and José Barbagelata. *Evolución Urbana de la Ciudad de Lima*. Lima: Consejo Provincial de Lima, 1945.

Burkholder, Mark A., and D. S. Chandler. *Biographical Dictionary of Audiencia Ministers in the Americas, 1687–1821*. Westport, Conn.: Greenwood Press, 1982.

Burns, Kathryn. *Colonial Habits: Convents and the Spiritual Economy of Cuzco, Peru*. Durham: Duke University Press, 1999.

Bustíos Romaní, Carlos. *Cuatrocientos años de la Salud Pública en el Perú (1533–1933)*. Lima: Universidad Nacional Mayor de San Marcos, CONCYTEC, 2004.

Cabral, José Victoriano. *Lina Montalvan o El terremoto que destruyó el Callao y la Ciudad de Lima en 1746 con una reseña sobre el descubrimiento del Perú a que se agrega algunas reminiscencias históricas acerca de su independencia*. Buenos Aires: Imprenta del Porvenir, 1880.

Cahill, David. "Colour by Numbers." *Journal of Latin American Studies* 26 (1994): 325–46.

———. "Financing Health Care in the Viceroyalty of Peru: The Hospitals of Lima in the Late Colonial Period." *The Americas* 52, no. 2 (1996): 123–54.

Calderón, Gladys. *La Casa Limeña: Espacios habitados*. Lima: NP, 2000.

Campbell, Leon. *The Military and Society in Colonial Peru, 1750–1810*. Philadelphia: American Philosophical Society, 1978.

Campbell, Peter R. *Power and Politics in Old Regime France, 1720–1745*. New York: Routledge, 1996.

Cañizares-Esguerra, Jorge. "Spanish America: From Baroque to Modern Colonial Science." In *The Cambridge History of Science, Volume 4: The Eighteenth Century*, edited by Roy Porter, 718–38. New York: Cambridge University Press, 2003.

———. *How to Write the History of the New World: Histories, Epistemologies, and Identities in the Eighteenth-Century Atlantic World*. Stanford: Stanford University Press, 2001.

———. "Eighteenth-Century Spanish Political Economy: Epistemology and Decline." *Eighteenth-Century Thought* 1 (2003): 295–314.

———. "Postcolonialism avante la lettre? Travelers and Clerics in Eighteenth-Century Colonial Spanish America." In *After Spanish Rule: Postcolonial Predicaments of the Americas*, edited by Mark Thurner, 141–75. Durham: Duke University Press, 2003.

Cascajo Romero, Juan. *El pleito de la curación de la lepra en el hospital de San Lázaro, de Lima*. Seville: EEH-A, 1948.

Cervantes, Fernando. *The Devil in the New World: The Impact of Diabolism in New Spain*. New Haven: Yale University Press, 1994.

Céspedes del Castillo, Guillermo. *Lima y Buenos Aires: Repercusiones económicas y políticas de la creación del virreinato del Plata*. Seville: EEH-A, 1947.

234   Charney, Paul. *Indian Society in the Valley of Lima, Peru, 1532–1824.* Lanham, Md.: University Press of America, 2001.

Chartier, Roger. "Power, Space, and Investments in Paris." In *Edo & Paris: Urban Life and the State in the Early Modern Period*, edited by James L. McClain, John M. Merriman, and Ugawa Kaoru, 132–52. Ithaca: Cornell University Press, 1994.

Chatellier, Louis. *The Religion of the Poor: Rural Missions in Europe and the Formation of Modern Catholicism, c. 1500–c. 1800.* Translated by Brian Pearce. Cambridge: Cambridge University Press, 1997.

Chowning, Margaret. "Convent Reform, Catholic Reform, and Bourbon Reform in Eighteenth-Century New Spain: The View from the Nunnery." *Hispanic American Historical Review* 85, no. 1 (2005): 1–36.

Clark, Charles Edwin. "Science, Reason, and an Angry God: The Literature of an Earthquake." *New England Quarterly* 38 (1965): 340–62.

Clement, Jean-Pierre. "El nacimiento de la higiene urbana en la américa española del siglo xviii." *Revista de Indias* 171 (1983): 77–95.

Coakley, John. "Friars as Confidants of Holy Women in Medieval Dominican Hagiography." In *Images of Sainthood in Medieval Europe*, edited by Renate Blumenfeld-Kosinski and Timea Szell, 222–46. Ithaca: Cornell University Press, 1991.

Cogorno Ventura, Gilda. "Tiempo de lomas: Calidades del medio ambiente y administración de recursos." In *Lima en el siglo xvi*, edited by Laura Gutiérrez Arbulú, 19–102. Lima: Instituto Riva-Agüero, 2005.

Cope, R. Douglas. *The Limits of Racial Domination: Plebeian Society in Colonial Mexico City, 1660–1720.* Madison: University of Wisconsin Press, 1994.

Cosamalón Aguilar, Jesús. *Indios detrás de la muralla.* Lima: PUC, 1999.

Cruz de Amenábar, Isabel. *El Traje: Transformaciones de una segunda piel.* Santiago: Universidad Católica de Chile, 1996.

Cummins, Thomas. "A Tale of Two Cities: Cuzco, Lima and the Construction of Colonial Representation." In *Converging Cultures: Art and Identity in Spanish America*, edited by Diana Fane, 157–70. New York: Brooklyn Museum, Harry N. Abrams, 1996.

Dager Alva, Joseph. *Conde de Superunda, Colección Forjadores del Perú.* Lima: Editorial Brasa S.A., 1995.

Darnton, Robert. "It Happened One Night." *New York Review of Books*, June 24, 2004, 60–64.

D'Arrigo, Cosme. *El Callao en el Centenario. Historia Documentada del Callao.* Callao: Imp. E. Moreno, 1921.

Defourneaux, Marcelin. *Pablo de Olavide: El Afrancesado.* Translated by Manuel Martínez Camaró. Mexico: Editorial Renacimiento, 1965.

de la Barra, General Felipe. *Historic Monograph on the "Real Felipe" Fortress of Callao and Guide to the Museum of Military History.* Translated by Elda de Sagasti. Lima: CEHMP, 1968.

de Larreta, P. Francisco. "Letras Anuas de la Provincia del Perú de la Compañía de Jesús—1620 a 1724." *Revista de Archivos y Bibliotecas Nacionales* 5, no. 3 (1900): 35–142.

del Castillo Andraca y Tamayo, Fray Francisco. *Obras de Fray Francisco del Castillo An-*   235
draca y Tamayo. Edited by S. J. Rubén Vargas Ugarte. Lima: Studium, 1948.

Delumeau, Jean. *El miedo en occidente*. Translated by Mauro Armiño. Madrid: Taurus, 1989.

De Oré, Fray Luis Gerónimo. *Relación de la vida y milagros de San Francisco Solano*. Lima: PUC, 1998.

Descola, Jean. *Daily Life in Colonial Peru, 1710–1820*. Translated by Michael Heron. New York: Macmillan, 1968.

Deustua Pimental, Carlos. "Reminiscencias incaicas en el siglo xviii (sublevación de Indios de 1750)." In *Homenaje a Don Aurelio Miró Quesada Sosa*, edited by Héctor López Martínez, 143–50. Lima: Academia Peruana de la Lengua, Academia Nacional de Historia, Consorcio Nacional de Universidades, 1998.

de Zaballa Beascoechea, Ana. "Joaquinismos, utopías, milenarismos y mesianismos en la América colonial." In *Teología en América Latina: Desde los orígenes a la Guerra de Sucesión (1493–1715)*, edited by Josep Ignasi Saranyana, 613–87. Madrid: Iberoamerican, Vervuert, 1999.

de Zaballa Beascoechea, Ana, ed. *Utopía, mesianismo y milenarismo: Experiencias latinoamericanas*. Lima: Universidad San Martín de Porres, 2002.

Donahue, Darcy. "Writing Lives: Nuns and Confessors as Auto/Biographers in Early Modern Spain." *Journal of Hispanic Philology* 13 (1989): 230–39.

Dorbath, L., A. Cisternas, C. Dorbath. "Assessment of the Size of Large and Great Historical Earthquakes in Peru." *Bulletin of the Seismological Society of America* 80, no. 3 (1990): 551–76.

Dorta, Enrique Marco. "La Plaza Mayor de Lima en 1680." In *XXXVI Congreso Internacional de Americanistas, España 1964. Actas y Memorias*, 296–303. Seville, 1966.

———. *La arquitectura barroca en el Perú*. Madrid: Instituto Diego Velázquez, CSIC, 1957.

Durán Montero, María Antonia. *Lima en el Siglo XVII: Arquitectura, Urbanismo y vida cotidiana*. Seville: Diputación Provincial de Sevilla, 1994.

Durand, José. *Gaceta de Lima, de 1756 a 1762*. Vol. 1, *Gaceta de Lima*. Lima: COFIDE, 1982.

Durston, Alan. "Un régimen urbanistico en la américa hispana colonial: El trazado en damero durante los siglos xvi y xvii." *Historia* 28 (1994): 59–115.

Duviols, Jean-Paul. "Descripción de la ciudad de Lima Capital del Reyno . . ." In *Cultures et sociétés Andes et Méso-Amérique. Mélanges en hommage a Pierre Duviols*, edited by Raquel Thiercelin, 251–97. Provence: Université de Provence, 1991.

Earle, Rebecca. "'Two Pairs of Pink Satin Shoes!' Race, Clothing and Identity in the Americas (17th-19th Centuries)." *History Workshop Journal* 52 (2001): 175–94.

———. "Luxury, Clothing and Race in Colonial Spanish America." In *Luxury in the Eighteenth Century*, edited by Maxine Berg and Elizabeth Eger, 219–27. New York: Palgrave Macmillan, 2003.

Egaña S. I., Antonio de. *Historia de la Iglesia en la América Española desde el Descubrimiento hasta comienzos del siglo XIX*. 2 vols. Vol. 2, *Colección de Autores Cristianos*. Madrid: La Editorial Católica, 1966.

236 Eguiguren, Luis A. (Multatuli). *Las calles de Lima*. Lima: np, 1945.

Elliott, J. H. *Empires of the Atlantic World: Britain and Spain in America 1492–1830*. New Haven: Yale University Press, 2006.

Estabridis Cárdenes, Ricardo. "Lima a través del arte de los viajeros extranjeros." In *Redescubramos Lima: Grabados Colección Antonio Lulli*, 11–33. Lima: Fondo Pro-Recuperación del Patrimonio Cultural de la Nación, Banco de Crédito, 1997.

Estenssoro Fuchs, Juan Carlos. "Modernismo, estética, música y fiesta: Elites y cambio de actitud frente a la cultura popular, Perú, 1750–1850." In *Tradición y modernidad en los andes*, edited by Henrique Urbano, 181–96. Cuzco: CBC, 1992.

———. "Los colores de la plebe: razón y mestizaje en el Perú colonial." In *Los cuadros de mestizaje del Virrey Amat*, edited by Natalia Majluf. Lima: Museo de Arte de Lima, 2000.

———. *Del Paganismo a la Santidad: La incorporacion de los Indios del Perú al Catolicismo 1532–1750*. Translated by Gabriela Ramos. Lima: PUC, IFEA, 2003.

———. "Construyendo la memoria: La figura del inca y el reino del Perú, de la conquista a Túpac Amaru II." In *Los incas, reyes del Perú*, 94–173. Lima: Banco de Crédito, 2005.

Farriss, N. M. *Crown and Clergy in Colonial Mexico 1759–1821: The Crisis of Ecclesiastical Privilege*. London: Athlone Press, University of London, 1968.

Fernández, Roberto. *La España Moderna: El Siglo XVIII*. Vol. 4, *Manual de Historia de España*. Madrid: historia 16, 1993.

Fisher, John R. *Government and Society in Colonial Peru: The Intendant System, 1784–1814*. London: University of London, Athlone Press, 1970.

———. *Bourbon Peru, 1750–1824*. Liverpool: Liverpool University Press, 2003.

Fisher, John Robert, Allan J. Kuethe, and Anthony McFarlane. *Reform and Insurrection in Bourbon New Granada and Peru*. Baton Rouge: Louisiana State University Press, 1990.

Flores Araoz, José, et al. *Santa Rosa de Lima y su tiempo*. Lima: Banco de Crédito, 1996.

Flores Espinoza, Javier, and Rafael Varón, eds. *El hombre y los Andes: Homenaje a Franklin Pease G. Y.* 3 vols. Lima: PUC, BCP, IFEA, 2003.

Flores Galindo, Alberto. *Buscando un Inca*. Lima: Editorial Horizonte, 1994.

———. *Túpac Amaru II-1780: Sociedad colonial y sublevaciones populares*. Lima: Retablo de Papel Ediciones, 1976.

———. *Aristocracia y plebe: Lima, 1760–1830*. Lima: Mosca Azul, 1984.

Flores Guzmán, Ramiro. "El enemigo frente a las costas: Temores y reacciones frente a la amenaza pirata, 1570–1720." In *El Miedo en el Perú, siglos xvi al xx*, edited by Claudia Rosas Laura, 33–50. Lima: PUC, 2005.

Foucault, Michel. "Space, Knowledge, and Power." In *Power*, edited by James D. Faubion. New York: New Press, 2000.

Fraile, Pedro. "Putting Order into the Cities: The Evolution of 'Policy Science' in Eighteenth-Century Spain." *Urban History* 25, no. 1 (1998): 22–35.

Fuentes, Manuel A. *Lima: Apuntes Históricos, descriptivos, estadísticos, y de costumbres*. Lima: Banco Industrial del Perú, 1988 [1867].

Gálvez, José. *Calles de Lima y meses del año*. Lima: IPC, 1943.

——. *Una Lima que se va*. Lima: Editorial Euforion, 1921.

Ganster, Paul Bentley. "A Social History of the Secular Clergy of Lima During the Middle Decades of the Eighteenth Century." Ph.D. diss., UCLA, 1974.

García Acosta, Virginia, ed. *Historia y desastres en América Latina*. 2 volumes. Bogotá: CIESAS/La Red, 1996.

García Calderón, Ventura. *Para una Antología de la limeña*. Brussels, 1935.

García Cárcel, Ricardo. "Cuerpo y enfermedad en el antiguo régimen: Algunas reflexiones." In *Le Corps dans la Société Espagnole des XVI et XVII Siécles*, edited by Agustín Redondo, 131–39. Paris: Université de la Sorbonne Nouvelle-Paris III, 1990.

García Irigoyen, Manuel. *Historia de la catedral de Lima, 1535–1898*. Lima: El País, 1898.

García Jordán, Pilar. *Iglesia y poder en el Perú contemporáneo, 1821–1919*. Cuzco: CBC, 1991.

Garland Ponce, Beatriz. "Las Cofradías en Lima durante la Colonia: Una primera aproximación." In *La Venida del Reino: Religión, evangelización y cultura en América, Siglos XVI-XX*, edited by Gabriela Ramos, 199–228. Cuzco: CBC, 1994.

Garrett, David. *Shadows of Empire: The Indian Nobility of Cusco, 1750–1825*. Cambridge: Cambridge University Press, 2005.

Gasparini, Graziano. *América, Barroco y Arquitectura*. Caracas: Ernesto Armitano, 1972.

Giesecke, Alberto, and Enrique Silgado. *Terremotos en el Perú*. Lima: Rikchay, 1981.

Glave, Luis Miguel. *De Rosa y espinas: Economía, sociedad y mentalidades andinas, siglo xvii*. Lima: IEP, BCR, 1998.

Goldthwaite, Richard A. *The Building of Renaissance Florence*. Baltimore: Johns Hopkins University Press, 1980.

Gómez Canedo, O.F.M., Lino. "Franciscans in the Americas: A Comprehensive View." In *Franciscan Presence in the Americas*, edited by Francisco Morales, O.F.M., 5–45. Potomac: Academy of American Franciscan History, 1983.

Gómez Gómez, Margarita. *Forma y Expedición del Documento en la Secretaría de Estado y del Despacho Universal de Indias*. Seville: Universidad de Sevilla, 1993.

Gómez Urdáñez, José Luis. *El proyecto reformista de Ensenada*. Lleida, Spain: Milenio, 1996.

González, Frank I. "Tsunami!" *Scientific American*, May 1999, 56–65.

Graziano, Frank. *Wounds of Love: The Mystical Marriage of Saint Rose of Lima*. Oxford: Oxford University Press, 2004.

Guardino, Peter. *"The Time of Liberty": Popular Political Culture in Oaxaca, 1750–1850*. Durham: Duke University Press, 2005.

Guerra, Francois-Xavier, and Annick Lempériére. *Los espacios públicos en Iberoamérica: Ambiguedades y problemas, siglos XVIII y XIX*. Mexico City: Centro Francés de Estudios Mexicanos y Centroamericanos, Fondo de Cultura Económica, 1998.

Guibovich Pérez, Pedro. *En Defensa de Dios: Estudios y Documentos sobre la Inquisición en el Perú*. Lima: Congreso del Perú, 1998.

238   Guimerá, Agustín, ed. *El reformismo borbónico*. Madrid: CSIC, Alianza Editorial, 1996.

Günther Doering, Juan, and Guillermo Lohmann Villena. *Lima*. Madrid: MAPFRE, 1992.

Gutiérrez Arbulú, Laura, ed. *Lima en el siglo xvi*. Lima: Instituto Riva-Agüero, 2006.

Haenke, Tadeo. *Descripción del Perú*. Lima: Imprenta de "El Lucero," 1901.

Haitin, Marcel. "Late Colonial Lima: Economy and Society in an Era of Reform and Revolution." Ph.D. diss., University of California Berkeley, 1983.

Hamnett, Brian R. "Church Wealth in Peru: Estates and Loans in the Archdiocese of Lima in the Seventeenth Century." *Jahrbuch fur Geschichte Lateinamerikas* 10 (1973): 113–32.

Hardoy, Jorge. "Two Thousand Years of Latin American Urbanization." In *Urbanization in Latin America: Approaches and Issues*, edited by Jorge Hardoy, 3–55. Garden City, N.Y.: Anchor Books, 1975.

Harth-Terré, Emilio. "Bicentenario de un infausto suceso (El Terremoto del 28 de Octubre de 1746)." *Boletín Municipal* 1508 (1946).

Harth-Terré, Emilio, and Alberto Márquez Abanto. "Las Bellas Artes en el virreynato del Peru: Historia de la Casa Urbana Virreynal de Lima." *Revista del Archivo Nacional del Perú* 26, no. 1 (1962): 109–206.

———. "El artesano negro en la arquitectura virreinal limeña." *Revista del Archivo Nacional del Perú* 25, no. 3 (1961): 3–73.

———. "Nota para una historia del balcón en Lima." *Revista del Archivo Nacional del Perú* 23, no. 2 (1959): 3–59.

Heras, O.F.M., Fr. Julián. *Los franciscanos y las misiones populares en el Perú*. Madrid: Editorial Cisneros, 1983.

Herr, Richard. *The Eighteenth-Century Revolution in Spain*. Princeton: Princeton University Press, 1958.

Herzog, Tamar. *Defining Nations: Immigrants and Citizens in Early Modern Spain and Spanish America*. New Haven: Yale University Press, 2003.

Hidalgo Lehuede, Jorge. "Amarus y cataris: Aspectos mesiánicos de la rebelión indígena de 1781 en Cusco, Chayanta, La Paz y Arica." *Chungará* 10 (1983): 117–38.

Higgins, James. *Lima: A Cultural History*. Oxford: Oxford University Press, 2005.

Hill, Ruth. *Hierarchy, Commerce, and Fraud in Bourbon Spanish America: A Postal Inspector's Exposé*. Nashville: Vanderbilt University Press, 2005.

Hohenberg, Paul M., and Lynn Hollen Lees. *The Making of Urban Europe 1000–1950*. Cambridge, Mass.: Harvard University Press, 1985.

Hünefeldt, Christine. "El crecimiento de las ciudades: Culturas y sociedades urbanas en el siglo XVIII latinoamericana." In *Procesos americanos hacia la redefinición colonial*, edited by Enrique Tandeter and Jorge Hidalgo Lehuede, 375–405. Madrid: UNESCO, TROTTA, 2000.

Hunt, Alan. *Governance of the Consuming Passions: A History of Sumptuary Laws*. New York: St. Martin's Press, 1996.

Israel, Jonathan I. *Radical Enlightenment: Philosophy and the Making of Modernity 1650–1750*. Oxford: Oxford University Press, 2001.

Iwasaki, Fernando. "El pensamiento de Pablo de Olavide y los ilustrados peruanos." 239
Histórica 11, no. 2 (1987): 133–62.

——. "Mujeres al borde de la perfección: Rosa de Santa María y las alumbradas de Lima." Hispanic American Historical Review 73, no. 4 (1993): 581–613.

Izaguirre, Fray Bernardino. Historia de las Misiones Franciscanas y narración de los progresos de la geografía en el oriente del Perú. 12 vols. Vols. 1–2. Lima: Talleres Gráficos de la Penitenciaría, 1922.

Johns, Alessa, ed. Dreadful Visitations: Confronting Natural Catastrophe in the Age of the Enlightenment. New York: Routledge, 1999.

Jouve Martín, José Ramón. "En olor de santidad: Hagiografía, cultos locales y escritura religiosa en Lima, siglo XVII." Colonial Latin American Review 13, no. 2 (2004): 181–98.

——. Esclavos de la ciudad letrada: Esclavitud, escritura y colonialismo en Lima (1650–1700). Lima: IEP, 2005.

Kagan, Richard L. Lucrecia's Dreams: Politics and Prophecy in Sixteenth-Century Spain. Berkeley: University of California Press, 1990.

——. Urban Images of the Hispanic World, 1493–1793. New Haven: Yale University Press, 2000.

Kamen, Henry Arthur Francis. Empire: How Spain Became a World Power, 1492–1763. 1st American ed. New York: HarperCollins, 2003.

Kaplan, Stephen Laurence. "Provisioning Paris: The Crisis of 1738–1741." In Edo and Paris: Urban Life and the State in the Early Modern Period, edited by James L. McClain, John M. Merriman, and Ugawa Kaoru, 175–210. Ithaca: Cornell University Press, 1994.

Katzew, Ilona. Casta Painting: Images of Race in Eighteenth-Century Mexico. New Haven: Yale University Press, 2004.

Keenan, Philip C. "Astronomy in the Viceroyalty of Peru." In Mundialización de la ciencia y cultura nacional, edited by A. Elena A. Lafuente, M. L. Ortega, 297–305. Madrid: Doce Calles, 1993.

Kelemen, Pál. Baroque and Rococo in Latin America. 2d ed. New York: Dover Publications, 1967.

Kendrick, T. D. The Lisbon Earthquake. Philadelphia: J. B. Lippincott, 1955.

Knight, Alan. Mexico: The Colonial Era. Cambridge: Cambridge University Press, 2002.

Lafuente, Antonio, and Antonio Mazuecos. Los caballeros del punto fijo: Ciencia, política y aventura en la expedición geodésica hispanofrancesa al virreinato del Perú en el siglo xviii. Madrid: SERBAL/CSIC, 1987.

Larson, Brooke. Colonialism and Agrarian Transformation in Bolivia: Cochabamba, 1550–1900. Princeton: Princeton University Press, 1988.

Lastarria, José Victorino. El Manuscrito del Diablo. Edited by Luis Alberto Sánchez, Biblioteca Amauta. Santiago: Ediciones Ercilla, 1941.

Lastres, Juan B. "Terremotos, hospitales y epidemias de la Lima colonial." Archeion 22, no. 2, n.s. t, 1 (1940).

240   Lauer, Mirko. "Ruiz Cano: Espacio Colonial y Espacio Criollo en un esteta Limeño del siglo xviii." *Revista de Crítica Literaria Latinoamericana* 46 (1997): 177–90.

Lavallé, Bernardo. *Las promesas ambiguas: Criollismo colonial en los andes.* Lima: PUC, Instituto Riva-Agüero, 1993.

Lavrin, Asunción, and Rosalva Loreto L. *Monjas y beatas: La escritura femenina en la espiritualidad barroca novohispana.* Mexico City: AGN/Universidad de las Américas, 2002.

Leguía, Jorge Guillermo. "Lima en el siglo xviii." In *Monografías históricas sobre la Ciudad de Lima,* 169–86. Lima: Concejo Provincial de Lima, 1935.

Lewin, Boleslao. *La rebelión de Túpac Amaru.* 3d ed. Buenos Aires: SELA, 1967.

Liebersohn, Harry. *The Travelers' World: Europe to the Pacific.* Cambridge, Mass.: Harvard University Press, 2006.

Lima, Concejo Provincial de, ed. *Monografías Históricas sobre la Ciudad de Lima.* 2 vols. Lima: Gil, 1935.

Locke, Adrian Knight. "Catholic Icons and Society in Late Colonial Spanish America: The Peruvian Earthquake, Christs of Lima and Cusco, and Other Comparative Cults." Ph.D., diss., University of Essex, 2001.

Lockridge, Patricia. *Tsunamis in Peru-Chile.* Boulder: World Data Center A for Solid Earth Geophysics, Report SE-39, 1985.

Lohmann Villena, Guillermo. *El arte dramático en Lima durante el virreinato.* Madrid: EEH-A, 1945.

———. "La destitución del Oidor Limeño Pablo de Olavide." *Revista de Indias* 28–29 (1947): 497–500.

———. *Las relaciones de los virreyes del Perú.* Seville: EEH-A, 1959.

———. *Las Defensas Militares de Lima y Callao.* Seville: Academia Nacional de la Historia del Perú, EEH-A, 1964.

———. *Pedro de Peralta, Pablo de Olavide.* Vol. 15, *Hombres del Perú.* Lima: Editorial Universitaria, 1964.

———. *Los ministros de la audiencia de Lima en el reinado de los Borbones (1700–1821). Esquema de un estudio sobre un núcleo dirigente.* Seville: EEH-A, 1974.

———. "Victorino Montero del Aguila y su 'Estado Político del Reyno del Perú' (1742)." *Anuario de Estudios Americanos* 31 (1974): 751–807.

———. *Un Tríptico del Perú Virreinal: El Virrey Amat, El Marqués de Soto Florido y la Perricholi. El Drama de Dos Palanganas y su Circunstancia.* North Carolina Studies in the Romance Languages and Literature. Chapel Hill: University of North Carolina, 1976.

Lossio, Jorge. *Acequias y gallinazos: Salud ambiental en Lima del siglo XIX.* Lima, Perú: IEP, 2003.

Lowry, Lyn Brandon. "Forging an Indian Nation: Urban Indians under Spanish Colonial Control (Lima, Peru, 1535–1765)." Ph.D. diss., University of California, Berkeley, 1991.

Lynch, John. *Spanish Colonial Administration, 1782–1810.* London: University of London Press, 1958.

―――. *Bourbon Spain, 1700–1808.* Oxford: Basil Blackwell, 1989.

Macera, Pablo. *La imagen francesa del Perú.* Lima: INC, 1976.

―――. *Viajeros Franceses siglos xvi–xix.* Lima: Biblioteca Nacional del Perú, Embajada de Francia, 1999.

Majluf, Natalia, ed. *Los cuadros del mestizaje de Amat.* Lima: Museo de Arte de Lima, 2000.

Mannarelli, María Emma. *Pecados Públicos: La ilegitimidad en Lima, siglo xvii.* Lima: Flora Tristán, 1993.

Maravall, José Antonio. *Culture of the Baroque: Analysis of a Historical Structure.* Minneapolis: University of Minnesota Press, 1986.

Mariátegui Oliva, Ricardo. *El Rimac: Barrio limeño de abajo del puente.* Lima: Talleres Gráficos Cecil, 1956.

Marks, Patricia. *Deconstructing Legitimacy. Viceroy, Merchants, and the Military in Late Colonial Peru.* University Park: Penn State University Press, 2007.

Martin, Luis. *Daughters of the Conquistadores. Women of the Viceroyalty of Peru.* Albuquerque: University of New Mexico Press, 1983.

Martínez, María Elena. "The Black Blood of New Spain: Limpieza de Sangre, Racial Violence, and Gendered Power in Early Colonial Mexico." *William and Mary Quarterly* 61, no. 3 (2004): 479–519.

Massard-Guilbaud, Geneviéve. "Introduction: The Urban Catastrophe-Challenge to the Social, Economic, and Cultural Order of the City." In *Cities and Catastrophes, Villes et catastrophes*, edited by Geneviéve Massard-Guilbaud, H. Platt, D. Schott, 9–42. Frankfurt: Peter Lang, 2002.

Maxwell, Kenneth. "Lisbon: The Earthquake of 1755 and Urban Recovery under the Marqués de Pombal." In *Out of Ground Zero*, edited by Joan Ockman, 20–45. Munich: Prestel Verlag, 2002.

Maza, Sarah. *The Myth of the French Bourgeoisie. An Essay on the Social Imaginary 1750–1850.* Cambridge, Mass.: Harvard University Press, 2003.

McClain, James L., John M. Merriman, and Ugawa Kaoru. *Edo and Paris: Urban Life and the State in the Early Modern Period.* Ithaca: Cornell University Press, 1994.

Medina, José Toribio. *Historia del Tribunal del Santo Oficio de la Inquisición de Lima (1569–1820).* 2 vols. Santiago: Imprenta Gutenberg, 1887.

―――. *La Imprenta en Lima (1584–1824).* 4 vols. Santiago: Casa del autor, 1905.

Meléndez, Mariselle. "Visualizing Difference: The Rhetoric of Clothing in Colonial Spanish America." In *The Latin America Fashion Reader*, edited by Regina A. Root, 17–30. Oxford: Berg, 2005.

Merino, O. S. A., P. Luis. *Estudio crítico sobre las 'Noticias Secretas de América' y el Clero Colonial (1720–1765).* Madrid: CSIC, Instituto Santo Toribio de Mogrovejo, 1956.

Mignot, Claude. "Urban Transformations." In *The Triumph of the Baroque: Architecture in Europe 1600–1750*, edited by Henry A. Millon, 315–32. Milan: Rizzoli International, 1999.

Milhou, Alain. *Colón y su mentalidad mesiánica en el ambiente franciscanista español.* Valla-

242   dolid: Casa-Museo de Colón y Seminario Americanistas de la Universidad de Valladolid, 1983.

Millar Carvacho, René. *Inquisición y sociedad en el Virreinato Peruano*. Lima and Santiago: Instituto Riva-Agüero, Instituto de Historia, Ediciones Universidad Católica de Chile, 1997.

———. *La Inquisición de Lima (1697–1820)*. Vol. 3. Madrid: Editorial Deimos, 1998.

———. *La Inquisición de Lima: Signos de su decadencia 1726–1750*. Santiago: LOM, DIBAM, 2005.

Millon, Henry, ed. *The Triumph of the Baroque: Architecture in Europe, 1600–1750*. Milan: Rizzoli International, 1999.

Millones, Luis. *Las confesiones de don Juan Vázquez*. Lima: IFEA, PUC, 2002.

Mills, Kenneth, William B. Taylor, and Sandra Lauderdale Graham. *Colonial Latin America: A Documentary History*. Wilmington: SR Books, 2002.

Minchom, Martin. *The People of Quito, 1690–1810: Change and Unrest in the Underclass*. Boulder: Westview Press, 1994.

Miró Quesada S., Aurelio. *Lima, Ciudad de los Reyes*. Buenos Aires: Emecé Editores, 1946.

———. "Una descripción inédita de Lima en el siglo xviii." In *20 Temas Peruanos*, 317–33. Lima: P. L. Villanueva, 1966.

Moore, John Preston. *The Cabildo in Peru under the Bourbons: A Study in the Decline and Resurgence of Local Government in the Audiencia of Lima 1700–1824*. Durham: Duke University Press, 1966.

Moreno Cebrián, Alfredo. Introducción, Superunda, Conde de. *Relación de gobierno, Perú (1745–1761)*. Madrid: CSIC, 1983.

———. *El corregidor de indios y la economía peruana del siglo XVIII: (los repartos forzosos de mercancías)*. Madrid: CSIC, Instituto G. Fernández de Oviedo, 1977.

———. "Cuarteles, Barrios y Calles de Lima a fines del siglo XVIII." *Jahrbuch für Geschichte Lateinamerikas* 18 (1981): 96–161.

———. *El virreinato del Marqués de Castelfuerte, 1724–1736: El primer intento borbónico por reformar el Perú*. Madrid: Editorial Catriel, 2000.

———. "El Regalismo Borbónico frente al Poder Vaticano: Acerca del Estado de la Iglesia en el Perú Durante el Primer Tercio del Siglo XVIII." *Revista de Indias* 63, no. 227 (2003): 223–74.

Morgan, Ronald J. *Spanish American Saints and the Rhetoric of Identity, 1600–1810*. Tucson: University of Arizona Press, 2002.

Mörner, Magnus. *Race Mixture in the History of Latin America*. Boston: Little, Brown, 1967.

Morse, Richard. "Urban Development." In *Colonial Spanish America*, edited by Leslie Bethell. Cambridge: Cambridge University Press, 1984.

Mujica Pinilla, Ramón. *Rosa limensis: Mística, política e iconografía en torno a la patrona de América*. Lima: IFEA, Fondo de Cultura Económica, Banco Central de Reserva del Perú, 2001.

———, ed. *El Barroco Peruano: Colección Artes y Tesoros del Perú*. Lima: Banco de Crédito del Perú, 2002.

———. *El Barroco Peruano, II, Colección Artes y Tesoros del Perú*. Lima: Banco de Crédito del Perú, 2003.

Mumford, Lewis. *The City in History: Its Origins, Its Transformations, and Its Prospects*. New York: Harcourt, Brace and World, 1961.

Muro Orejón, Antonio. "La igualdad entre indios y españoles: La real cédula de 1697." In *Estudios sobre política indigenista española en América. I: Iniciación, pugna de ocupación, demografía, lingüística, sedentarización, condición jurídica del indio*, 365–86. Valladolid: Universidad de Valladolid, Seminario de Historia de América, 1975.

Navarro, José María. *Una denuncia profética desde el Perú a mediados del siglo XVIII: El Planctus indorum christianorum in America peruntina*. Lima: PUC, 2001.

Nieto Vélez, S. J., Armando. "Una Descripción del Perú en el siglo XVIII." *Boletín del Instituto Riva-Agüero* 12 (1982–83): 283–93.

———. "Testimonio sobre el Venerable Francisco del Castillo en el siglo xviii." In *Homenaje al R.P. Doctor Antonio San Cristóbal Sebastián*, edited by Ada Olaya Guillinta, 377–85. Arequipa: Universidad Nacional de San Agustín, 2000.

Noel, Charles C. "Missionary Preachers in Spain: Teaching Social Virtue in the Eighteenth Century." *American Historical Review* 90, no. 4 (1985): 866–92.

Nuñez, Estuardo. *Cuatro viajeros alemanes al Perú*. Lima: UNMSM, 1969.

———. *Viajes y viajeros extranjeros por el Perú*. Lima: CONCYTEC, 1989.

Núñez, Estuardo, and George Petersen. *Alexander von Humboldt en el Perú: Diario de viaje y otros escritos*. Lima: BCR, 2002.

Ockman, Joan, ed. *Out of Ground Zero: Case Studies in Urban Reinvention*. Munich: Prestel, 2002.

Oeser, Erhard. "Historical Earthquake Theories from Aristotle to Kant." In R. Gutdeutsch, G. Grünthal, and R. Musson, eds. *Historical Earthquakes in Central Europe*. Vol. 1. Vienna, 1992.

Olaechea, Juan B. "Sacerdotes indios de América del Sur en el siglo XVIII." *Revista de Indias* 29 (1969): 371–91.

———. "Los indios en las órdenes religiosas." *Missionalia Hispánica* 29, no. 86 (1972): 241–56.

Oliver-Smith, Anthony. "Anthropological Research on Hazards and Disasters." *Annual Review in Anthropology* 25 (1996): 303–28.

———. "El terremoto de 1746 de Lima: El modelo colonial, el desarrollo urbano y los peligros naturales." In *Historia y desastres en América Latina*, edited by Virginia García Acosta, 2:133–61. Lima: La Red-CIESAS, 1997.

O'Phelan Godoy, Scarlett. "'Ascender al estado eclesiástico': La ordenación de indios en Lima a mediados del siglo XVIII." In *Incas e indios cristianos: Elites indígenas e identidades cristianas en los Andes coloniales*, edited by Jean-Jacques Decoster, 311–29. Cuzco: CBC-IFEA, 2002.

———. *Un siglo de rebeliones anticoloniales: Perú y Bolivia 1700–1783*, Archivos de historia andina 9. Cuzco: CBC, 1988.

———. *La gran rebelión en los Andes de Túpac Amaru a Túpac Catari*. Archivos de historia andina, 20. Cuzco: CBC, 1995.

————. "Una rebelión abortada. Lima 1750: La conspiración de los indios olleros de Huarochirí." *Varia Historia (Belo Horizonte)* 24 (2001): 7–32.

————. "El vestido como identidad étnica e indicador social de una cultura material." In *El Barroco Peruano*, edited by Ramón Mujica Pinilla, 99–133. Lima: Banco de Crédito, 2003.

O'Phelan Godoy, Scarlett, ed. *El Perú en el siglo XVIII: La Era Borbónica*, Instituto Riva-Agüero no. *179*. Lima: PUC, Instituto Riva-Agüero, 1999.

————. *La independencia en el Perú: De los Borbones a Bolívar*. Lima: PUC, Instituto Riva-Agüero, 2001.

Ortega, Francisco A. "Catastrophe, Ambivalent Praises, and Liminal Figurations in Pedro de Oña's *Temblor de Lima de 1609*." *Colonial Latin American Review* 13, no. 2 (2004): 213–41.

Orti Belmonte, Miguel A. *Los Ovando y Solis, de Cáceres*. Badajoz: Tip. Artes Gráficas, 1932.

Ortiz de la Tabla Ducasse, Javier. *El Marqués de Ovando Gobernador de Filipinas (1750–1754)*. Seville: EEH-A, 1974.

Osorio, Alejandra. "The King in Lima: Simulacra, Ritual, and Rule in Seventeenth-Century Peru." *Hispanic American Historical Review* 84, no. 3 (2004): 447–74.

Palma, Ricardo. *Anales de la Inquisición*. Lima: Congreso de la República, 1997 [1897].

Panfichi, Aldo. "Urbanización temprana de Lima, 1535–1900." In *Mundos interiores: Lima 1850–1950*, edited by Aldo Panfichi and Felipe Portocarrero. Lima: Universidad del Pacífico, 1995.

Patrón, Pablo. "Lima Antigua." In *Monografías Históricas sobre la ciudad de Lima*. Lima: Concejo Provincial de Lima, 1935.

Paz, Octavio. *Sor Juana or, The Traps of Faith*. Cambridge, Mass.: Belknap Press of Harvard University Press, 1988.

Pearce, Adrian J. "Early Bourbon Government in the Viceroyalty of Peru, 1700–1759." Ph.D. diss., University of Liverpool, 1998.

————. "Huancavelica 1700–1759: Administrative Reform of the Mercury Industry in Early Bourbon Peru." *Hispanic American Historical Review* 79, no. 4 (1999): 669–702.

————. "The Peruvian Population Census of 1725–1740." *Latin American Research Review* 36, no. 3 (2001): 69–104.

Peña Prado, Mariano. *Lima y sus murallas*. Lima, 1935.

Peralta, Manuel José de. "El terremoto de 28 de octubre de 1746." *Revista de Lima* I (1860).

Peralta Ruiz, Víctor. "Tiranía o buen gobierno: Escolasticismo y criticismo en el Perú del siglo XVIII." In *Entre la retórica y la insurgencia: Las ideas y los movimientos sociales en los Andes, Siglo XVIII*, edited by Charles Walker, 67–88. Cuzco: CBC, 1996.

————. "Las razones de la fe: La iglesia y la ilustración en el Perú, 1750–1800." In *El Perú en el siglo XVIII: La Era Borbónica*, edited by Scarlett O'Phelan Godoy. Lima: PUC, Instituto Riva-Agüero, 1999.

Peralta Ruiz, Víctor, and Charles F. Walker. "Viajeros naturalistas, científicos y dibu-

jantes." In *De la ilustración al costumbrismo en las artes (siglos XVIII y XIX)*, edited by   245
Ramón Mujica Pinilla, 243–72. Lima: Banco de Crédito del Perú, 2006.

Pérez Cantó, María Pilar. *Lima en el siglo xviii*. Madrid: Universidad Autónoma de Madrid, ICI, 1985.

Pérez-Mallaína Bueno, Pablo Emilio. "La utilización interesada de un desastre natural: El terremoto de Lima en 1746." *Jahrbuch für Geschichte Lateinamerikas* 35 (1998): 73–99.

———. "La fabricación de un mito: El terremoto de 1687 y la ruina de los cultivos de trigo en el Perú." *Anuario de Estudios Americanos* 57, no. 1 (2000): 69–88.

———. *Retrato de una ciudad en crisis: La sociedad limeña ante el movimiento sísmico de 1746*. Seville: EEH-A-CSIC/Instituto Riva-Agüero, 2001.

Phelan, John Leddy. *The Millennial Kingdom of the Franciscans in the New World*. 2d ed. Berkeley: University of California Press, 1970.

Pimentel, Juan. *Viajeros científicos: Tres grandes expediciones al nuevo mundo, novatores*. Madrid: Nivola, 2001.

Poole, Deborah. *Vision, Race, and Modernity: A Visual Economy of the Andean Image World*. Princeton: Princeton University Press, 1997.

Porras Barrenechea, Raúl. *Pequeña Antología de Lima (1535–1935)*. Madrid: Galo Sáez, 1935.

———. *Perspectiva y panorama de Lima*. Lima: Entre Nous, 1997.

Pratt, Mary Louise. *Imperial Eyes: Travel Writing and Transculturation*. New York: Routledge, 1992.

Premo, Bianca. *Children of the Father King: Youth, Authority and Legal Minority in Colonial Lima*. Chapel Hill: University of North Carolina Press, 2005.

Preuss, Jane, and Julio Kuroiwa. "Urban Planning for Mitigation and Preparedness: The Case of Callao, Peru." Paper presented at the Fourth U.S. National Conference on Earthquake Engineering, Palm Springs, Calif., 1990.

Quiroz, Alfonso W. *Deudas olvidadas: Instrumentos de Crédito en la Economía Colonial Peruana, 1750–1820*. Lima: PUC, 1993.

Quiroz Chueca, Francisco. "Movimiento de tierra y de piso: El Terremoto de 1746, la corrupción en el Callao y los cambios borbónicos." *Investigaciones Sociales* 4 (1999): 37–50.

Ramírez, Casteñada, Ricardo, and Charles Walker. "Cuentas y cultura material: La reconstrucción del Real Palacio de Lima después del terremoto de 1746." *Anuario de Estudios Americanos* 49, no. 2 (2002): 657–96.

Ramón Joffré, Gabriel. "Urbe y orden: Evidencias del reformismo borbónico en el tejido limeño." In *El Perú en el siglo XVIII*, edited by Scarlett O'Phelan Godoy, 295–324. Lima: PUC, 1999.

———. *La muralla y los callejones: Intervención urbana y proyecto político en Lima durante la segunda mitad del siglo XIX*. Lima: SIDEA/Prom Peru, 1999.

Ramos, Demetrio. *Trigo chileno, navieros del callao y hacendados limeños entre la crisis agrícola del siglo xvii y la comercial de la primera mitad del xviii*. Madrid: CSIC, Instituto Gonzalo Fernández de Oviedo, 1967.

Ramos Sosa, Rafael. *Arte Festivo en Lima Virreinal*. Seville: Junta de Andalucía, 1992.

246   Restall, Matthew, ed. *Beyond Black and Red: African-Native Relations in Colonial Latin America*. Albuquerque: University of New Mexico Press, 2005.

Reynolds, D. T. M. *Terremoto de 1746: Destrucción total del Callao y parte de Lima. Escrito en Ingles por el Sr. DTM Reynolds, Durante su Viaje Al Rededor del Mundo en la Fragata de Guerra Norte-Americana Potomac y traducido por El Playero*. Callao: Tipografía de Estevan Dañino, 1852.

Richter Prada, O.F.M., Mons. Federico. *Presencia Franciscana en el Perú en los siglos xvi al xx*. 2 vols. Lima, 1995.

Rico, Juan. "Criptoburguesía y cambio económico en la ilustración española." *Cuadernos Hispanoamericanos* 408 (1984): 25–55.

Riva Agüero, José de la. "Añoranzas." In *Monografías históricas sobre la ciudad de Lima*. Lima: Concejo, 1935.

———. *La Historia en el Perú*. Madrid: Imprenta y Editorial Maestre, 1952.

———. *La conquista y el virreinato*. Vol. 6, *Obras completas de José de la Riva-Agüero*. Lima: PUC, 1968.

Rizo-Patrón Boyle, Paul. *Linaje, Dote, y Poder: La nobleza de Lima de 1700 a 1850*. Lima: PUC, 2000.

Roberts, Marie Mulvey. "Pleasure Engendered by Gender: Homosociality and the Club." In *Pleasure in the Eighteenth Century*, edited by Roy and Marie Mulvey Roberts Porter, 48–76. London: Macmillan, 1996.

Roche, Daniel. *France in the Enlightenment*. Translated by Arthur Goldhammer. Cambridge, Mass.: Harvard University Press, 2000.

Rodríguez-Camilloni, Humberto. "Tradición e innovación en la arquitectura del virreinato del Perú: Constantino de Vasconcelos y la invención de la arquitectura de quincha en Lima durante el siglo xvii." In *Arte, Historia e Identidad en América: Visiones Comparativas*, edited by Gustavo Curiel et al., 386–403. Mexico City: UNAM, Instituto de Investigaciones Estéticas, 1994.

Rodríguez Casado, Vicente, and Florentino Pérez Embid. *Construcciones militares del Virrey Amat*. Seville: EEH-A, 1949.

Rodríguez Villa, Antonio. *Don Zenón de Somodevilla, Marqués de la Ensenada*. Madrid: Librería de M. Murillo, 1878.

Romero, Carlos A. "Rebeliones indígenas en Lima durante la Colonia." *Revista Histórica* 9, no. 4 (1935): 317–35.

Romero de Tejada, Pilar, ed. *Frutas y castas ilustradas*. Madrid: Museo Nacional de Antropología, 2004.

Rosas Lauro, Claudia, ed. *El miedo en el Perú, siglos xvi al xx*. Lima: PUC, 2005.

———. "Jaque a la Dama: La imagen de la mujer en la prensa limeña de fines del siglo xviii." In *Mujeres y género en la historia del Perú*, edited by Margarita Zegarra, 143–71. Lima: CENDOC-Mujer, 1999.

Rostworowski de Diez Canseco, María. *Señoríos indígenas de Lima y Canta*. Lima: IEP, 1978.

———. *Pachacamac y el Señor de los Milagros: Una trayectoria milenaria*. Lima: IEP, 1992.

Rubial García, Antonio. "Los Santos Milagreros y Malogrados de la Nueva España."

In *Manifestaciones religiosas en el mundo colonial americano*, edited by Clara García   247
Ayluardo and Manuel Ramos Medina, 51–88. Mexico City: Universidad Ibero-
americana, 1997.
———. *La ciudad barroca*. Mexico City: El Colegio de México, FCE, 2005.
Sáenz-Diez, Juan I. *Los Riojanos en América*. Madrid: MAPFRE, 1992.
Said, Edward. *Orientalism*. New York: Vintage, 1979.
Saiz Diez, O.F.M., Félix. *Los Colegios de Propaganda Fide en Hispanoamérica*. Madrid:
Raycar, 1969.
Sala Catalá, José. *Ciencia y técnica en la metropolización de América*. Madrid: Doce Calles,
CSIC, 1994.
Sala i Vila, Nuria. *Y se armó el tole tole: Tributo indígena y movimientos sociales en el virreinato
del Perú, 1784–1814*. Lima: IER José María Arguedas, 1996.
Salvat Monguillot, Manuel. "En torno a la fundación de San Felipe el Real (1740)." In
VI Congreso Internacional de Historia de América, 187–98. Buenos Aires, 1982.
Sánchez Bella, Ismael. *Iglesia y Estado en la América Española*. Pamplona: Universidad
de Navarra, 1990.
Sánchez Ortega, María Helena. "Women as Source of 'Evil' in Counter-Reformation
Spain." In *Culture and Control in Counter-Reformation Spain*, edited by Anne J. Cruz
and Mary Elizabeth Perry, 196–215. Minneapolis: University of Minnesota Press,
1992.
Sánchez Rodríguez, Susy. "La ruina de Lima: Mito y realidad del terremoto de 1746."
Masters degree, PUC, 2001.
Sánchez-Concha B., Rafael. *Santos y santidad en el Perú virreinal*. Lima: Vida y espiritu-
alidad, 2003.
San Cristóbal Sebastián, Antonio. *Lima: Estudios de la arquitectura virreinal*. Lima:
Patronato de Lima, Epígrafe Editores, 1992.
———. *La Catedral de Lima: Estudios y Documentos*. Lima: Museo de Arte Religioso de
La Catedral de Lima, 1996.
———. "La reconstrucción de la iglesia de Nuestra Señora de Copacabana después
de 1746." *Histórica* 24, no. 2 (2000): 441–57.
———. *La Casa Virreinal Limeña de 1570 a 1687*. 2 vols. Lima: Fondo Editorial del
Congreso del Perú, 2003.
Schutte, Anne Jacobsen. *Aspiring Saints: Pretense of Holiness, Inquisition, and Gender in the
Republic of Venice, 1618–1750*. Baltimore: Johns Hopkins University Press, 2001.
Scott, H. M., ed. *Enlightened Absolutism: Reform and Reformers in Later Eighteenth-Century
Europe*. London: Macmillan, 1990.
Sekora, John. *Luxury: The Concept in Western Thought, Eden to Smollett*. Baltimore: Johns
Hopkins University Press, 1977.
Serulnikov, Sergio. *Subverting Colonial Authority: Challenges to Spanish Rule in the
Eighteenth-Century Southern Andes*. Durham: Duke University Press, 2003.
Sifuentes de la Cruz, Luis Enríque. *Las murallas de Lima en el Proceso Histórico del Perú:
Ensayo acerca de la historia y evolución urbana de la ciudad de Lima entre los siglos XVII y
XIX*. Lima: CONCYTEC, 2004.

248   Silgado, Enrique. "Historia de los sismos más notables ocurridos en el Perú (1513–1970)." *Geofísica Panamericana* 2, no. 1 (1973): 179–243.

———. *Historia de los sismos más notables ocurridos en el Perú (1513–1974)*. Lima: Instituto de Geología y Minería, 1978.

Sotelo, Hildebrando R. *Las Insurrecciones y Levantamientos en Huarochirí y sus Factores Determinantes*. Lima: "La Prensa," 1942.

Spalding, Karen. *Huarochirí*. Stanford: Stanford University Press, 1984.

Stavig, Ward. *The World of Tupac Amaru: Conflict, Community, and Identity in Colonial Peru*. Lincoln: University of Nebraska Press, 1999.

Steele, Arthur Robert. *Flowers for the King: The Expedition of Ruiz and Pavon and the Flora of Peru*. Durham: Duke University Press, 1964.

Steinberg, Ted. *Acts of God: The Unnatural History of Natural Disaster in America*. Oxford: Oxford University Press, 2000.

Stern, Steve, ed. "The Age of Andean Insurrection, 1742–1782." In *Resistance, Rebellion, and Consciousness in the Andean Peasant World, 18th to 20th Centuries*, edited by Steve Stern, 34–93. Madison: University of Wisconsin Press, 1983.

———. *The Secret History of Gender: Women, Men, and Power in Late Colonial Mexico*. Chapel Hill: University of North Carolina Press, 1995.

Suárez, Margarita. "El poder de los velos: Monasterios y finanzas en Lima siglo XVII." In *Estrategia de desarrollo: Intentando cambiar la vida*, edited by Patricia Portocarrero Suárez, 165–74. Lima: Flora Tristan, 1993.

———. "Ciencia, ficción e imaginario colectivo: La interpretación de los cielos en el Perú colonial." In *Historia, memoria y ficción*, edited by Luis Millones and Moises Lemlij, 312–19. Lima: Biblioteca Peruana de Psicoanálisis, 1996.

Tandeter, Enrique, and Jorge Hidalgo Lehuede, eds. *Historia general de América Latina*. Madrid: Editorial Trotta/Ediciones UNESCO, 1999.

Taylor, John Gates. "Eighteenth-Century Earthquake Theories: A Case History Investigation into the Character of the Study of the Earth in the Enlightenment." Ph.D. diss., University of Oklahoma, 1975.

Taylor, William B. *Magistrates of the Sacred: Priests and Parishioners in Eighteenth-Century Mexico*. Stanford: Stanford University Press, 1996.

Thomas, Keith. *Religion and the Decline of Magic*. Oxford: Oxford University Press, 1997.

Tilly, Charles. *Coercion, Capital and European States, A.D. 990–1992*. Malden: Blackwell, 1990.

Tobriner, Stephen. "Earthquake Planning in the 17th and 18th Centuries." *Journal of Architectural Education* 33, no. 4 (1980).

———. "La Casa Baraccata: Earthquake-resistant Construction in 18th-Century Calabria." *Journal of the Society of Architectural Historians* 42, no. 2 (1983).

Turiso Sebastián, Jesús. *Comerciantes españoles en la Lima Borbónica: Anatomía de una elite de poder (1701–1761)*. Valladolid: Universidad de Valladolid, PUC, 2002.

Twinam, Ann. *Public Lives, Private Secrets: Gender, Honor, Sexuality, and Illegitimacy in Colonial Spanish America*. Stanford: Stanford University Press, 1999.

Ugarte Eléspuru, Juan Manuel. *Lima y lo limeño*. Lima: Editorial Universitaria, 1966.

Urdiain Martínez, María Camino. *Archivo Provincial de Alava, "Fondos Especiales," Tomo 1,* 249
Fondo Samaniego (inventario de documentos). Alava: Diputación Foral de Alava, 1984.

Valdizán, Hermilio. *Locos de la Colonia*. Lima: INC, 1988.

Vale, Lawrence J., and Thomas J. Campanella. *The Resilient City: How Modern Cities Recover from Disaster*. Oxford: Oxford University Press, 2005.

Van Deusen, Nancy. *The Souls of Purgatory: The Spiritual Diary of a Seventeenth-Century Afro-Peruvian Mystic, Ursula de Jesús*. Albuquerque: University of New Mexico Press, 2004.

———. *Between the Sacred and the Worldly: The Institutional and Cultural Practice of Recogimiento in Colonial Lima*. Stanford: Stanford University Press, 2001.

Varese, Stefano. *Salt of the Mountain: Campa Asháninka History and Resistance in the Peruvian Jungle*. Translated by Susan Giersbach Rascón. Norman: University of Oklahoma Press, 2002.

Vargas Ugarte, Rubén. *Historia del Perú, Fuentes*. 2d. ed. Lima: Librería e Imprenta Gil, 1945.

———. *Historia de Santo Cristo de los Milagros*. Lima: Lumen, 1949.

———. *Concilios Limenses (1551–1772)*. Vols. 2, 3. Lima, 1952.

———. *Historia de la Iglesia en el Perú*. Vol. 4. Burgos: Aldecoa, 1961.

———. *Ensayo de un diccionario de artífices de la América meridional*. 2d ed. Burgos: np, 1968.

———. *Historia General del Perú, Virreinato (Siglo XVIII) 1700–1790*. Vol. 3. Lima: Librería e Imprenta Gil, 1956.

Vegas de Cáceres, Ileana. "Una imagen distorsionada: Las haciendas de Lima hacia finales del siglo XVIII." In *El Perú en el siglo XVIII: La era Borbónica*, edited by Scarlett O'Phelan Godoy, 97–125. Lima: PUC, Instituto Riva-Agüero, 1999.

Velarde, Hector. *Arquitectura peruana*. Mexico City: Fondo de Cultura Económica, 1946.

Velázquez Castro, Marcel. *Las máscaras de la representación: El sujeto esclavista y las rutas del racismo en el Perú (1775–1895)*. Lima: UNMSM, BCR, 2005.

Vélez, César. *Memoria y utopía de la vieja Lima*. Lima: Universidad del Pacífico, 1985.

Vergara Ormeño, Teresa. "La población indígena." In *Lima en el siglo xvi*, edited by Laura Gutiérrez Arbulú, 175–226. Lima: Instituto Riva-Agüero, 2005.

Vicuña Mackenna, Benjamín. "Lima en 1810." In *Pequeña Antología de Lima*, edited by Raúl Porras Barrenechea, 248–56. Madrid: Galo Sáez, 1935.

Vidler, Anthony. "The Scenes of the Street: Transformations in Ideal and Reality, 1750–1871." In *On Streets*, edited by Stanford Anderson, 29–106. Cambridge: MIT Press, 1978.

Viqueira Albán, Juan Pedro. *Propriety and Permissiveness in Bourbon Mexico*. Translated by Sonya Lipsett-Rivera and Sergio Rivera Ayala. Wilmington: SR Books, 1999.

Vivanco, Carmen. "Bandolerismo colonial peruano, 1760–1810: Caracterización de una respuesta popular." In *Bandoleros, abigeos, montoneros*, edited by Carlos Aguirre and Charles Walker, 25–56. Lima: Instituto de Apoyo Agrario, Pasado y Presente, 1990.

250   Voekel, Pamela. *Alone Before God: The Religious Origins of Modernity*. Durham: Duke University Press, 2002.

Walker, Charles. "Introducción: Dossier, Los andes en el siglo xviii." *Anuario de Estudios Americanos* 61, no. 1 (2004): 19–29.

———. *Smoldering Ashes: Cuzco and the Creation of Republican Peru, 1780–1840*. Durham: Duke University Press, 1999.

———. "Civilize or Control? The Lingering Impact of the Bourbon Urban Reforms." In *Political Culture in the Andes*, edited by Cristóbal Aljovín de Losada and Nils Jacobsen, 74–95. Durham: Duke University Press, 2005.

Warren, Adam. "Piety and Danger: Popular Ritual, Epidemics, and Medical Reforms in Lima, Peru, 1750–1860." Ph.D. diss., University of California, San Diego, 2004.

Weber, Allison. *Teresa of Avila and the Rhetoric of Femininity*. Princeton: Princeton University Press, 1996.

Whitaker, Robert. *The Mapmaker's Wife: A True Tale of Love, Murder, and Survival in the Amazon*. New York: Basic Books, 2004.

Wuffarden, Luis Eduardo. "Los lienzos del virrey Amat y la pintura limeña del siglo xviii." In *Los cuadros de mestizaje del Virrey Amat*, edited by Natalia Majluf. Lima: Museo de Arte, 2000.

———. "La ciudad y sus emblemas: Imágenes del criollismo en el virreinato del Perú." In *Los Siglos de Oro en los Virreinatos de América 1550–1700*, 59–75. Madrid: Museo de América, Sociedad Estatal para la Conmemoración de los Centenarios de Felipe II y Carlos V, 2000.

———. "La plentitud barroca y el arte mestizo (1680–1750)." In *Enciclopedia temática del Perú, Arte y Arquitectura*, 39–50. Lima: El Comercio, 2004.

Index

CHARLES F. WALKER is professor of history at the University of California, Davis. He is the author of *Smoldering Ashes: Cuzco and the Creation of Republican Peru, 1780–1840* (Duke, 1999).

Library of Congress Cataloging-in-Publication Data

Walker, Charles F.
Shaky colonialism : the 1746 earthquake-tsunami in Lima,
Peru, and its long aftermath / Charles F. Walker.
p. cm.
Includes bibliographical references and index.
ISBN-13: 978-0-8223-4172-7 (cloth : alk. paper)
ISBN-13: 978-0-8223-4189-5 (pbk. : alk. paper)
1. Lima (Peru)—History—18th century.
2. Earthquakes—Social aspects—Peru—Lima.
3. Earthquakes—Peru—Lima—Psychological aspects.
I. Title.
F3601.3.W35 2008
985'.25033—dc22
2007043971